THE CLOCKWISE HOUSE SYSTEM

THE CLOCKWISE HOUSE SYSTEM

A TRUE FOUNDATION FOR SIDEREAL AND TROPICAL ASTROLOGY

JACQUES DORSAN

LINDISFARNE BOOKS

2011

LINDISFARNE BOOKS
An imprint of Anthroposophic Press, Inc.
610 Main Street, Great Barrington, MA 01230
www.steinerbooks.org

Translation from the French by Lesley Spring;
edited and revised by Wain Farrants and Robert Powell

Cover image: "The Prague Astronomical Clock"
Copyright © Ladislav Bihari (shutterstock.com)
Book and cover design: William Jens Jensen

LIBRARY OF CONGRESS CATALOGING-IN-PUBLICATION DATA

Dorsan, Jacques.
[Le véritable sens des maisons astrologiques. English]
The clockwise house system : a true foundation for sidereal and
tropical astrology / Jacques Dorsan.
p. cm.
Includes bibliographical references.
ISBN 978-1-58420-095-6
1. Astrology. 2. Houses (Astrology) I. Title.
BF1708.2.D6613 2011
133.5—dc22

2010051972

eBook ISBN 978-1-58420-102-1

Contents

Index of Charts

Preface to the English Edition

Jacques Dorsan

So that readers may benefit fully from the present work, as I sincerely hope you will, I must make it clear that I am a *siderealist*. I am an ardent advocate of the practice stating that the planets, as well as the cusps of the houses, be considered according to the natural zodiac, structured on the constellations, or groups, of fixed stars.

However, the practitioners and students who remain tied to the tropical zodiac, which starts March 20 or 21 under the pretext that this date marks the beginning of spring, will also benefit from my recommendations. The theory exposed in the following pages does not depend in any way on which zodiac is used; it works with any system of domification you apply. In my previous book, *Retour au zodiaque des étoiles* ("Return to the Stellar Zodiac"), I state that I have demonstrated the supremacy of the natural zodiac of ancient times through arguments arising from history, logic, analogy, observation, cosmography, experience, and statistics. Moreover, the statistics are not mine, nor are they extracted from my personal collection of horoscopes. Through the practice of the sidereal zodiac, I have discovered the reasons for which the seven classical planets known to the ancients are exalted to a certain degree. Thus, exaltations and the corollary of these have again found their significance and, as a result of this, their use.

Once again, in this work I have followed the same path. The twelve signs of the zodiac, owing to the analogy between a day and a year, have given birth to the twelve houses. However, if you stop and think and check your thoughts through simple observation, you will quickly realize that the unfolding of the houses should be considered to take place in a rotation contrary to that of the succession of the signs. If you give the same direction to both signs and houses, do you realize that what you call the twelfth house—to which you attribute hidden sickness, secretiveness, and obscurity and occurs more in the dark—corresponds to the first two hours or so following sunrise, which is fully in the light of day? When the ancients described the four Quadrants of the celestial sphere, they regularly enumerated them as follows. The first one covers the part of the chart from Ascendant to Midheaven; the second goes from Midheaven to Descendant; the third from Descendant to Imum Coeli; and the fourth from Imum Coeli back to the Ascendant. Thus, because of diurnal movement, they noticed and stated that, for the observer, the celestial sphere rotates contrary to the succession of the zodiacal signs.

Therefore, for heaven's sake, why should we give the opposite direction of rotation to these four Quadrants once we divide each of them into three parts to obtain a number of sections of the ecliptic equal to that of the twelve signs? Moreover, if you follow my suggestion, you will admit that the second house, to which we attribute gains, does not correspond any more to the quietest part of the night—from roughly 2 a.m. to 4 a.m.—but rather to the beginning of the working day, around 8 a.m. to 10 a.m., during which time we may be more efficient in our professional activities.

The third house, which corresponds to short trips, will remain above the horizon; while the end of the ninth house, that of long journeys, reaches the I.C., which perfectly symbolizes the antipodes.

And finally, I offer a natural solution to the problem raised by the contradictions we find among different authors—that is, what are the exact houses we should assign to the native's father and mother?

I am not asking you to accept my recommendation blindly, inasmuch as my proposition might seem too revolutionary to many. On second thought, however, you will realize that the significations we give to the four angles are not dramatically invalidated; they are only slightly modified.

In conclusion, I am inviting you to test the method I have been using to my complete personal satisfaction for more than a quarter of a century. This technique has allowed me to improve my interpretation of celestial charts, and I feel sure that it will permit you to do likewise. Nothing can compete with one's own personal experience.

To my cousin Madame Jean Mayoux, née Marie-Adèle Quintin, who, during the forties, intuitively furnished proof, through the rectitude of her interpretation, of the certitude of the principles expressed in these pages, while I, through the rigorous and mathematical application of what was then considered to be classical theories, did my utmost to demonstrate to her that she was entirely wrong.

> *A thousand pardons and just as many thanks.*
> *Most affectionately yours,*
> Jacques Dorsan

Editor's Introduction

Wain Farrants

Sidereal Zodiac

The horoscopes displayed in this book show the visible stars in the zodiac in the outer concentric circle, the positions of the planets in the sidereal zodiac in the middle circle, and the aspects between the planets in the center. Note that we use the Babylonian sidereal zodiac in which the star Aldebaran is at 15°3' of Taurus and Antares at 15°1' of Scorpio. This differs slightly from the various sidereal zodiacs used by different schools of Indian astrology, so that even Indian astrologers should be able to study this book, making a small adjustment. The horoscopes are all cast by the computer program *Astrofire*.[1]

Aspectogram

The names of the aspects with their respective angles, which I have chosen to use, follow.

Major Aspects	Minor Aspects
☌ Conjunction (0°)	∠ Semi-square (45°)
☐ Square (90°)	✳ Septile (51° 26')
△ Trine (120°)	✶ Sextile (60°)
☍ Opposition (180°)	Q Quintile (72°)
	⚏ Sesquiquadrate (135°)
	⚻ Quincunx (150°)

---

1   Treadgold. *Astrofire* (astrological computer program; see bibliography, p. 309).

To avoid clutter, I have often omitted most of the minor aspects even when they exist in a particular horoscope.

RULERS OF THE SIGNS OF THE ZODIAC

Beginners in astrology should be aware that each sign of the zodiac has a planetary ruler. Before the discovery of Uranus, Neptune and Pluto, ten of the signs shared the five planets while the ruler of Cancer was the Moon and the ruler of Leo was the Sun. Following their discovery, Uranus has frequently been substituted for Saturn, ruling Aquarius; Neptune for Jupiter, ruling Pisces; and Pluto for Mars, ruling Scorpio. If the zodiac signs are arranged sequentially in something like the following way, then you can clearly see the rulers in a logical sequence.

CLASSICAL PLANETARY RULERS OF THE ZODIAC

ZODIAC SIGN	SINGLE RULER	COMMON RULER	SINGLE RULER	ZODIAC SIGN
Leo	Sun		Moon	Cancer
Virgo		Mercury		Gemini
Libra		Venus		Taurus
Scorpio		Mars		Aries
Sagittarius		Jupiter		Pisces
Capricorn		Saturn		Aquarius

MODERN PLANETARY RULERS OF THE ZODIAC

ZODIAC SIGN	SINGLE RULER	SINGLE RULER	ZODIAC SIGN
Leo	Sun	Moon	Cancer
Virgo	Mercury	Mercury	Gemini
Libra	Venus	Venus	Taurus
Scorpio	Pluto	Mars	Aries
Sagittarius	Jupiter	Neptune	Pisces
Capricorn	Saturn	Uranus	Aquarius

Jacques Dorsan, on the whole, preferred the classical rulers but he also referred to the modern rulers and even ascribed Pluto not only to Scorpio, but also to Aries; Neptune not only to Pisces, but also to Sagittarius; and Uranus not only to Aquarius, but also to Capricorn. As he used the classical rulers, however, some houses could be ruled by three zodiac signs.

Since most houses encompass two zodiac signs, houses are ruled by the planets, which rule both signs. A very narrow house may contain only one sign, and a very wide house may contain two or even more signs. For example, if Gemini is on the cusp of the fifth house and Taurus is on the cusp of the sixth house (remember, the house progresses backward through the zodiac), then both Mercury and Venus will be rulers of the fifth house. Bill Herbst writes:

> Some astrologers believe that the sign on the cusp is dominant, while the intercepted sign indicates a more subtle meaning. Others contend that the cuspal sign is conscious, while the intercepted sign represents a more subconscious motif.... I recommend the first approach—cuspal dominance and intercepted subtlety.[2]

> In the early years of his astrological practice, Dorsan used the Placidus house system, later the Campanus system, and then the Equal house system for the latter part of his life. However, in most of his examples the Placidus system agrees with his conclusions. One of the foundation stones of his work is Michel Gauquelin,[3] who emphasised the Midheaven axis, and whose sectors correspond "fairly closely to the Placidean house system."[4]

Although Dorsan disliked Placidus, the editors nevertheless chose to cast the horoscopes using Placidus. The main editor has found that planets transiting Placidus House cusps (with a very narrow orb) often announce a notable event. The Equal House system, we feel, ignores the significant role played by the MC–IC axis in more clearly distinguishing between the third and fourth houses as well as the ninth and tenth houses.

---

2   Herbst. *Houses of the Horoscope.*

3   Gauquelin. *Neo-astrology: A Copernican Revolution.*

4   Powell. *History of the Houses.*

ACCURACY OF THE HOROSCOPES

Some of Dorsan's birth times were found to be completely wrong, owing to more up-to-date birth data or to errors he made in relation to time zones. I have either assigned the horoscope to a different section (e.g. Charles de Gaulle, Howard Hughes) or discarded it. I have also added many additional examples. I think it will be obvious whether it is Dorsan or me speaking. I have also embellished many of Dorsan's delineations.

I rectified every horoscope by the Tritune of Hermes. We are aware that the Hermetic Rule has gone out of fashion. However, we believe that the horoscope of conception is just as important as the horoscope of birth for human destiny.

The astrology program that I use to work out the conception chart is *Astrofire*. The concept behind the Hermetic Rule is that between conception and birth the Ascendant–Descendant axis swaps places with the Moon. For example, if you have 10° Aries rising at birth and the Moon is in 15° Leo, then there are four possible positions at conception. The Moon is either 10° Aries or 10° Libra, and the Ascendant is either 15° Leo or 15° Aquarius. You have to know whether the individual was born late or premature and, ideally, the place where that person was conceived if it was some distance from the place of birth. It is also worth noting that ten lunar months (that is, the month from New Moon to New Moon) is equal to about nine calendar months.

As the Ascendant moves through the zodiac in approximately twenty-four hours, then on any possible day of conception there are two possibilities averaging about twelve hours apart. However, the Moon will have passed through about 6° to 7° between the two possible times and as the

Moon corresponds to the Ascendant at birth it will make a fair difference to the birth time.

I checked the accuracy of my rectifications by taking transits to the conception chart and comparisons with significant events in the person's life, which are not easily explicable by the birth chart. I find the sidereal zodiac to be more accurate. One can also add on precession to tropical positions.

The computer program *Astrofire* also includes a facility for progressing the conception chart discovered by Willi O. Sucher,[5] which takes one lunar month between conception and birth equal to seven years in your life.[6]

---

5   Willi Sucher (1902–1985) encountered the work of Rudolf Steiner in 1919 at the age of seventeen. He devoted his life to Anthroposophy, working closely with Dr. Elizabeth Vreede, a leader in the spiritual research of astronomy and mathematics in the Anthroposophical Society. Sucher devoted almost sixty years to developing the new "star wisdom" called *astrosophy*, which he considered the form of astrology most appropriate for modern humanity.

6   Sucher. *Practical Approach to a New Astrosophy 1972–1974*. For an extensive exposition concerning this discovery by Willi Sucher, see also Powell, *Hermetic Astrology, Volume II: Astrological Biography*.

CHAPTER 1

INTRODUCTION

I fell madly in love with astrology right from the beginning. I realize why one of my masters, Alan Leo, called it his cherished mistress of long-standing. My first chart of the heavens was drawn, a little before sunrise, with the aid of my index finger on the sand at Grand Bassam beach, on the Ivory Coast. It was at that particular hour that I could spot Mercury from time to time. "How on Earth," one of my friends complained one day, "can you claim to have seen Mercury, when certain astronomers lament the fact that they have never seen it." It was, however, absolutely true. Nevertheless, the right time and moment must be chosen. Generally, it is more readily visible when it rises in the morning, before the Sun, than when it sets in the evening, after the Sun. In the mornings, there is less mist, less water evaporation from the sea than after a long hot day. The time to choose is when it is, for our eyes, the furthest from the Sun, when it reaches its maximum elongation.

I must make it clear, however, that I observed the heavens and compared my findings with what I studied in my first books. It is this particular frame of mind that gave rise to the following remark made to me by Gustav-Lambert Brahy, the Dean of French-speaking astrologers: "Ah! You really do live your astrology."

My second chart of the heavens was traced by means of a simple wooden compass. I was delighted to have come across it in the possession of one of the religious fathers at the nearby mission, who was prepared to relinquish ownership for the sum of one franc. Such memories are never forgotten.

I often returned to the beach very early in the morning in order to regularly compare theory and practice. Consequently, one of the things that really set me thinking, right from the beginning, was the fact that the astrologers counted the houses—twelve sections of roughly 30° each—from the Ascendant in the same direction as the signs of the zodiac. I bowed, nevertheless, to their superior knowledge. I had not been reared in an atmosphere of student dissension. It was obviously the teachers who were right.

The years went by. Within one year, I had already absorbed the second volume of Henri-Joseph Gouchon's famous dictionary on the Primary Directions.[1] What experiences! What encouragement!

When I left the Ivory Coast, I had been given the occasion to draw up twenty-five percent of the celestial charts pertaining to the births of the population, both European and assimilated, as recorded in the census of 1936, the year of my arrival. Not that I dealt with a quarter of this population, as it had increased considerably during my stay, that is to say, during the first part of the war. I must admit I was greatly assisted by circumstances. A man can be demolished by slander. But it also happens that legends can be based on erroneous information. How could I have predicted that a certain Lemaître was going to have an airplane accident when I was ignorant of the fact that he had an airplane? However, it is true that it was the same Lemaître who spread the news concerning a prediction that was true this time. He spent a Sunday afternoon with me. I drew up his horoscope and warned him of an impending fracture. "I do not know if it will be an arm or a leg, owing to the severe oppositions of the planets from Gemini to Sagittarius." The following day, he was hospitalized with an open fracture of the femur. The fact that this accident took place on the bicycle—which I had lent him so that he could stay a little longer with me in Abidjan (before returning to his nearby plantation)—gave rise to my first reflections on the mysterious links that go to make up the tapestry of our existence.

---

1   Gouchon and Reverchon. *Dictionnaire astrologique: Supplément technique pour simplifier ou supprimer tous les travaux mathématiques concernant la carte totale, les révolutions solaires et surtout les directions* (Paris, 1947).

Still, I think the most powerful stimulant from which I drew gratification during this period, especially as it concerned mundane astrology (a field considered to be difficult), was the fact that I predicted, nine months in advance, the exact day when the civil war in Spain would end. I participated in a competition sponsored by the weekly *Gringoire*. "When will the Spanish civil war cease?" I was careful enough to mention in the form of a postscript that the date had not been determined purely by chance, but as a result of scientific astrological calculations. I drew my inspiration from a book by Léon Lasson [1901–1989] on mundane astrology, in which he dealt at great length with the initial effects of eclipses and their subsequent duration. I began with the premise that this terrible war would not cease before spring of 1939. I searched for a deadly date on the Spanish Republic's horoscope that coincided with military (Mars) success (Jupiter) based on the horoscope of General Franco. The month of March seemed to fit perfectly. In fact, an exact Jupiter–Uranus sextile was in force; Jupiter crossed the exact degree of Mars at the birth of the Generalissimo.

It was indeed a brief and sudden (Uranus) military success. The new Moon of March 21 was strongly Martian. Quite simply I chose the date March 29, 1939, owing to the fact that on that day the moon made a trine to the General's natal Mars. This meant that, on this very same day, there was a transmission of light in operation on the Jupiter–Uranus sextile mentioned. That very day, pro-Franco troops entered Puerta del Sol in Madrid and brought an end to the war.

"So you won the competition" is what you are thinking of me. Well, no. When attempting to predict the future with a certain amount of success, one must be in a highly receptive state, and above all (in fact, most important of all), one must be totally impartial. This is difficult to attain. This certainly was not the case where the organizers of the competition were concerned. They had stated, "We consider the civil war to be over when the pro-Franco troops take Barcelona." Indeed, there had been fighting there for months. Finally the town fell January 26, 1939. However, the Republicans continued to resist in several towns, with the last to surrender being Madrid. Indeed, the satisfaction I drew from this was personal, but great nonetheless. In fact, quite to the contrary, that particular day I received quite a shock. I told Louis Gastin, a local newspaper astrologer, about it. I did not think at the time that I could possibly be helped by unknown forces. I was too young and I attributed this success entirely to myself. Later on, however, further precise successes followed—of note, at Darlan I provided the exact date of the first bombardment of Paris (which involved the Renault factories at Billancourt) by the Royal Air Force during the night of March 2 and 3, 1942, as noted in the appendix to my *Retour au zodiaque des étoiles* (Return to the Stellar Zodiac). I wondered if, unknown to myself, I was not being "guided." To this day, the question remains unanswered.

After seven years of preparation, I opened my consulting rooms. My first consultation was quite an event. Two women entered. I guessed that the younger of the two was her stepfather's mistress. "Ah," you say, but in fact they were mother and daughter.

Seven more years went by ... One evening I held a conference at Cannes on the French Riviera. It was announced by means of publicity posters, as others of its kind had been. The little posters in question contained a promise at the end of the announcement: "The conference [astrological, of course] will be illustrated by flash horoscopes of audience members."

A few local inhabitants, deeply interested in the subject, agreed among themselves to come along and jeer the author of this pledge, so much did they consider it to be fallacious. Once my usual explanation of astrology was over, I continued on to put it into practice. One could think that for me this would be the most harrowing part of the evening. It would be the moment when I was put to the test. Not at all. This was the time I enjoyed the most, and for good reason. One of the men in the front row threw me the date, time, and place of his birth. In less than three minutes, his horoscope came into being, on an enormous sheet more than a meter wide. I remember having mentioned the subject's artistic propensities, that he could earn money selling his works abroad (there having been links between Venus, the arts, the native financial indications and faraway lands), and I noticed his neighbors nodding approval. But the stranger tried to put me on the spot. Making everybody in the hall laugh (which revealed to me that he was far from unknown in the locality and that people were quite familiar with him), he asked me, "Will I get married once or twice?"

This charming Venusian heard the reply: "It is more likely to be three times than twice," and the audience burst into laughter…while I, of course, remained ignorant of the fact that he had already undergone a marriage annulment. However, I became bolder and was unable to resist mentioning the dominant element of earth. So I added, "I have the impression that you could be greatly interested in agriculture and that you could undertake a course of studies in this field."

At last, the mocking laughter, so long awaited by some, rang around the hall. But I maintained my point of view and even went on to develop it further. At this point, to the general astonishment of all present, Auguste Pasteur, a well-known pianist composer, stood and announced that he was a fully trained agricultural engineer.

Dazzled by the footlights, I was unable to see the faces of those who addressed me, especially those in the back rows. It was then, from the farthest end of the hall, that I heard a man's voice fling me his birth date. From the accent, I guessed that my interlocutor was of Asian origin. Mars and Saturn in Aries revealed to me a facial wound, which I was unable to see, but I remember this configuration, having seen it already in a man who fought in a duel, and I shouted out to him, "I'd rather have you as a counsel than as an enemy." Maître Quah Van Giao, former president of the bar at Grasse, would later become my legal counselor.

Indeed, both these people became my friends. That very evening, several others joined our group. At one o'clock in the morning, we celebrated with champagne at my home. They immediately asked me to set up a training course in astrology, which half a dozen or so of my previous candidates in disparagement would follow with diligence. Several of them, however, hesitated at the setting up of a celestial chart, before conforming with the rule, which stipulated that the houses must be followed in the order of the signs. This was not the first time that a perspicacious student took a nosedive over this particular issue. It is true that I insisted, above all, on cosmography. It was then that I took it upon myself to study this question profoundly and to sift it through the fingers of experiment.

A full seven years later, after having practiced intensely in South America, I was absolutely, entirely, definitively convinced. For me it was an unconditional certitude: the rotation of the twelve houses must be accomplished by taking diurnal movement, cosmographical reality, into account. They could move only in the direction opposite to that of the zodiacal signs.

What I am presenting here to the reader is not, by any means, new to me. I have been testing this system for more than twenty years before revealing it to you now. Once this idea was firmly imprinted in my mind, I wished to bear witness to it. Then, and only then, did I reveal it to my friend Müller of São Paulo in 1959, just prior to my return to France. This revelation took place in a large hotel in Rio de Janeiro during one of the many breakfasts we shared together. This psychologist, sufficiently well versed in astrology, immediately seized the implications of my discovery. He exclaimed, *"Mas que confusão! Não e possível!..."* Then we laughed for a long time like two kids, followed by a long silence that we did not bother to explain to each other, but that said everything in itself. For the seven years during which we knew each another, Alfredo had already formed a high opinion of me as an astrologer, but from that day onward, he saw me in an entirely new light. He was, indeed, most enthusiastic about this technique.

It is fully justified in the Northern Hemisphere to lay out the twelve signs of the zodiac on our horoscope sheets in a counterclockwise direction. It is not, however, an error for a practitioner in the Southern Hemisphere to lay them out in a clockwise fashion.

THE TWO DIRECTIONS OF ROTATION

How great was my stupefaction, at Campos do Jordão in Brazil, when I leaned over the balcony of my hotel room to see the signs laid out in this fashion in the mosaic of the hotel patio. The architect had not made an error there by any means.

Imagine yourself hovering over the North Pole in an almost stationary helicopter, and you would see the Earth (you could also, at least, imagine the equator), turning counterclockwise. Now transplant yourself to the South Pole to carry out the same operation; it is clear that you would contemplate our Earth turning in a clockwise direction, even though it always turns in the same direction. Yes indeed, it does, but you see it from a different point of view.

I am not a journalist short of work who, one fine morning, has conscientiously scratched his head with his ballpoint pen and decided to write a book on astrology, indiscriminately throwing a heap of information that has been picked up "any old place."

I know all about putting one's trade into practice after the initial apprenticeship period, and I know what all these years of practical experience have brought me. It is not the slightest exaggeration when I say that I have practiced astrology in ten different countries. It is this that has opened my mind. If you wish to know the details, I gladly provide them in chronological order: the Ivory Coast, Morocco, New York City, the Principality of Monaco, France, Luxembourg, Belgium, Zaire, Brazil, and New Caledonia.

Go and tell a Brazilian or a New Caledonian that the zodiac begins with Aries on March 21, because that is the first day of the spring and that person will laugh in your face.

CRITICIZED FOR ATTEMPTING TO PUT WRONGS RIGHT

Over the years, I have brought this aberration to the attention of many different astrologers. I have made it clear that, in the name of all that is logical, according to the only path traced out by cosmography, we should in fact display the twelve houses in the direction opposite to that of the signs. On many different occasions I proposed to publish articles in the astrological press to correct what I then considered (and still consider) to be a very serious mistake. I have, however, been practically censured. As for my censors (critics), I thank them. I bless them everyday. It is precisely because of their attitude toward me that I have become a writer-astrologer. To remain silent would have been worse than simply abandoning this idea completely. It would be an act of treason against the world of astrology, against all those students who, in their great numbers, are sincerely taken by astrology, who are keen on progressing in their studies, and who question their elders in search of guidance. Real creators must communicate their singularity.

The conditions imposed on me by my censors were so rigorous that they were completely impracticable. We must, nevertheless, understand these critics and forgive them. During the last few decades, it is true that a number of new methods have come into being before our very eyes. It is also a fact that some of them have contributed to the progress of astrology and have furthered the cause for its official recognition; however, others have simply been valid solely to their instigators. On occasion, we meet sincere people engaged in research but who also lack a certain scientific discipline and are completely unfamiliar with the laws of numerical reckoning. I am no stranger to the case of a highly esteemed author who wrote a whole book to present her own unique idea, which I recognize to be extremely valid (I told her so).

In *Mars and Aries,* Janduz offers the hypothesis that, if it is true that Mars in Aries suits men, this combination is harmful to women, as it causes them to lose their femininity. Please note that the author is a woman. Imagine my surprise when Janduz announced to me during the course of our exchange of correspondence that I was extremely fortunate, being the young student that I was, to have among my cases a greater number that displayed this particularity than she had herself. Supposing that you have roughly as many horoscopes of men as you do of women, it stands to reason that only one in twenty-four—roughly four percent—will be that of a woman under the influence of Mars in Aries at birth. It is essential, therefore, to have a large collection of horoscopes in order to draw conclusions, which come exclusively from such a small percentage. Luckily, this does not in any way detract from Janduz's worthiness, probably guided by intuition, in having made such a fascinating discovery. This example is only one of many.

What can be said about those who are authors of the most whimsical methods, so far removed from cosmography that they bear a relation to astrology in name only?

How to establish the statistics that were asked of me? On what basis? According to what criteria? Above all, who could speak out and have the final word, given the fact that astrologers have firm ideas on the subject, having practiced and taught that the sequence of the twelve houses follows that of the signs? Moreover, some statisticians do not even know astrology. What to do? All the more, let us not forget that statistics satisfy only those who are already convinced of the validity of the rule which one wishes to demonstrate.

In addition, the more that statistics stir up astrological factors, the more difficult it becomes to apply them. One factor has to be isolated among so many others. It is possible to arrive at a roughly identical conclusion by treating astrological configurations that are different and alien to the one that has been isolated. A few examples will better illustrate my line of thinking.

Consider, for example, a native of August 3 (I am thinking with regret about Michel Ponge-Helmer as I write these lines) who, according to the tropical zodiac, believed himself to be a Leo. Such a subject will perhaps raise doubts about the validity of the sidereal zodiac under the pretext that he has a cardiac weakness and will claim that he could not be Cancer (sidereal). However, the fact that he was born under the influence of a Sun–Mars conjunction is, in my eyes, amply sufficient to provide a satisfactory explanation of his cardiac weakness. Moreover, the Sun in sidereal Cancer corresponds more closely to the role of the family, the mental climate, the native country, politics, not forgetting history, and all of these things were of paramount importance to our late colleague.

Another will claim that he feels particularly Martian and will personally attribute this to the fact that he has an Ascendant in Scorpio. (Just in passing, this illustrates the common confusion that often arises over a sign and its ruler.) In fact, this particular characteristic could just as easily be attributed to the aspect of Mars to the Ascendant. A close aspect from the Moon to Mars would do just as well.

At first, a great number of astrologers cast a scornful eye on the theory I presented in my book *Return to the Stellar Zodiac*, which urges a return to using the sidereal zodiac. They justified their opinion by saying that they felt they did not belong to the preceding sign, only to soon become enthusiastic advocates of sidereal astrology, making clear public declarations to this effect. Missing characteristics, caused by changing the solar sign, were found again in configurations other than that of the Sun within the sign.

In my opinion, statistics have their role to play and serve a purpose when they question a single, well-defined configuration and when it is possible to apply to this same configuration a particular influence or precise fact. This was the case insofar as the 2,492 eminent clergymen were concerned in relation to the position of the Sun within the sign, as described in detail in my book *Return to the Stellar Zodiac,* quoted earlier.

To cut a long story short, it was extremely difficult to furnish the "proof" required of me—and justly required, I must admit. It would have been a lengthy business, an arduous task, that I was not prepared to take up for a multitude of reasons. As I have said, it was uncertain whether I would end up convincing my interlocutors, who were initially rather daunting, especially in the face of any suggestions from someone who dared to disturb the established order. It would have been possible to assert simply that a certain choice had been made. In any case, I maintain that in this kind of research nothing can equal personal experience, and I propose this very thing a little further on.

OTHER TOOLS OF DEMONSTRATION

In addition to statistics, we have other tools at our disposal. These include, among others, reasoning, logical observation, the history of astrology, and cosmography, especially the latter. We must remain faithful to analogy, the traditional key to interpretation. Besides, on reading what is exposed in these pages, we shall have many opportunities to establish undeniably that reasoning by analogy is the procedure most often adopted. It goes without saying that the supreme argument in the debate (if indeed there is a debate, and as far as I am concerned there is none) will be that of the results obtained by this observation—results that lead in turn to a constant amelioration and enrichment of the interpretation of the celestial chart. Upon my return from South America a little more than twenty years ago, I had occasion to discuss my discovery with Alexandre de Volguine, which also meant I had to face his line of argument, his doubts, and his demands for proof. I was able to shake him significantly in his convictions with the following line of reasoning.

"You say that the third house is that of short journeys; it corresponds perfectly, as I see it, with the sign of Gemini, which is often represented by two children or adolescents of different sexes, walking hand-in-hand along the way. According to our predecessors, you also teach that the ninth house is the one of long voyages; this corresponds perfectly, as far as I can see, with the sign of the centaur (Sagittarius), which travels more quickly and over greater distances. It is quite true that a horse, especially at a gallop, can travel farther than a mere pedestrian. But how can you explain that those on short trips disappear very rapidly from sight under the horizon, whereas those who travel long distances remain visible, above the horizon? There is yet worse to come, Monsieur Volguine. You are ready to admit, no less than I do, that the cusp of the ninth house represents the beginning of a long voyage, and that the end of the ninth denotes the termination of a long voyage. If you count the houses as I recommend, in the direction opposite to that of the signs, the end of the long voyage reaches the I.C. (the tenth house cusp). What better way to represent it than by this angle of the horoscope, which symbolizes, and actually is, the Antipodes?" The founder of *Les cahiers astrologiques* remained opened-mouthed, dumbstruck.

Let us not make a mistake. I do not in any way hold statistics in contempt. I simply say (and many of my fellow astrologers will go along with me) that statistics are rather difficult to apply in the field of astrology. Do I need statistics to prove to you, dear reader, without any fear of being contradicted, that it is dark during the two hours before sunrise, that it is light when the Sun rises, that this act of the Sun brings light, warmth, and the stirring of life with it. Well now, it so happens that the Sun is found in the twelfth house, to which secret things are attributed, representing obscurity and decreased vitality.

Without taking cosmography into account in any way, it being allied to analogy, the keys to interpretation, according to tradition, the manuals teach that the first house, that of the Ascendant, represents the subject more than the others especially as far as his physical body, health and life are concerned, whereas your first house, the one you call the Ascendant, is the sector of the heavens which is in fact located under the horizon and which corresponds to the last hours of the night. When the Sun, in actual fact, rises and brings light you say that it is in the twelfth house which is the source of information on secret, obscure and hidden things.

Statistics? Well, friends, there are statistics based on more than 50,000 cases, with hours of birth not in any way proposed or imposed by my person, which we will examine further along.

REVOLUTION IMPOSED BY COSMOGRAPHY

Certain authors, in efforts to modernize astrology, unfortunately tend to move further from tradition, adulterating it in the process. (We shall bring proof of this to light in the pages to come.) I am persuaded that, regardless of what one may think, rather than running headlong into the exploration of whimsical new methods (which hardly stand in the face of experience, let alone statistics), it is necessary to turn toward the past to study in greater depth what has brought this tradition to us.

In my previous work, *Return to the Stellar Zodiac*, I quoted from citations spread out over twenty-three centuries to back up my argument that the planets exercise the influences over us that we attribute to them only when we place them in the twelve signs of the sidereal zodiac structured on the fixed stars. Now I propose reversing the direction you give to the twelve astrological houses. If you consider only the form, it is a matter of revolution. True enough, but more simply it is a question of recognizing the reality of diurnal movement—that is, to remain very closely attached to the cosmography from which an astrologer who wishes to be scientific should never ever stray.

What I am proposing is instead a *renovation* of astrology. I am willing to admit that, clearly, this project is ambitious. However, the people around me who thought that my first work would provoke a general outcry of indignation and who, let me tell you, criticized me most harshly even before reading my work, have now become passionate advocates of the sidereal zodiac after reading my work and coming to understand my line of reasoning. Indeed, as a result of all this, I received correspondence from five continents over a period of eighteen months. The record was broken by an isolated Israeli research worker who sent me a twenty-four-page letter in which, alas, he asked me an overwhelming number of questions. For the most part, those who wrote to me were not content simply to pass on their compliments, but often asked me for additional help in the interpretation of their celestial charts. This is, therefore, the object of the work you now have in your hands. My objective is, no less, with the help of these two books, to put astrology back on track. Presumptuous? That is very quickly said. However, it must be pointed out that ninety percent of astrology as taught in the West rests on Ptolemy, for whom the Earth was flat and immobile.

Morin de Villefranche—and how many others like him—knew that those theories are completely false. They admitted, and even declared through their writings, that astrology no longer works as well as it had in the past, simply because the zodiac's starting point was vernal. No sooner had they made these observations than they nonetheless carried on, continuing to work according to those same erroneous principles, as their works clearly show beyond any doubt. Are we going to stand by, arms folded, and do absolutely nothing about it?

All of this reminds me of a conversation I had with a prospective client about the management of his portfolio in transferable securities. He told me, "I bought Bazard de l'Hotel de Ville (investment bonds) at four hundred francs. Today they are worth one hundred."

"Sell them," I told him.

"You've got to be kidding," he said. "You will make me lose three hundred francs per share, and I have quite a number of them."

"But I am not making you lose anything. It is just that, in my opinion, they are going to fall even further." In fact, they fell to fifty francs and, of course, my interlocutor had insisted on holding on to them.

From this little anecdote, we can conclude that a grave error is extremely difficult to correct, given the extent of its consequences. This is no excuse for closing our eyes and remaining passive. To put it in a nutshell, astrologers have, from generation to generation, continued to operate under the premise that the twelve houses follow the signs of the zodiac, simply because it was so stated and repeated in the manuals. This is the saddest part of all. Young students are bound to this set of rules, without question, examination, or discussion, and often go on to perpetrate the error when they, in turn, become teachers.

George I. Gurdjieff was quite right when he taught that one of the great human weaknesses is the lack of critical sense and that this can in fact hinder personal advancement. As far as I am concerned, counting the twelve astrological houses in the same direction of succession as that of the signs constitutes a contradiction in the face of the two fundamental elements of astrology (cosmography and analogy), since we end up relying on these two elements to reach a correct interpretation. Cosmography, in that it is descriptive astronomy, particularly as far as our solar system is concerned, should constitute the essential makeup of any astrologer who wishes astrology to be considered as a science. After all, anatomy is the common root of all medical practitioners, whatever their speciality, whatever therapeutic methods they choose to use. As for analogy, this means the relationship which exists between two essentially different things. Later on we shall come back to look at these questions in greater detail.

THE IMPORTANCE OF THE HOUSES

It would seem that there is an enormous disparity between the importance of the houses as we understand them and the amount of literature which exists in relationship to them. When I was a student, right at the very beginning, my main source of reference (as was most other people's) were the Tables of Houses by Placidus. At that stage I was even ignorant of the name and the fact that there were various methods of domification. Quite quickly I came to realize that they had been universally adopted simply because the English editor Foulsham had widely broadcast them. Very often, the name of Placidus was not even quoted. Then I began to realize that working as we do, continually bent over our worksheets, engrossed in our celestial charts, we tend to forget that we work in a three-dimensional world.

We should come to consider these twelve houses not simply as duodecimal divisions within the range of the ecliptic, but rather as twelve lunes in orange-slice formation, which have different thicknesses according to the methods adopted. We are not, however, going to spend too much time on this question, as it could be the subject of an entire book in itself. Despite this hiatus, most astrologers recognize the fact that the houses have an important role to play. As we shall see, they are extremely important and revealing when it comes to the study of someone's destiny. Indeed, the planets in the signs relate mainly to the internal human being—his character, his innate temperament, his latent possibilities—whereas the houses reveal the external human being, the events which are strewn along his path of destiny, the lucky breaks that he is likely or unlikely to have, and the different areas throughout his life in which these events will be manifested. All this can be discerned by studying the directions and transits through the houses.

The student does not lack the necessary information required to assign a well-defined domain of life to a certain house or the overall pattern concerning the different fields of life in connection with people or activities, which are dependent on each of the twelve houses. Most of the manuals are quite explicit on these matters. However, what they do not explain is the origin and the foundation of the houses. Everyone is very quiet on the subject of the establishment of the houses and, more often than not, the manuals do not breathe a word about this. In this way we have been led to make use of the Placidian house system, at the same time causing the twelve houses to turn in the same direction as that attributed to the twelve signs.

Nevertheless, in the case of some demanding practitioners this hiatus has brought about certain consequences. Given that the houses did not always line up to expectations, there has been a total rejection of the houses on the part of some, notably those of the German school. However, in the case of the four angles within the boundaries fixed by the horizon and the meridian, there have never been any great problems.

The Ascendant frequently represents the personality, the Lower Meridian domestic and family life, the Descendant, the spouse or declared enemies. This association of ideas has always made me stop and think. Why should your spouse necessarily become your first, deadly enemy? However, do not let us get ahead of ourselves. We shall come back to this problem later on. The Midheaven stands for the social and professional life. However, opinions are greatly divided over the question of the intermediate houses. It really is of the utmost importance, therefore, to bring about a necessary rectification, as this is essential to correct interpretation of the horoscope. Let us recall that a slow planet often remains in the same sign for years. It follows that it will change houses roughly every two hours. We can never insist too much on the direct consequences of this fact when we are working out the horoscope. The numerous births which take place around the same day are distinguished from one another in relation to the scenario acted out by the houses. The fundamental influences of each planet in the signs together with their interplanetary aspects are manifested in the different fields of each life, that is, each destiny will differ considerably according to the houses in which the various planets are based. This goes to show the paramount importance of the role played by the houses.

"The main source of error lies in the use of rules of interpretation—whether traditional or not—that are totally erroneous." This is what Henri-Joseph Gouchon tells us in *Les cahiers astrologiques* of September 1957 (p. 181–186), a special edition devoted to interpretation. He even adds with considerable insistence, "A rule is exact only when it can be verified by experience. If this is not the case then the rule is erroneous."

In the eyes of some, this remark appears to be self-evident, but it is worthwhile underlining and spending time on it. Consequently we must be wary of accepting some axioms at face value without first subjecting them to the test of experience. The danger seems to be greater in the case of an ancient aphorism as we tend to consider it to be classical and, therefore, totally true. During the course of almost half a century of the daily practice of astrology, the author has learned to be more and more skeptical in the face of widely accepted affirmations of this sort. I must again point out to the reader that I have been interpreting celestial charts for over twenty years now, according to the principle that the houses revolve in the opposite direction to that of the twelve signs. This practice has brought complete satisfaction to myself and my clients.

In truth, you are not really born under one particular sign as we hear so often, but under *seven* signs. Above the horizon five full signs can be counted; moreover, the first part of one sign is cut by the Ascendant and the last part of the opposite sign is cut by the Descendant. For the layman or the ill-informed it will be the realm of these six houses which will be the most visible and apparent. Whereas it takes the special skill of a psychologist and observer to discern the signification of the houses which are placed under the horizon.

The planets and their positions in the signs reveal possibilities. However, they act passively whereas their positions within the houses become actual events. The planets in the houses have direct effects on what we like to call luck or bad luck, on fate (in the Latin sense of the term), and on the different realms of life; in short, they form destiny. It is impossible to engage in a serious interpretation, real or scientific, without a true and intense study of the meaning given to each house. This is exactly what these pages offer through the process explained herein. Let us add that the more an individual is evolved, the more he will be dependent only on the influence of the planets in the sign. However, the greater the distance he has to cover along the path leading to his spiritual development the more he will be subjected to the role attributed to the planets in the houses.

If you spend time studying the impact of a luminary or a particular planet in the sign, it is absolutely necessary, in the event of your following our teaching and adopting our viewpoint, to take the Ayanamsa into account and to consider it solely in the light of the sidereal zodiac. In this way the houses will be considered as replicas of the signs but on a terrestrial basis.

Note by Robert Powell

Ayanamsa, or *Ayanamsha,* is the Sanskrit term in Indian astronomy for the angle by which the sidereal ecliptic longitude of a celestial body is less than its tropical ecliptic longitude. To convert from a tropical horoscope to a sidereal horoscope, it is necessary to know the value of the Ayanamsa. This value increases by 1° every 72 years, since the vernal point shifts backward through the sidereal zodiac (precession of the equinoxes) at a rate of 1° in 72 years. The Ayanamsa was 0° in 221 C.E., when the vernal point was at 0° Aries in the sidereal zodiac (as defined in Powell's book, *History of the Zodiac*). In the meantime, the vernal point has shifted back through the sign of Pisces by 25°. Because the vernal point is currently at 5° Pisces in the sidereal zodiac, the present value of the Ayanamsa is 25°—this being the angular distance from 5° Pisces to 0° Aries. Note that this value of 25° for the Ayanamsa will be exact in 2019, but it is already very close to 5° Pisces in 2011. By definition, the starting point of the tropical zodiac is called 0° Aries and is equated with the vernal point. It is evident that, since the vernal point is at 5° Pisces, there is a constant difference of 25° between the longitudes of celestial bodies measured in the tropical zodiac and those measured in the sidereal zodiac at the present time. To convert a tropical horoscope to a sidereal horoscope, for a birth at the present time (2011), 25° (Ayanamsa) must be subtracted from everything in the tropical horoscope. For example, if the Moon is at 26° Aries in the tropical horoscope, its position in the corresponding sidereal horoscope for a birth around the present time would be 1° Aries. However, because of the precession of the equinoxes, the value of the Ayanamsa changes constantly. For example, for a birth in 1947 (seventy-two years prior to 2019), the Ayanamsa was 24° (rather than 25°), and this value of 24° would be the amount for a horoscope from that time (1947) to subtract from the tropical longitudes to convert them to their corresponding sidereal longitudes.

CHAPTER 2

COSMOGRAPHY

A TRICK QUESTION

During a starry evening you contemplate the waxing Moon high in the sky. The Sun, beneath the horizon, has just set in the west, on your right. A little to the left of the Moon you observe a large planet. Let us suppose it is Jupiter.

Question: Does the Moon move in the direction of arrow A or arrow B? Think hard and reply before turning the page. It is in fact a trick question and one I regularly put to each person to whom I teach Cosmography. First, may I remind you that usually astrologers draw their celestial charts

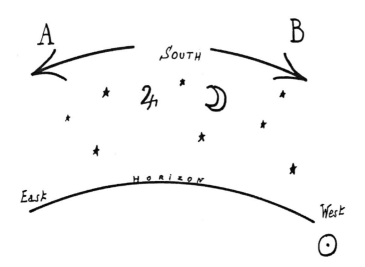

in such a way as to orientate the Ascendant to the left and the Descendant to the right. This allows the MC, the highest point of the ecliptic, to find its position, quite naturally, toward the top. In this way all that we see in the upper portion of the chart, above the Ascendant–Descendant line, is placed in the upper half of the celestial sphere, above the horizon. Just in passing, I point out to you that this is a quick and practical way of finding out if you have made a gross error in the calculation of the sidereal time of birth. The best known of these errors is that of 12 hours, due to the fact that our Astronomical Ephemerides are computed either for zero hours midnight or for twelve hours noon. By holding your chart computed in this way and having a look at the position of the Sun, taking into account your hour of birth, it is obvious that if your consultant tells you he was born at midday, and you see that the Sun is joined to the Lower Meridian, you know that a mistake of 12 hours has been made in the calculations.

I am assuming that the reader lives in the Northern Hemisphere. This being so, then the MC indicates the south. In French, for example, the words for "midday" (*midi*) and "south" (*sud*) are in fact synonyms. Indeed, when the Sun reaches its highest point, in conjunction with the MC, the Sun, in consequence, shows you the direction of the south. If you are not in the equatorial zone, the Sun will never be at the Zenith, exactly over your head, even on June 21 at noon. This is due to the inclination of 23°26' of the Earth's equator in relation to the ecliptical plane. However, on this day, the date of the summer solstice, if you are in Bhopal, India, which is 23°17' north of the equator, the Sun will appear directly over-head at midday.

Editorial insertion: This also explains why horoscopes in the Northern Hemisphere are opposite to geographical maps. On maps, north is at the top, east is on the right, south is at the bottom and west is on the left. But horoscopes are the other way around because you have to face south in order to see the zodiac. In the Southern Hemisphere you have to look north to see the zodiac so geographical maps and observation will be similar. Of course the horoscope could be reversed but in the equatorial zone and the tropics it would be a conundrum.

Answer: The Moon appears to follow the path of arrow B toward the right and, so doing, it sets in the west. However, it is only a question of appearances. Behind this very word lies the truth. This apparent movement to the right is due to diurnal movement (the Earth's rotation on its axis from the west to the east in the course of 24 hours). The Moon daily appears to move in the east–west direction 27 times faster than it really does in its path around the Earth which is in 27.32 days in the west–east direction, a journey which in fact takes place toward the left in the direction of arrow A.

During the course of its actual journey the Moon moves in the direction of arrow A, proceeding through the zodiac roughly a degree or more every two hours. Its apparent movement in the same time is through an entire house in the direction of arrow B. The waxing Moon seems to run toward the Sun in the diagram whereas the waxing Moon is actually moving further away from the Sun. This explains the tendency to reply to the previous question incorrectly.

If you were to repeat your observation the next day you would note that the Moon has moved further in relation to the background of fixed stars by about 12° to 15°. Clearly the moon has also moved away as much as this from the Sun. What you are also able to see is that the Moon is closer to Jupiter by that same arc of 12° to 15° than it was previously.

YOUR PERSONAL CONCLUSION

What might your conclusion be? It could only be the following: Yes, you have found it yourself. That is the main thing. The houses, because of diurnal movement, rotate in the opposite direction to that of the advancement of the planets through the signs, the latter being in the same direction as that of the succession of the zodiac signs.

A scientific mind sometimes takes heed of the imagination as well as taking note of what the eyes behold. In this present example we find an explanation which encompasses all that we are able to conclude while appearing to deny it all at the same time.

THE OBSERVATION OF DIURNAL MOVEMENT

Diurnal movement takes place in the opposite direction to that of the planets' journey across the ecliptic. The implications of this are enormous for an astrologer, especially when he attacks the problem of the houses with all the seriousness that such an undertaking deserves. Let us consider, first of all, the path of the Sun, since we are used to its daily journey, although it is the same for the planetary bodies and the Moon.

> First house: The Sun rises in the east, bringing with it light, heat and life. You call it the twelfth house. For us it is the first house. The Sun remains here for roughly two hours.
>
> Second house: According to chronological order, this is the second. The Sun climbs in the southeast. You say it is in the eleventh house. We consider it to be in the second house.
>
> Third house: The Sun terminates the last third of its course climbing toward the meridian. You say it is in the tenth house. We continue to follow the chronological journey which is unfolding before our eyes. It is in the third house and reaches the MC at real noon.
>
> Fourth house: The Sun begins its descent toward the south-southwest. You say it is in the ninth house. For us it is in the fourth house.
>
> Fifth house: The Sun continues its descent in the middle of the afternoon toward the southwest. You say it is in the eighth house. Mid-afternoon. We see it in the fifth section counted from the first house (Ascendant=start of the first house).
>
> Sixth house: Then the Sun reaches the western horizon at the end of the afternoon. You say it is in the seventh house. We say that it is in the sixth.
>
> Seventh house: The Sun begins its descent below the horizon. You say it is in the sixth house. For us it is in the first of the nocturnal houses in the seventh house.
>
> Eighth house: The Sun pursues its descent below the horizon to the northwest. You say it is in the fifth house. For us it is in the eighth house.
>
> Ninth house: The Sun reaches the Imum Coeli at real Midnight. You say it is in the fourth house. For us it is in the ninth house.

Tenth house: From the Lower Meridian the Sun begins its journey upward below the horizon. You say it is in the third house, we say it is in the tenth house.

Eleventh house: The Sun climbs upward to find itself at the northeast. You say it is in the second house. For us, it is in the eleventh house.

Twelfth house: The Sun terminates its journey below the horizon and at the end of its course comes to merge once again with the Ascendant. When the Sun is in the twelfth house, it is the last part of the night. You say it is in the first house. We have followed the chronological order. For us it has terminated the last twelvefold division. Logically, therefore, it is in the twelfth and last house.

THE HOUSES AND SIGNS ROTATE IN CONTRARY DIRECTIONS

If we use the order explained beforehand on our celestial chart, it is clear that we give the houses an order of progression totally opposite to that of the succession of the signs.

When it comes to interpretation, the most important thing as far as the houses are concerned is the significance we attach to each one rather than the name we give it. Rather than calling them the house of the subject, the house of material gains, the house of short trips, and so on, we prefer to refer to each one with the aid of a number from I to XII, or one to twelve. We could just as easily give them the first twelve letters of the alphabet. But why not just call them by the numbers which have always been used?

We can even say it does not really matter if we place them in a clockwise or a counterclockwise direction—yes, it is true. The most important thing is that we draw them on our blank chart so that they travel in the opposite direction to that of the twelve signs of the zodiac.

It is, moreover, the diurnal movement which is at the basis of the Primary Directions. According to Primary Directions, each planet is directed or steered by the rotation of the Earth as it turns on its own axis. Things are greatly simplified by the clockwise house system if we really think about it. Authors have put forward elaborate philosophical theories to try and explain the contrary nature of Primary Directions. Here we see it is simply a question of the application of logic in consideration of the one or the other direction of rotation.

Further, there have been other authors who have thought of these two opposite, complementary directions. The Greek commentators of Ptolemy's *Tetrabiblos* tell us that the order "Aries to Pisces" is that of the signs following each other in a direct sense. From "Pisces to Aries" on the other hand is in the reverse sense.

The astrologer Don Néroman in *Planets and Signs*[1] speaks of material evolution in the direction of Aries, Taurus, Gemini, Cancer, and so on, and spiritual evolution in the direction Aries, Pisces, Aquarius, Capricorn, and so on. The planets act physically in the first direction. We know that Aries is the symbol of life, Taurus of nourishment, Gemini of infancy, Cancer of conception, Leo being the child that Virgo carries on her hip, and so on.

Above all, the houses reveal events. They clarify the domains of life in which the planetary influences are manifested. In this way the experiences that we live through invite us toward spiritual evolution.

When Don Néroman elaborates upon his theory of spiritual evolution we can well understand why he has the natal MC move in the opposite direction to that of the Planets in the signs of the zodiac.

THE ANCIENTS REFERRED TO NATURAL ORDER

Through reading these authors attentively, we are shown that they considered the houses according to their natural unfolding, that is to say what you call the twelfth, eleventh, tenth and so on.

Let us look at it this way. Manilius left us one of the oldest known documents on the subject of astrology. It is called *Astronomica*. It was written in about 10 A.D. It is therefore older by one and a half centuries than the *Tetrabiblos* of Ptolemy. Manilius tells us:

---

1   Néroman. *Traite d'astrologie rationnelle* (1943), his best-known book.

INTERVALS BETWEEN THE ANGLES RULE THE VARIOUS PARTS OF LIFE	
Between the Ascendant and Midheaven	The first years
Between the Midheaven and the Descendant	The years of youth
Between the Descendant and the Imum Coeli	Maturity
Between the Imum Coeli and the Ascendant	Old age

Concerning the house that astrologers normally call the tenth house, he goes on to say, "At the highest point of the heavens, this place where the stars cease to climb and begin to descend, is the house that is equidistant from the place of rising and setting."

You can clearly see that the house that occupies the highest point of the heavens certainly is not the tenth portion of the ecliptic, which starts from the MC toward the Ascendant, and that you call the tenth house if you count them from the Ascendant in the same direction as the signs. This house really starts from the Midheaven to travel toward the Descendant.

Let us look at what the astrologers call the "Ascendant." Manilius expresses himself in this way: "Whence the stars are reborn, as they begin again to travel their customary path, whence the Sun rises from the bosom of the ocean, its feeble rays strengthening by degrees, transformed into warmth and golden light."

The first house is well established by these first degrees that the Sun crosses on rising toward the MC, given that they are "transformed into warmth and golden light." What you call the twelfth house is, as a result of this, really the first house.

Incontestably, Manilius takes note of the direction of diurnal movement in his observations.

Alan Leo[2] tells us:

When the Sun rises it is carried by the revolution of the Earth through the twelfth and eleventh houses to the cusp of the tenth, or Midheaven, traversing three houses from sunrise to noon.

Literally, the Ascendant is the rising point.

---

2   Leo. *Mars, the War Lord*, p. 36.

In our astrological jargon, we often confuse the Ascendant as a point of the ecliptic (intersected by the plane of the horizon) with some 30°, which go to make up an entire house. We are very tempted to believe that this first house which rises is in fact the first of the twelve. I tell you in our system "it is precisely that."

If, by extension of the term, you give to the word *Ascendant* the meaning "first house," this is exactly what happens when you say there is such and such a planet in the Ascendant. One could think that this planet is above the horizon, but what is meant is that it is still in what you call the first house; that is, it is still below the horizon.

To summarize, the overall description, according to these texts, is as follows: The Sun, Moon, planets and stars are included in the same description. They rise (Ascendant), culminate (Midheaven) and set (Descendant). Nothing could better depict that their journey, owing to diurnal movement, is in the opposite direction to the course of the signs of the zodiac.

The Hindus counted the houses in the desired direction and may still continue to do so. However, they have also inverted the direction of the course of the twelve signs. In my opinion, by so doing, they have made the mistake of causing the houses to rotate in the same direction as the signs. Moreover, in this part of the world, the Northern Hemisphere, the signs of the zodiac do in fact turn in a counterclockwise direction. They arrive, therefore, at the same erroneous result: houses and signs rotating in the same direction. In a Hindu astrology manual, widely distributed in the West, the author of the manual happened to make a parallel between the four Cardinal Points and the angles of the horoscope and gave MC as being the north. I pointed out this error to him, making it clear that in the Northern Hemisphere whether one practices Western tropical, sidereal, or Hindu astrology, the MC can point only to the south. I wonder if this error was not generated by the fact that at some earlier stage in time the Hindus decided to invert the order of the houses, thereby causing them to move in the same direction as the signs. Whatever the case may have been, given that according to their present schema the houses follow one another in accordance with the diurnal movement, they turn in the same direction that we advocate. Nonetheless we cannot insist strongly enough that the signs and houses must turn in opposite directions to each other if we wish to remain faithful to cosmography.

For a long time now I have been placing the abbreviation *Asc* next to the point of the Ascendant, but I have always been careful to place them next to the right wing of the arrow which, on my celestial charts, marks the Ascendant. An acutely observant person could have noticed this strange little habit whose only purpose, as far as I am concerned, is to make it very clear that the first house, synonymous with the Ascendant, is above the eastern horizon.

PLANETS IN STRONG LATITUDE

A planet with a marked northerly latitude and close to the Ascendant, appearing beneath the horizon in the horoscope because it has been placed according to its longitude at the commencement of what you call the first house (counting in a counterclockwise direction), may be actually above the horizon, if it has just risen.

This is also a valid consideration for other houses in certain methods of domification. A planet near to a cusp and which we believe to be in one house could be actually in the neighboring house owing to its celestial latitude. It should be pointed out that this sort of difficulty will arise in the case of nearly every house method which rests on the division of space, of which those of Campanus and Regiomontanus are the best known. However, Morin de Villefranche's method escapes this difficulty, owing to the fact that for the great Morin the Ascendant does not indicate the beginning of the first house. Nevertheless, his method does not attract us despite the patronage accorded to him by Cardinal Richelieu himself.

THE DIFFERENT METHODS OF DOMIFICATIONS

As for those methods of domification based on the division of time, we prefer to reject them as a matter of principle, the most well known being that of Placidus.

We consider astrology, on the whole, to be dynamic. However, since a celestial chart is a representation of the celestial state at a precise moment, seen from a given point, it is in fact essentially static.

For this reason astrologers must admit that according to various methods of domification, the cusps of the succedent and cadent houses are determined according to factors which are posterior to the time of birth, since, in order to arrive at the cusps of the intermediate houses, the time it took for the Ascendant to reach the MC has been calculated and divided into three parts. This means that if a celestial chart is established for the nativity of a child born alive and who dies two hours later, the chart will be arrived at by using factors which took place well after death. We find that illogical. However, it must be recognized that the great majority of practitioners are quite unaware of this anomaly.

Without spending too much time on the question of domification—the different methods of calculating the houses—let us say a few introductory words on the subject. Authors agree among themselves on the two principal planes, the horizon and the meridian, that mark out the Ascendant and MC, which play the main role in many of the different domification procedures. However, we know that this is not so in the case of the intermediate houses. (It was mentioned in the preceding chapter why the Placidian method of domification was the one most widely used.)

Campanus was an Italian astronomer, geometrician and mathematician of the thirteenth century. His methods were the subject of renewed interest at the outbreak of World War II. Indeed, from the end of the forties onward, there was (particularly in the United States) an efflorescence of astrologers who possessed a profound knowledge of astronomy, owing to the fact that many students had to rapidly become naval officers where they were on active wartime duty. They found Campanus's method to be more scientific, being more in keeping with the local division of the celestial sphere.

Regiomontanus was a German astronomer and mathematician of the fifteenth century who, it is worth noting, translated Ptolemy. He perfected a method of domification which is considered by many to be close to that of Campanus—so much so that the two methods are often confused with one another. In fact they are very different because only Campanus determines the points of the houses 11, 12, 2, and 3 through truly local factors, owing to the fact that he does this by dividing the prime vertical into three equal portions. The prime vertical is the large circle of the celestial sphere which passes through the zenith and is at the same time perpendicular to the circle of the meridian and to the horizon.

Placidus was an Italian monk who came to the fore only in the seventeenth century. His method of domification was widely propagated, as already explained. It can be added that for purely mathematical reasons his method was more easily presented in the form of tables than the other methods known until then. There lies the error: To suppose that Placidus's house system was nearer to the truth than that of his illustrious predecessors simply because he was closer to our era. In fact, instead of perfecting the system of domification, he further deformed astrologers' charts. Why was this? More than likely it was because he was unable to draw any great satisfaction from the interpretation of the Horoscope using the methods of his predecessors. Once again why was this? Well, in this matter we agree with the astrologer P. E. A. Gillert. Moreover, we are inclined to think that the problem was caused by the time lag caused by the phenomenon of the precession of the equinoxes, which grew with the centuries. Be that as it may, in our opinion the remedy which Placidus proposed did more harm than good.

To summarize, some eminent astrologers wanted to correct the faults which had come to their attention. New systems multiplied... Some rare astrologers denounced these mistakes but they were not heeded. In this way, numerous house systems arose which served to alienate us further from a tradition that was ready and willing to reveal all its marvels to us.

CHAPTER 3

HISTORY

What history? The story of the twelve houses? There is none; well, I guess there was one, but it remains unknown to us. The houses themselves and their utilisation constitute one of the most important branches of astrology. In any case, as things stand presently, we are unable to quote authentic writings dating from two thousand years ago. For each affirmation on the part of one there exists a denial on the part of another, often without sufficient proof. Over the last forty years, Europeans, particularly the French, have really let fly on the subject. All this fervor has resulted in very serious quarrels during which they have torn strips off one another to the extent that it really has overstepped the limits of decency.

Some time ago, in Toronto, Canada, during 1976, there was a seminar whose sole subject was the question of the division of the houses. This same seminar was attended by the most illustrious figures of the astrological world. It almost ended in fisticuffs. There was total discord, not really because of the facts but mainly because of the lack of any real proof. This is the point which interests us the most. Facts for us are convincing from the moment they can be backed by experience. We remain steadfast in the belief that there is an equal number of houses and signs, that there is an analogy between these two kinds of division, and that they rotate in opposite directions to each other. The origin of the houses is not exactly precise. The ancients had divided the heavens into four quadrants whose boundaries were dependent on the horizon and the meridian. This was the spring board off which a number of modern authors jumped into the idea of twelve houses, which were, in fact, a product of their imagination. Although they quoted the quadrants as being their source of inspiration, they were not able to quote authentic, reliable sources for the houses. If we stick to the facts, during the course of time the quadrants were divided into two, just like a compass card, which in turn gave us a division into eight. As we shall see for ourselves later on, these divisions into four were counted according to the astrologers' observations, according to diurnal movement—in other words, in the direction opposite to that of the signs. Later, to strengthen the idea of an analogy between the houses and the signs, a further four houses were added to make them equal in number. It would seem that this desire to bring the two elements closer together eventually led to their being considered as rotating in the same direction.

Confusion over Vocabulary

One cause of confusion which led contemporary astrologers into believing that the ancients used the houses, let us say over two thousand years ago, arises from vocabulary. The ancients' writings were often mistranslated, so that we encounter such expressions as "the house of Jupiter." Here the word *house* really means "sign," or more precisely, "the sign of Jupiter's domicile." It is the same in French, in which the word *maison* should, according to the context, be translated as "sign," not "house."

Ptolemy tells us in *Tetrabiblos* I:18:[1]

> Of the triangles…the first of these, which passes through Aries, Leo and Sagittarius, is composed of three masculine signs and includes the houses of the Sun, of Mars, and of Jupiter.

It is in this way that a great many authors noticed that the judgments they were able to draw from the houses did not always comply with the facts observed in the destiny of the subject. A number of authors suggested that the house be made to begin 5° before its starting point, counting as only part of the house the 25° that followed its cusp. Others suggested that the cusp be considered not as the beginning point but as the center of the

1   Ptolemy. *Tetrabiblos*, p. 83.

house (despite the fact that from the etymological point of view cusp quite clearly means tip). You will notice in all those cases that the authors clearly perceived that the planet expressed itself effectively within the significance of the house in question, only if it was considered as developing in the other direction. This endless discussion over the fixing of a house's starting point can be likened in complexity only to the difficulties encountered when trying to set precise and certain boundaries in the ecliptic sectors having a bearing on the father and mother respectively. A solution to the latter problem will be given in due course.

In the French astrologer's journal *Les cahiers astrologiques* of 1971 (pp. 25–29), one can read an article on the "System of Equal Houses" by Aldo Lavignani, translated under the name of Gemini. We know the aforementioned person very well, having spent time in his company during the early sixties up until his departure from the French Riviera for England.

He left because England offered him greater possibilities to practice his Roulette method, due to the fact that he took personal factors into account which moved at a rate of four minutes every twenty-four hours. In England, he was able to frequent the casinos twenty-four hours a day nonstop.

WHERE DOES THE HOUSE BEGIN?

For the moment we are not dealing with domification systems. Here are a few extracts which serve to illustrate the disarray into which astrologers have plunged, especially in the case of new students or beginners. As far as the correct starting point goes, Lavignani says,

> The divisions are envisaged from another angle—the dividing line or limit between two adjacent houses for Western astrologers represents for their Eastern counterparts the middle of the following house which begins, consequently, with the second half of the preceding house. This is confirmed by experience. At least a third and probably the entire second half of the twelfth house really belong to the first house. Astrologers have insisted on this but not with the clarity desired of them. This means that most students

and practitioners are still led astray by the material divisions of the houses such as we find in the tables.

Thus, the only rational conception of domification consists in seeing the cusp not as a demarcation line but rather as the active center and the area of maximum influence within the house. This cusp belongs completely to the house in question, in that the house spreads out in one way or another from the cusp.

Certain astrologers take into consideration a "no-man's land" section within each house preceding the cusp; this would seem to corroborate the above conception.

M. F. Xavier Kieffer's[2] insistence on the subject of showing the cusp to be at the middle of the house comes back to the idea which we have just expressed. We could call your attention to a great many similar quotations at the risk, however, of contributing very little to the reader. What we really wish to impress on the reader's mind is the following conclusion, that the cusps are the boundaries, which both start and finish the house. This house reveals to us what we expect of it if it is included with its eleven sisters, in a rotation which moves in liaison with diurnal movement. Then, and only then, does all become orderly once more.

As far as we are concerned, all the rest is a matter of idle discussion. All the names and quotations which I could present would do more harm than good to the cause of astrology. We shall therefore limit ourselves to presenting another precise case which better illustrates our opinion since it is a question of a forgery—perhaps an unconscious one—in "quoting" from Ptolemy. In any case we are not going to quote one authority to uphold our thesis. The only judge on the subject should be the reader himself, who can conduct a series of personal experiments once he has put our theory into practice.

A FORGED QUOTATION

In the astrological publication *Les cahiers astrologiques* (Nov. 1947), there is an article by J. Hieroz. In reading page *329*, one might believe that Ptolemy used—as many have said—twelve astrological houses.

---

2   Kieffer. "Truth on Domification" (*Les cahiers astrologiques*).

Nothing could be further from the truth. Here with the relevant text by Ptolemy, quoted from chapter 10 of book 3 of the *Tetrabiblos*. Ptolemy was an advocate of the general significators and did not pay much attention to the houses. Apart from a few rather contestable attributions such as the tenth to the mother and children, the fifth to sicknesses, it is only in his third book where he goes into the question of *"hyleg"* places, that we find a few lines devoted to the houses. Hieroz attributes the following to Ptolemy:

> These different places are the sign situated on the angle of the Ascendant from 5° above the horizon to 25° below, the 30° in the right sextile which constitutes the eleventh house named Good Daemon; also the 30° in square dexter which form Midheaven; that part in trine dexter which makes up the ninth house called God; and lastly those opposite which form the angle of the Occident. (See below for an accurate translation into English of this passage from *Tetrabilbos* III.10 by F. E. Robbins.)

Here the author lets us suppose that Ptolemy used the houses, since he refers to the eleventh and the ninth. I declare with all my remaining force without any fear of being contradicted, that nothing could be further from the truth. Ptolemy did not write that. The phrases "that constitute the eleventh," and "that make up the ninth" are pure fabrication. As both of them are followed by the word *house,* the reader naturally assumes that it is a question of the eleventh house on the one hand and of the ninth house on the other. I do not accuse Hieroz of deliberately misleading the reader. This I have not said at all. I simply want to provide proof that one can be led astray.

On the lower portion of the relevant pages from the *Tetrabiblos* (pp. 272–273), we find a note (no. 2). This is not Ptolemy's note but that of F. E. Robbins as a modern commentator. Here we find mention of the twelve houses. These few lines point out the extent to which the houses are used in present-day calculations of nativities. This confirms our way of thinking and should further provide warning of the need to be doubly cautious when using ancient texts. Unwary readers would very quickly jump to the conclusion that Ptolemy already used the twelve houses.

Note by Robert Powell

Herewith the translation of the relevant passage from *Tetrabiblos* III.10 by F. E. Robbins,[3] where Robbins uses the word *horoscope* for the Ascendant:

> The twelfth part of the zodiac surrounding the horoscope, from 5° above the actual horizon up to the 25° that remains, which is rising in succession to the horoscope; the part sextile dexter to these 30°, called the house of the Good Daemon; the part in quartile, the midheaven; the part in trine, called the house of God; and the part opposite, the Occident (Descendant).

The entire passage by Ptolemy is dedicated to determining astrologically the length of life by way of the *hyleg*, or "prorogator of life," which is a highly complex astrological doctrine. Note that Magini (1555–1617), professor of mathematics at the University of Bologna, originated the house system that was later attributed to Placidus. Magini believed that he had found the house system intended by Ptolemy.

---

3   Ptolemy. *Tetrabiblos*, p. 273.

CHAPTER 4

THE FOUR QUADRANTS

We are well aware of the fact that the first division of the celestial sphere is established on the basis of the horizon and the meridian, to which it is more or less perpendicular. Both the horizon and the meridian are great circles. The eastern horizon denotes the Ascendant, the Upper Meridian is the Midheaven (MC). The western horizon is the Descendant and the Lower Meridian constitutes what we call the Imum Coeli (IC).

Well before psychoanalysis seized astrology (or perhaps it was the opposite), Alan Leo had in 1905 already drawn the following conclusions on the subject of the first division, as this quotation from chapter 15 of his *Progressed Horoscope*, illustrates:

> The lower part of the horoscope mainly concerns the personality—the aspect according to which a person (persona, mask) esteems or judges himself; whereas the upper portion relates rather to individuality, the human being, in terms of unity and outward identity.[1]

Before going any further, I would like to draw your attention to the following. The Midheaven corresponds exactly to what you have found in your tables of houses, because the straight line descends from the MC, goes through the observer's feet (or those of the native) to the center of the Earth and to the IC. This is not the case insofar as the longitude of the Ascendant goes. This is because the tables of houses are calculated from the center of the Earth and, all too often, we tend to confuse these two straight parallels, one being the horizon, the other the Ascendant, which

---

1   Leo. *The Progressed Horoscope*, p. 276.

passes through the center of the Earth. Whereas, so far as I know, you were not born in the center of the Earth, it is not a mistake to consider that the real Ascendant's longitude is slightly less than the one that appears in our tables, and that the Descendant's longitude is in fact greater than we generally presume. This is caused by the phenomenon of parallax[2] or, if you prefer, the thickness of one-half of the terrestrial sphere. This has no bearing on the faraway planets, which will always be considered in the light of the longitude found. However, for a celestial body as near as the Moon, it could raise difficulties, especially for those practitioners who are smitten by precise calculations, and even more so for those who believe they can obtain a correct rectification of the hour of birth based on the angles, notably the Ascendant. Actually, this would have a significant bearing only if the Moon were very close to the line of the horizon or, more precisely, if it occupied the first, sixth, seventh, or twelfth house.

The four angles of the horoscope are, therefore, of paramount importance to our celestial chart. Inasmuch as their role is not only to delineate the four quadrants (which we are now going to examine closely), but also to mark the commencement of the cardinal houses, which we shall consider later while examining the twelve houses.

Let us note that the word *cardinal* comes from *cardo, cardinis,* Latin for "hinge." This clearly demonstrates that everything hinges directly on these four points, the two main points being the Ascendant, which stands for the subject, or personality, and the Midheaven, which provides an insight into one's destiny. The most important quadrant, therefore, is quite naturally marked out by the two points which we have just singled out as being primordial, that is, the Ascendant and the MC. It is this very quadrant (which starts with the Ascendant and rises up to the MC) that is the chief element insofar as interpretation is concerned. Marcus Manilius's, in his five books of *The Astronomicon* (written one-and-a-half centuries before Claudius Ptolemy's *Tetrabiblos*), states clearly that the "four great spaces" of the heavens follow the same that we advocate—that is, in the direction opposite to that of the twelve signs of the zodiac. This is in direct agreement with what we have already seen in the chapter dealing with

2   See Bradley, *The Parallax Problem in Astrology.*

cosmography. In the extract that follows, he takes up the question, and again you will see for yourself that he follows the quadrants in the same order that we recommend. He also develops the resulting interpretation.

> The curve that stretches from the orient to the topmost point of the circle claims the earliest age and infant years. The slope that sinks down from the summit of the sky till it reaches the occident succeeds to the years of childhood and includes in its province control of tender youth. The portion that appropriates the setting heaven and descends to the bottom of the circle rules the period of adult life, a period tested by incessant change and checkered fortunes. But the part by whose return to the orient heaven's course is done and that with enfeebled strength slowly ascends the back-bent arc, this part embraces the final years, life's fading twilight, and palsied age.[3]

We realize from this that the ancients enumerated the four quadrants according to their observation—in the direction of diurnal movement: Ascendant, MC, Descendant, IC, and back to the Ascendant. The Sun rises, passes through the meridian, descends and sets. Why, for goodness sake, do we modern astrologers reverse the order of rotation in dividing each Quadrant into three to obtain the twelve houses? Since the houses succeed one another more rapidly than do the planets in their journey through the signs, we could possibly compare the small hand of a watch with the Sun's movement through the twelve signs, and the rapidly moving larger minute hand with the pace of the Ascendant in its journey through the signs. If we cause the twelve houses to adopt the same order and direction as that of the signs under the pretext that the big hand of the watch follows the same direction as that of the small hand, then so be it. However, I think this argument somehow lacks substance.

THE POLARITY OF THE QUADRANTS

On page 71 of Ptolomey's *Tetrabiblos* (in the edition quoted), after explaining that six of the zodiacal signs are masculine and that the other six are

---

3   Manilius. *Astronomica*, 2. 844–855, p. 149.

feminine, Ptolomey also gives the quadrants a masculine–feminine polarity. He goes on to say,

> …designating as matutinal and masculine signs those of the quadrant from the horoscope to the midheaven and those of the opposite quadrant from the occident to the lower midheaven, and as evening and feminine the other two quadrants.

If I may be so bold, this indicates that even Ptolemy, in his description of the first quadrant, gives the same direction of rotation as that upon which we so heavily insist.

We know that the odd zodiacal signs—that is, those of *fire* and *air*— are said to be positive and masculine, whereas the even signs of *earth* and *water* are negative and feminine. It is clear that, if we pass from the tropical zodiac to the sidereal zodiac with a lag of roughly 25° in the early part of the twenty-first century, the polarities are reversed in eighty-three percent of cases. This could place us in rather an awkward situation.

However, I point out to the practitioner that this difficulty does not arise in the polarities we attribute to the quadrants of the horoscope if we count them, beginning with the Ascendant, in the opposite direction to that of the signs as they succeed one another. In this way, the positive polarity is given to the first and third quadrants, while the negative polarity is attributed to the second and fourth ones. It would be in your interest to search among those horoscopes familiar to you to locate those that demonstrate the clear domination of a particular polarity. You will find them more easily if you are satisfied with only the seven classical planets. However, I shall provide examples in which I consider even the three invisible planets.

A positive quadrant emphasis will produce men and women of action, dynamic people who seek to assert themselves and who influence and dominate their peers. In the outside world, they manifest a centrifugal force, which proceeds outward from the center. They react strongly to events; they strive to control their destiny and even that of others.

A dominant negative quadrant expresses a centripetal force, which gives rise to introspective beings who look inward. They are receptive, register impressions, and have a rich inner life. They will submit to their destiny and allow themselves to be influenced by those around them and by events. As is generally the case in such categories, the archetype does not actually exist in its pure form.

Presidents Richard Nixon, Valery Giscard d'Éstaing, and Ronald Reagan have, respectively, nine, eight, and seven of ten planets in the positive Quadrants. For a long time, Nixon was labelled a born loser until he received the supreme honor, the US presidency. Valery Giscard d'Éstaing was not reelected president in 1981, although after having digested his defeat, he went on to hold his own again in the struggle in the political arena. These individuals certainly offer proof of their ability to go beyond the realms of ordinary endeavor to assert themselves.

On the other hand, Carl G. Jung, Maître Philippe de Lyon, and Dr. John Adams (the latter having been accused of a number of murders through the administration of poison) have, respectively, seven, nine, and ten planets gathered in the negative Quadrants. Each, in his own unique field, seems to demonstrate quite satisfactorily what we expect of this anomaly in the distribution of the planets around the two main axes. The first of the three, through his theory on the collective unconscious; the second by his knowledge and mastery of the invisible realms. As for the third and last, through his very discretion he almost certainly did not seek in any way to bring notice to himself or to be conspicuous.

Earlier mention was made of the four major ages of life that have, moreover, been continually taken into account from antiquity to the present day. I wish to bring to your attention the fact that the MC is related to youth and that by adopting our direction of rotation the fourth house has its point of departure from the MC. By analogy, this house is connected to the fourth sign of Cancer, that of motherhood. We shall later look in detail at the subject of the boundaries which involve the sectors related to motherhood and fatherhood. Without further delay, let us add that the tenth house, which proceeds from the IC and provides information relevant to the end of life, represents according to the new law of analogy the tenth sign Capricorn whose ruler is Saturn, the patron of the elderly. All this goes to show to what extent a harmonious pattern can be obtained in the realm of interpretation, thanks to the consistent analogy that exists between the signs and the houses when the latter unfold according to the clockwise direction, which we are recommending.

A Rough Outline on Interpretation

When it comes to interpretation, this first division allows us to detect a rough first draft of a certain quality that is, almost always, confirmed by the facts. The eastern portion of the horoscope is focused on the subjective side of existence, and the Ascendant as the central point should be examined with great care according to the exact aspects that it receives. If the majority of the planets are eastern, those born here are often those who forge ahead but work mainly on their own behalf. This figure also usually announces a very full life.

The western portion of the celestial chart represents the objective side of human nature, expressed through contacts with others. If the majority of the planets are western, the person born here is often altruistic, insofar as comportment, actions, and gestures are concerned. Such individuals will easily consider the viewpoints of others and will often think of others and act on their behalf. (Moreover, we can consult Libra and Aquarius, as well as the seventh and eleventh houses, since these sections of the heavens inform us as to the quality of the relations that the subject maintains within his family group and his professional environment.)

If the majority of the planets are found above the horizon, then we are usually dealing with an extrovert. The planets then strongly manifest outwardly. Occidental practitioners are generally of the opinion that planets above the horizon act more forcefully. Without a doubt, this is valid for Mars and the Sun. However, this theory will most certainly be questioned by anyone who has studied and put to the test the *Graha Bala* (force of the planets) technique, in accordance with Hindu astrological theories. This says that Mercury and Jupiter gain more force toward the Ascendant, and Saturn near the Descendant, while the Moon and Venus acquire greater strength when they are in a position near the Imum Coeli. If the majority of the planets are above the horizon, this indicates many activities in the outside world, positive realizations, and a life full of experiences. If, by contrast, the majority of the planets are found below the horizon, the subject is generally an introvert. Such individuals tend toward reflection and meditation. Their experiences are more on a soul level, and they enjoy a rich inner life. The opportunities for achievement on the material level will be less, and they must rely on sustained activity for success. Such a makeup does not necessarily rule out long-term success, but it will come more slowly and as the result of persistent personal effort.

ROYAL YOGA

In Hindu astrology, the Raja Yoga, or Royal Yoga, is taken into account. There is Royal Yoga only in certain cases and under very precise conditions. We say that the Royal Yoga reveals a horoscope that is out of the ordinary. Among the rules that define the Royal Yoga, one is determined by the Ascendant and, at the same time, by a mutual aspect that must have two planets between them for that Ascendant.

Editor: Jacques Dorsan based his examples on Professor B. V. Raman's book[4] and arrived at a complicated solution. After wrestling with his system, I almost abandoned this section from the English version, until I consulted a more contemporary book on Vedic astrology.[5] Ronnie Gale Dreyer explains that "Raj yogas are specific planetary combinations promising prosperity, success, and generally fortuitous circumstances" (page 176). After discussing a number of different yogas, Dreyer states:

> One of the most potent yet simplest Raj yogas to compute is the association of the fifth and ninth house rulers by conjunction, mutual aspect or mutual reception. Because this particular combination also constitutes a *Dhana*, or wealth-producing yoga, it will produce financial as well as professional success. (p. 178)

---

4   Raman. *Hindu Predictive Astrology*, chapter 17.

5   Dreyer. *Vedic Astrology: A Guide to the Fundamentals of Jyotish*, p. 178.

First, I have to say that Vedic astrology uses an equal-house system. Second, it makes no difference whether you use the traditional house direction or the clockwise houses, because the fifth and ninth house cusps simply trade places. Third, it is much simpler to understand Royal Yoga if we stick to the traditional planetary rulers of the sidereal zodiac signs, which are in grand trine to the sign on the Ascendant. The Western sidereal zodiac and the Hindu zodiac differ by less than 1°, so there will be some doubt in only a few cases. The following table should make it clear.

Ascendant	Sign in Trine and Planetary Ruler	Sign in Trine and Planetary Ruler
Aries	Leo – Sun	Sagittarius – Jupiter
Taurus	Virgo – Mercury	Capricorn – Saturn
Gemini	Libra – Venus	Aquarius – Saturn
Cancer	Scorpio – Mars	Pisces – Jupiter
Leo	Sagittarius – Jupiter	Aries – Mars
Virgo	Capricorn – Saturn	Gemini – Mercury
Libra	Aquarius – Saturn	Gemini – Mercury
Scorpio	Pisces – Jupiter	Cancer – Moon
Sagittarius	Aries – Mars	Leo – Sun
Capricorn	Taurus – Venus	Virgo – Mercury
Aquarius	Gemini – Mercury	Libra – Venus
Pisces	Cancer – Moon	Scorpio – Mars

For example, if the Ascendant is Aries, for a Royal Yoga look for an aspect like a conjunction between the Sun and Jupiter. I will give some examples as we look at individual horoscopes in chapter 10.

CHAPTER 5

OCTUPLE DIVISION

HERMES TRISMEGISTUS, THE GREEKS, AND THE CHINESE

Greek philosophy was dominated by the axiom of Hermes Trismegistus: "That which is above is as that which is below, and that which is below is as that which is above, for the fulfilment of the miracle of the one thing."[1]

Eight is synonymous with entirety, finality, and death, as we shall soon see. The division of each quadrant into two equal parts led the ancients to an eightfold division of the celestial. Greek literature of the first and second centuries BCE includes illustrations that show the celestial sphere divided into eight equal parts. This implies something identical for human events, corresponding to the celestial phenomena. The division of space into eight parts reminds us of the compass points. Certain authors have erroneously interpreted the ancients by affirming that the twelve houses were already used in antiquity. However, we lack documents that irrefutably demonstrate this. Some have confused the eight semi-quadrants with the eight succedent and cadent houses. If we add the four quadrants to the latter eight we obtain the number twelve, but certainly not through a duodecimal division of the ecliptic. The Chinese also divided the heavens into eight segments, and these are found in the form of the eight trigrams of the I Ching.

These eightfold divisions are found again with the Feast of Tet, which marks the first day of the New Year according to the Chinese calendar. It is in fact the day of the New Moon closest to midwinter or, if you prefer, to

---

1   *Tabula smaragdina*, 2 ("The Emerald Table of Hermes Trismegistus"), pp. 41–57, especially p. 42.

the mid-point of the tropical zodiac sign of Aquarius. Let us say that *eight* is associated with the idea of final accomplishment. According to certain sources, this is the source of the octagonal shape of many baptismal fonts. According to ancient tradition, *eight* symbolizes the course of death and rebirth into a new spiritual life. *Eight* thus represents the end of an evolution, and *nine* brings the idea of renewal. In the relationship between planets and numbers in India, the number *eight* is regularly attributed to the planet Saturn, implying the idea of finality, old age, and death. It is almost superfluous to add that Saturn's day is Saturday, the Sabbath, the last day of the week.

In many languages (French for instance), *nine* (*neuf*) is synonymous with *new* (*neuf*). As a point of interest, the English *nine* is from the Old English *nigon*, from the Old Norse *niu* cognate with the Latin *novem*.

In his book *L'esoterisme de l'astrologie*, Volguine[2] called the attention of those engaged in research to the importance of the eightfold division of the zodiac. Interested readers could, therefore, refer to this work.

In an article entitled "Les huit sentiers de l'idéal inscrits dans le zodiaque,"[3] Genevieve Creusat treats these eight sections, relating them to the eight trigrams of the I Ching. Note that this octuple division of the zodiac begins at the first degree of Cancer. In this brief summary, the eight trigrams are given with the names attributed to them by Creisat.

The trigram of Ch'ien	The Key of Love	0° Cancer
The trigram Sun	Pardon	15° Leo
The trigram K'an	Union	0° Libra
The trigram Ken	Truth	15° Scorpio
The trigram K'un	Faith	0° Capricorn
The trigram Ch'en	Hope	15° Aquarius
The trigram Li	Light	0° Aries
The trigram Tui	Joy	15° Taurus

We shall not go any further into the interpretation of these octuple divisions, as we have found so many contradictions herein that a more

2   Volguine. *L'esoterisme de l'astrologie.*

3   Creusat. *Les cahiers astrologiques* (March 1958).

extensive study is pointless and of interest only to certain specialists, who are very welcome to consult the works quoted here. However, as for those authors whose starting point for this octuple division of the zodiac is from the first degree of Aries, their interpretation is ill-fated, since the eighth trigram will go from the fifteenth degree of Aquarius to the end of Pisces and, for that very reason, evokes "the Hell of the Horoscope" instead of joy.

We must insist on the fact that it is a matter of the divisions of the zodiac. It will be noticed that the two divisions to which we have just referred go in the direction of the zodiac; this is quite normal, as they represent only a small portion thereof. We shall, above all, retain the fact that the eighth is the last division, and that the number *eight* represents death because of Saturn.

Therefore, when we add four more divisions to the first eight (making twelve in all to obtain a number equal to that of the signs of the zodiac), we cannot help but notice that the eighth of the twelve houses retains this idea of death that is attributed, on the one hand, to Saturn, ruler of the eighth and final octuple division beginning at 15° from Aquarius, and on the other hand to the sign of Scorpio, eighth sign of the zodiac, which represents death. Rather curiously, now that we use the twelve houses, although the cusp of the seventh is called the Point of Death, since it is in opposition to the Ascendant, and that the twelfth seems to justify its inauspicious character, the eighth of the twelve has conserved this deadly character, as can be verified in practice.

THE HOURLY WATCHES

In dividing the zodiac into eight sections of 45° each, commencing at sunrise, a planet can be attributed to each three-hour period, according to the sequence of the planets, following the days of the week. Each day begins and ends with the planet of the day: Sun (Sunday, *Dimanche*); Moon (Monday, *Lundi*); Mars (Tuesday, *Mardi*); Mercury (Wednesday, *Mercredi*); Jupiter (Thursday, *Jeudi*); Venus (Friday, *Vendredi*); and Saturn (Saturday, *Samedi*). The days of the week in English often correspond to a Roman or Norse god who manifests a planet. This division of time is what the ancients referred to as the "watches." They are mentioned in the Bible, notably in Matthew 14:25: "And in the fourth watch of the night, Jesus came to them, walking on the water."

Your attention is drawn to the fact that two-hour watches exist, each corresponding to one house in the system of the twelve houses. However, we have been alluding to the three-hour watches in the preceding pages.

While taking into account the hour and the day of the week, the following table will allow the reader to work out quickly the planets that rule these three-hour watches. Of course, as we can clearly see, the hours placed in the first column are only approximate points of reference. The hour of sunrise depends on a number of factors, most notably the geographical latitude, the time of the year, and the official times designated as so-called daylight saving time or standard time. Scientific practitioners will operate as follows. Take the lengths of the day and night into account and give the rulership of the fifth watch from sunrise (that is, what is for us the first night watch) only from the moment the Sun sets, and this for a period of time not equal exactly to three hours, but rather to the quarter of the exact length of time of the night. Of course, you will have operated in such a way as to attribute to each day watch a period of time equal to one-sixth the length of the actual day.

TABLE OF THE HOURLY WATCHES

Hours	Sunday	Monday	Tuesday	Wednesday	Thursday	Friday	Saturday
6–9	Sun	Moon	Mars	Mercury	Jupiter	Venus	Saturn
9–12	Moon	Mars	Mercury	Jupiter	Venus	Saturn	Sun
12–15	Mars	Mercury	Jupiter	Venus	Saturn	Sun	Moon
15–18	Mercury	Jupiter	Venus	Saturn	Sun	Moon	Mars
18–21	Jupiter	Venus	Saturn	Sun	Moon	Mars	Mercury
21–24	Venus	Saturn	Sun	Moon	Mars	Mercury	Jupiter
0–3	Saturn	Sun	Moon	Mars	Mercury	Jupiter	Venus
3–6	Sun	Moon	Mars	Mercury	Jupiter	Venus	Saturn

CHAPTER 6

ANALOGY

The word *Analogy*, from the Greek *analogia*, means relationship. It rests on the establishment of a relationship between things that are essentially different from one another. The ancients raised this process of reasoning from parallel cases to the level of a science.

In this commentary on the magic of *Timaeus* by Plato, according to Helena P. Blavatsky, Proclus gives the following explanation:

> In the same manner as lovers gradually advance from that beauty, which is apparent in sensible forms, to that which is divine; so the ancient priests, when they considered that there is a certain alliance and sympathy in natural things to each other, and of things manifest to occult powers, and discovered that all things subsist in all, they fabricated a sacred science from this natural sympathy and similarity. Thus they recognized things supreme in such as are subordinate, and the subordinate in the supreme; in the celestial regions, terrene properties subsisting in a causal and celestial manner; and in earth celestial properties, but according to a terrene condition....
>
> Now the ancients, having contemplated this mutual sympathy of things (celestial and terrestrial) applied them for occult purposes, both celestial and terrene natures, by means of which, through a certain similitude, they deduced divine virtues into this inferior abode.[1]

Evidently, Proclus does not advocate simple superstition, but a science.

---

1   Blavatsky. *Isis Unveiled*, vol. 1 (Science), pp. 243–4.

Analogy is of very great interest to astrologers. In the path of the ancients, we use it to translate the symbols of the signs and planets. Thus Libra, by means of its two scales, represents equilibrium, hesitation, correlation, relationships with society, and, by extension, associations, agreements, contracts, marriage, and possibly the breakdown of marriage, trials, and justice. The Sun is represented by a circle with a dot that marks the center (☉). The center itself becomes the symbol of the Sun, and the circumference is reminiscent of the ecliptic and the planets that revolve around it. Thus, through the law of analogy, the Sun represents the center, the chief, the king, the head of state, authority, highly placed jobs, success, all that shines brightly, both literally and figuratively, as well as hot countries.

Thus, it can be seen that in astrology that analogy is the key to interpretation. It is also used to localize events or, at the very least, to time and describe the nature of an astral climate. Dating the hoped for or feared event is the basic art of the astrologer.

The fundamental law of analogy in this domain is provided by the two principal movements of the Sun: the Earth system, *the day,* or rotation of the Earth on its own axis, by which the celestial sphere seems to revolve around the Earth (diurnal movement in astronomy); and *the year,* or revolution of the Earth around the Sun. This gives us the following equation: 1 year = 1 day. Moreover, this key is called to memory by the Bible: "I have appointed you each day for a year" (Ezekiel 4:6).

This movement is translated in astrology, generally geocentric, by the apparent movement of the Sun around the Earth. In this apparent path, the Sun seems to proceed 1° per day. Thus our equation becomes:

$$1 \text{ year} = 1 \text{ day} = 1°$$

The Earth revolves around its own axis every twenty-four hours. The celestial sphere, therefore, appears to make a complete circular trip in twenty-four hours, at the rate of one degree every four minutes. Our equation therefore becomes:

$$1 \text{ year} = 1 \text{ day} = 1° = 4"$$

In other words, upon considering the Earth's orbit around the Sun, a degree corresponds to a day; and in its rotation on its own axis, this degree corresponds to four minutes in time.

FOUR MINUTES TO SAVE YOUR UNION

Let us jump forward twenty-five centuries, from the time of Ezekiel and, again, astrology will be the means by which we explain an unusual discovery recently made by an American psychiatrist. The Parisian monthly magazine *Marie-Claire* of August 1974 published an article entitled "Tirez plus de votre couple" ("Get more out of your union"). It bore the following *précis:* Four minutes decide the success of a love affair. This is what the American psychiatrist Leonard Zunin explains to you. So, be careful of your early morning gestures… Here we find the period of four minutes—that is, twenty-four hours of the ecliptic divided by 360.

The American psychiatrist, Leonard Zunin, after countless interviews, psychodramas, and case studies, established that the first four minutes of any encounter, of any contact that is new or renewed, is enough to determine the climate of the future relationship. Four minutes is the time human destiny takes to create the links that unite two individuals or, by contrast, to refuse to create these links or even break them.

Doctor Zunin writes, "Why four minutes?"

> It is not an arbitrary period of time. It is a question of the average time, established by meticulous observation, that it takes for two strangers in each other's presence to react to each other and to decide if the relationship is worth pursuing any further or not.[2]

In time, without any doubt, there is an analogy between four minutes and a longer measure of time or a whole. Thus, Dr. Zunin advises married couples to take great care of their emotional reactions, right from the first four minutes after awakening in the morning, as the tone for the whole day will be established at that moment. We are in absolute agreement. In

---

2　Zunin. *Contact: The First Four Minutes.*

astrology there has always been an analogy between four minutes and a day. One degree equals four minutes.

I am anxious to assure you (and in this I particularly address the layperson and young student), since for the most part practitioners are already aware that astrologers obtain satisfactory results when it comes to research into the delimitation of time within the nature of astral climates. I would like you to pardon me for this euphemism but I have purposely refrained from using the expression "prediction of the future," since it is this shameful and diabolical practice by which our detractors bring us into disrepute. These people, for the most part, pseudo-scholars, are totally ignorant of astrology, never having put it to the test themselves.

CHALLENGE TO ASTROLOGY'S DETRACTORS

About ten years ago, Volguine informed me that it was UNESCO that had been conspicuous in taking up the campaign against astrology.

It is enough to make you double over with laughter when you reflect on the fact that not a single critic has ever accepted the following challenge: Quote the name of one man whose honesty and reliability are renowned (anyone, but just one), whether a mathematician, astronomer, philosopher, theologist, novelist, or scientist, past or present, who has ever studied and put astrology to the test, and who, afterward, has ever declared it to be a false science. People do not believe or disbelieve in astrology any more than they believe or disbelieve in algebra or chemistry. It is a question of knowledge or ignorance. According to Raymond Abellio:

> One either practices it or does not practice it; that's all. Moreover, if one practices it, that is, after having learned the rules of the game, one begins to use it with a certain continuity, and in all honesty one cannot help but take it seriously, and one is even forced to make it one of the principal subjects of reflection in life. (no reference provided by the author)

On many different occasions, I have read in the press that, in France alone, more than 60,000 astrologers and clairvoyants can be counted. I have no idea how these different journalists arrived at this figure, and I do not intend asking them to provide the names of even 600 astrologers. All I ask is the name of one reliable detractor. The great Galileo devoted himself to astrology; we have written traces of the horoscope he made for his nephew. Newton was an astrologer.

Out of discretion, I shall remain silent as to the identity of a French astronomer (he is still practicing his profession) who, for years, could not refrain from adding a little sally, often very severe, against astrologers, at the end of his interesting and very informative articles on astronomy published in a leading daily. I was cohost at a Mensa dinner party at which he was the guest of honor. That is the very reason I did not wish to embarrass him publicly by throwing a few bitter comments in his direction. I knew that he studied astrology. I could quite easily have revealed the name of someone who had lent him a particular book, and the fact that he had not returned the book in the given time because he had wanted to study it further. But I remained silent. Well, let me tell you, I do not regret having remained silent, although it was painful to me at the time. This astronomer continues to publish his articles in the same press, but now he no longer allows himself to conclude with wounding statements about us.

However, I have allowed myself to wander from the subject; it is high time we come back to it, more precisely, to Aries and the eleven others. There is an analogy between the two principal movements of the Earth, so much so that astrologers have quite naturally and justifiably established an analogy between the twelve signs and the twelve houses. However, I have learned through experience that this analogy in particular will provide us with the results we expect when we follow the advice given in these pages. Indeed, we are more often asked about destiny than personality, the latter being dependent on the planets in the signs that reveal hereditary, fundamental, innate, and native frames of mind. However, it is the houses, if correctly interpreted, that reveal the domains of life in which these influences are felt: work, finance, unions, travels, and so on. The planets give out, the houses receive.

RECTIFYING ANOMALIES

There was nonetheless an improvement that could be brought to all this. This is the goal we hope to have attained. We have spoken about the anomaly that became very clear to us concerning the first and twelfth houses and how they lived up to our expectations so much better when we inverted them. We shall provide illustrations of this in chapter 10.

The reader would have arrived at this conclusion independently, armed only with the powers of reflection and common sense. It so happens that health-care professionals confirm our theories. Indeed they think that sick people clearly and openly regain their energy after sunrise, that is in the first house, the one we call the "house of life." They affirm, without any doubt, that feelings of distress, fear of the dark, grip sick people, especially those suffering from insomnia, during the first part of the night. This corresponds to our eighth house, a house of misfortune. However, if you count the houses in the same direction as the signs, this part of the night corresponds to the fifth house, said to be a house of fortune. And finally, cardiologists are categorical: blood pressure drops very noticeably toward the end of the night. The Sun (the heart) reaches the twelfth and last house in our system, fatigued by its long journey below the horizon.

In our introduction, we quoted the case of the third and ninth houses, which corresponded much better to the law of analogy when we inverted them—if you will recall, it was in connection with physical travel. The law of analogy requires that short trips belong above the horizon, whereas the end of a very long journey blends itself into the Imum Coeli. It is the same for spiritual journeys in the context of intellectual life. Concrete intellect and intellectual activities, which are attributed to Gemini and the third house, are well placed above the horizon and merge intellectual tasks with the action of making arrangements. On the other hand, abstract intellect, philosophy, deep spiritual speculations, ideals, and dreams, all of which are attributed to Sagittarius and by analogy to the ninth house, are better placed below the horizon rather than above.

Moreover, do you realize that what the traditional astrologers call the second house (when you count the houses in the same direction as the signs) corresponds to the most inactive period of the twenty-four-hour cycle, since it covers the period 2 a.m to 4 a.m? It would not be unseemly for me to insist heavily on this strange paradox. It would be better for me to be positive and emphasize the harmony that will be attained once I have convinced you of the need to count the houses in a clockwise direction. So doing, the house that is said to be the one of material gains would then correspond to the second third of the morning, the period that marks the beginning of the work day. How much better that this house is suited to a period during which a materially rewarding activity is practiced.

THE FATHER AND THE MOTHER

Just to determine their respective significators, relations as close as the parents of the native have become the object of the greatest possible differences of opinion. Usually, the fourth house is the father's house, whereas the tenth house is the mother's. However, more often than not, the results obtained are disappointing. In the case of some authors, it was thought that the difficulties could be solved by inverting the houses normally attributed to each parent, so that the mother's house becomes the father's house and vice versa, especially in female nativities.

Other authors, still with the same praiseworthy purpose in mind, sought to correct the errors discovered by retaining the normal attributions in the case of diurnal nativities and inverting them in the case of nocturnal nativities, thereby attributing the fourth house to the mother and the tenth house to the father. However, if we are four billion individuals according to the most recent scientific calculations [in 1984], then there are about one billion women who really are a nuisance in that they make it very awkward for learned astrologers, having the audacity to have been born at night. As far as these authors are concerned, there were hardly any problems, as they are not the same ones who recognized the two solutions. However, for my part, there were and very quickly, too.

Indeed, if we consult the most reliable authors, we can read in Antares' manual: "The fourth house represents the father in a masculine nativity, and the tenth house the mother, in a masculine nativity." In the chapter titled "The Relations," the author adds "According to certain authors, the fourth house relates to the mother and the tenth house to the father, in the case of feminine nativity."

Gouchon, in his dictionary, attributes the fourth house to the father and the tenth house to the mother.[1] However, he adds under the word *mother,* "Certain authors attribute to the fourth house an influence on the mother." And under the word *mourning,* he states, "The fourth house influences mainly the father, the tenth house the mother; however authors do not agree entirely on the matter."

Sepharial, the famous English author, says the opposite.[2] In his *Manual of Astrology* in four books (like Ptolemy), he says very clearly in chapter 5 of the first book, "house 4: the mother in a man's horoscope, the father in a woman's horoscope, the mother-in-law in a man's horoscope, and the father-in-law in a woman's; house 10: the father or the mother, according to the sex of the horoscope." If horoscopes have different sexes then quite clearly our problems are only just beginning.

It is true that the French drive on the right and the English on the left. It is hardly surprising that here they should be so strongly in total opposition to one another. After all, it is only a matter of differentiating between the father and the mother. Is it a mere trifle?

We encounter the same difficulties insofar as the designation of the eyes is concerned. It is thought that the Sun governs the right eye, whereas the Moon governs the left, at the very least in masculine nativity. Certain authors think that the contrary applies in feminine nativity.

We do not claim to suddenly make everyone agree with one another— in so doing, we would be jumping to conclusions concerning the possible reception of our proposition. However, we do claim to provide a solution to this very important problem. Which house, which twelfth of the ecliptic, corresponds to the father? Which house must be attributed to the mother? The reply is simplicity itself; it flows forth naturally and imposes itself on

---

1   Gouchon and Reverchon. *Dictionaire astrologique.*

2   Sepharial. *Manual of Astrology,* pp. 28–9.

our minds. We insist upon the fact that it is simple—the most striking feature in all this.

The House Corresponding to the Mother

Just how does a newborn baby behave? Animated by the Creator, driven by a powerful impulse to suck, it is pushed toward the mother's breast. This impulse ensures our survival. I said very clearly: it is pushed toward the mother. There is no exception to this, whether a boy or a girl. Newborn babies do not wonder whether they are male or female. In fact in English *it* has no gender. We refer to a baby using the neuter pronoun *it*. A baby does not know if it is born at night or during the day; it even confuses them both for a while. How many young parents can tell us all about their baby when it confuses night with day.

Well now, the sign of maternity is Cancer. The symbol used to represent this sign (♋) symbolizes, among other things, the two breasts of the woman. The fourth sign of the zodiac, Cancer, is that of maternity. In our eyes, therefore, the fourth house is indisputably that of the mother, both generally and definitively, for all natives, without any doubt and without any hesitation whatsoever, with no exceptions. Experience will show you that it works. Of course, you must count the houses in the direction opposite to that of the signs. This is obvious.

Consequently, the house of the mother is the one that commences at the MC. Well, tradition justly attributes private, secret family life to the IC invisible to the public, while the MC refers to public affairs, career, and professional matters, all of which are visible. Without being facetious, it is clear that the mother is known. Her pregnancy is physically evident for all to see, not just to her immediate family. If the MC is the point from which the house attributed to one of the parents commences, it is obvious that it is the one related to the mother. Thus, we have attributed to the mother the fourth house, which corresponds to the fourth sign, Cancer, the most feminine sign, the most maternal of the zodiac, the sign of lactation.

THE HOUSE CORRESPONDING TO THE FATHER

It does not necessarily follow that the father be designated by the tenth house. If we have given the mother a feminine sign par excellence, why should the father be designated by a feminine sign and, according to the law of analogy, by a feminine house—that is, an even house?

Jupiter is the *pater familias*. According to the Greeks, he is the father of the gods and human beings. He governs Sagittarius ($\nearrow$). This sign is represented by the centaur, the man who leaves for the hunt, armed with his bow to provide for his family. Astrologers insist on the fact that this sign is half man, half animal. Quite obviously, one of its most animal functions is that of reproduction. Moreover, I do not go along with the idea that Libra governs the internal genital organs (understood to be feminine), given that it is a masculine sign and that Scorpio governs the external genital organs (read masculine), given that it is a feminine sign. Libra, with its two scales ($\triangleq$), governs the kidneys. Let us tarry a while on the subject of Sagittarius and let us note that its arrow symbolizes the erection of the phallus and the stretched out bow the outline of the scrotum. Finally, Scorpio, which is always represented with its sting erect ($\mathfrak{m}$), smaller than that of Sagittarius's arrow, symbolizes the phallus in miniature, the clitoris, which is also erectile.

Here we find perfect harmony, especially if you now consider that Scorpio is not only the sign of general sexuality, but also and more particularly that of the female sex. It is a feminine water sign, whereas Sagittarius is exclusively a masculine fire sign. We need to recall that all our poets speak of lovers asking their lady loves to extinguish their flames? I had already noticed that those so-called cold Capricornians, born between December 22 and January 20, were not really as cold as all that. However, when I began to practice the sidereal zodiac, twenty-four out of thirty of these natives were in fact real Sagittarians for the siderealist—this explained a good many behavior patterns.

There is more. It must be known that, for many Hindus (we do not delude ourselves, the art of interpretation in astrology is difficult, and differences of opinion exist among them, too), the ninth house is the father's house—not only that of the spiritual father, as one might think. In Hindu astrology, Jupiter is more often taken to be the general indicator of father-hood than he is in Western astrology. In the latter, Saturn and the Sun are more often considered to be the general indicators of fatherhood, more frequently the Sun in a diurnal nativity and Saturn in nocturnal nativity. Recall that the general indicators are those that refer to such and such a planet or planets, whereas particular indicators are the rulers of such and such a house, which varies according to the orientation of the horoscope and the planets that are in the house in question. Only *Jupiter* is known as "Guru" in Sanskrit, and means "spiritual father." Given that we cannot comprehend the Hindus if we leave religion aside, it is understood, by analogy, that they attribute the ninth house to the father, since the ninth sign, that of Sagittarius, is that of religion.

By attributing the ninth house to the father, Jupiter, we have applied a very similar set of reasoning to what led us to give the fourth house to the mother, since the fourth sign is governed by the Moon, the mother.

You will find confirmation of these principles in interpretation by counting the houses clockwise—that is, in the direction opposite to that of the signs.

THE BENEFITS OF THIS SOLUTION

The fourth and ninth houses of the horoscope describe much more the nature of the relationship with the mother and father respectively, than a description of both parents. Finally and above all, these two houses must be consulted for a great number of other domains besides simply that of family relationship. Career, honors, social life for the fourth house; long trips, idealism for the ninth. It is quite obvious that brothers and sisters will have fourth and ninth houses of a different nature, despite the fact that they are engendered by the same parents.

We come to understand that certain authors wanted to give the fourth house to the father, that is, to the IC that, by its very position, symbolizes perfectly the innermost, secret and mysterious origins from which the native has been brought forth. In the same way, we begin to understand why they wanted the tenth house to represent the mother—when counting the houses in the same direction as the signs—that is to represent the MC. The mother controls the child; she is the dominant factor in formative years. She raises him and is generally in charge of his initial education. However, by doing this, the fourth house was attributed to the father, to the sign of maternity and the tenth, by analogy, to Capricorn, which rather than representing a young mother usually represents old men. It just did not fit.

Moreover, the house that leaves from the IC enlightens us about real estate matters and it is difficult to conceive the idea of a house built on the fourth sign, Cancer, that is on the sea, on moving water. Consequently, we willingly admit that it was thought that an intervention was necessary in that the fourth house was attributed to the mother so that it corresponded to Cancer, the sign of breastfeeding. However, this meant that the mother was represented by an invisible sector under the heavens, whereas the authors always tried to bring the father into relationship with the IC, and quite rightly so. This is why it was not confirmed either in interpretation.

Moreover, if we return to the four Quadrants of the chart of the heavens, and my proposition is adopted, we shall no longer see the IC simultaneously providing information on the one hand about origins, the beginnings of life, and on the other hand, concerning the end of the things and old age. Any person engaged in research, who is dedicated to the truth, will willingly admit that one cannot hope to find in the same place within the heavens indications concerning two periods of life, which are so obviously in discord with one another. If the authors preferred to give the fourth house to the father, it was probably because they wished to give him a sector placed beneath the heavens; once again, quite justifiably so. However, they were sometimes also helped in this by a rather fortunate circumstance. Indeed, the 30° or so counted from IC in the direction of the signs of the zodiac are the same ones that go to make up the ninth house if we count the houses in a clockwise direction. If one or several planets are found to be placed there, they certainly concern the father, whatever method is used.

But that is not so as far as rulerships are concerned, especially if we pass from the tropical zodiac to the sidereal one. In addition, the same advantage cannot be applied to the particular significators of the mother.

CHAPTER 7

STATISTICS

Léon Lasson

Now, let us come down to statistics. However, before talking about Gauquelin's, let us render unto Léon Lasson what belongs to Léon Lasson. As early as 1946, the astrologer Léon Lasson revealed the fruit of his observations, using figures and graphs, nonetheless eloquent.[1] In one single circular figure, the author counted the house position of Mars of 158 military chiefs (other than Gustave Adolphe), 144 marshals or generals, four admirals, and nine superior officers. He found two abnormal accumulations of planets, when Mars had just risen or when it had just culminated. Moreover, Lasson provides the names, dates, times, and places of birth of all those great soldiers. Straight away this allowed all skeptics to check his research and discoveries.

Then he did the same with 134 politicians on the theme "La lune et la popularité" ("The Moon and Popularity") and obtained the same results— that two characteristic accumulations were situated precisely in the same zones that Mars abnormally frequented in the case of military men.

He observed the same anomaly in a similar case study involving Venus and 190 artists, then with "Mercure et la diffusion des idées" ("Mercury and the Broadcast of Ideas"), which considered 209 lawyers, actors, preachers, novelists, journalists, storytellers, and philosophers. Lasson found that thirty-four of them had Mercury in the counterclockwise

---

1 Lasson. *Ceux qui nous guident* ("Those Who Guide Us").

twelfth section of the ecliptic, situated just above the eastern horizon, whereas the expected average was only seventeen.

Let us add that all the data, complete with times of birth and the names of those celebrities, were furnished without exception. It was therefore already clear that both these twelfths of the ecliptic—that is, the two houses that start from the two principal points of the Horoscope, the Ascendant and the MC—do not live up to our expectations in relation to interpretation unless they are counted in a clockwise direction.

At this point, it is worthwhile recalling, as we have already pointed out, that there is more than one author who has suggested taking 5° or even half of a house backward from the point in relation to the habitual gyration given to the houses.

In a contribution to the book *Greek Astrology*,[2] Bouché-Leclercq quite clearly states that a considerable number of authors in antiquity argued together over what proportions of the Ascendant's house should be shared between the upper and lower positions (below and above the horizon, some opting for a half-and-half basis, others for a third and two-thirds). Ptolemy had adopted the practice of situating this house entirely below the Ascendant, thus refusing to follow those who, before him, had situated it entirely above. Yet again Ptolemy, while taking the liberty of correcting his predecessors, led us astray and onto a false road.

Lasson, underlining "the error of astrologers, which can be attributed to Ptolemy and be called *Ptolemy's inversion*," drew the following conclusions from his works: The space occupied by a house goes in the same direction as diurnal movement. However (regrettably in my opinion), he left the succession of the houses, from first to twelfth, so that they continued to be counted in the same direction as the signs.

On the whole, he was neither heeded nor followed. The few who did in fact study his proposition found nothing better than to make him the object of the greatest sarcasm, to such an extent that the man was deeply marked by their criticism.

---

2   Bouché-Leclercq. *Astrologie grecque.*

MICHEL GAUQUELIN

Michel Gauquelin was only seventeen years old and already smitten by astrology. He has devoted himself to statistics since his early beginnings right to this day [he died in 1991]. His results are exactly the same as those obtained by Lasson; they emphasize the importance of the same two sectors, but they are based on a greater number of case studies. The statistical works of Gauquelin, aided by his wife, Françoise, constitute an authority on the matter.

However, his relationships with astrological circles are irregular. He refutes traditional astrology; he is, above all, a statistician. It is in this vocation that he is known and appreciated in international scientific circles.

From page 52 onward in his book,[3] Gauquelin brings out the significance between the births of 3,647 great doctors and scientists; 3,438 warriors of great renown; 2,088 sports champions; 1,409 famous actors; 1,003 politicians; 1,352 writers; 903 journalists; and 202 company directors of large firms—in other words 14,042 case studies in all.

Insofar as doctors are concerned, there is a cluster of births that have Mars either soon after its rising or straight after its culmination (724 instead of an expected average of 626). There is one chance in 500,000 that such an excess in births could be caused by chance alone. For the 3,438 warriors, Jupiter and Mars are found to exceed in the regions that follow the rising and the culmination. With athletes, Mars alone dominates in a surprising fashion, 452 instead of 358, leaving one in five million to chance. With the actors, it is Jupiter. With the politicians Jupiter is counted 205 times instead of 166, the probability being therefore one in a hundred. It is pleasing, though not surprising, that actors and politicians are dominated by the same planet. This reminds me of the parallel that I made in my book *Return to the Stellar Zodiac* between Hitler and Charlie Chaplin, who were born four days apart.[4] With writers, the Moon is very prominent and it is always a question of the position after its rising or after its culmination. With journalists, it is again Jupiter, which occupies

---

3   Michel Gauquelin. *Dossier des influences cosmiques.*

4   Pp. 89–91.

privileged positions. Finally, with the 202 company directors Mars is the dominant planet.

The privileged sectors are those that correspond to what traditional astrologers call the ninth and twelfth houses, if you count the houses in the same direction as the signs. For the attentive reader who is conscious of the apparent rotation of the celestial sphere, due to diurnal movement, it is painfully obvious that the planet in question is dominant when it has just risen, that is to say just when it is found slightly above the eastern horizon, or when it has just gone past the MC. In other words, if one admits by analogy that the houses that start from the Ascendant and from the MC be called cardinal, as are the signs Aries and Cancer, the houses must be counted clockwise, that is in the opposite direction to that of the signs.

Michel Gauquelin also compared the analogous positions occupied by the Moon, Venus, Mars, Jupiter and Saturn in 32,074 births, that is 16,037 comparisons between each of the parents (father or mother), and the child.[5] The result of these labors shows that at the birth of the child the same planet rises or culminates as either of the parents.[6]

This ideal timetable was arrived at by grouping the observations made in connection with the births of professional celebrities. There are four moments of maximum intensity: after the horizon and after the meridian. Those of rising and the upper culmination are of a greater intensity than the two others. It will be seen during the course of this book that the same law is found again when temperaments and cosmic heredity are studied.[7]

Gauquelin perseveres seriously with his labors as related quite recently in the *Cahiers AFIS* (of the *Agence française d'information scientifique*), September 1982. He has also taken up the challenge, which was launched in his direction by *Comité français pour l'etude des phenomènes paranormaux* (CFEPP). Once again it is a question of the effect of Mars on athletic champions.

---

5   Gauquelin. *L'hérédité planétaire* ("Planetary Heredity").

6   Reproduction of page 55 of Gauquelin's *Dossier des influences cosmiques,* or the equivalent British edition, *Neo-astrology: A Copernican Revolution.*

7   Gauquelin. *Les hommes et les astres,* p. 195, fig. 2.

As we can see, even within the space of one generation, all the statistics cross-check one another. Thus they reveal a law.

We saw in chapter 4 on the quadrants

1. that the four angles are the hinges on which the horoscope rests;
2. that, according to the ancients, the angles moved along in the direction opposite to the rotation of the signs;
3. and that these four angles are also the beginning of the Cardinal[8] houses, each Quadrant having been divided into three sections in order to arrive at the concept of the twelve houses. It thus follows that these same houses, all of them, from the first to the twelfth, must follow the direction of diurnal movement.

The statistics provided by Lasson and Gauquelin have just confirmed the recommendation that we have been making right throughout these pages, and in so doing we quite simply confirm the observation made by Marcus Manilius[9] more than twenty centuries ago:

Of all the places in the heavens, the Sun prefers the house where it enters after the hour of noon, when, while descending from the heights of the heavens, it begins its downward journey toward sunset.

---

8 *Cardinal* usually refers to four signs of the zodiac: Aries, Cancer, Libra, and Capricorn. Cardinal houses are usually called "Angular houses" (1st, 4th, 7th, 10th), followed by Succedent houses (2nd, 5th, 8th, 11th) and Cadent houses (3rd, 6th, 9th, 12th), regardless of the direction of the houses. But in the clockwise house system, the Angular and Cadent houses will now exchange places.

9 Manilius. *Les astrologiques or astronomico*, p. 166.

CHAPTER 8

THE MEANINGS OF THE TWELVE HOUSES

We obtain the following meanings for each of the twelve houses when we take these considerations into account:

- cosmography;
- diurnal movement;
- the fact that the ancients considered the unfolding of the four quadrants to be directly in relation to diurnal movement;
- the twelve houses are drawn along according to this same one-way circular traffic;
- owing to the law of analogy, there is a correspondence between signs and houses;
- it is night when the Sun is under the Earth;
- day occurs when the Sun rises;
- the fourth house leaves from MC and corresponds to the sign of Cancer, the sign of maternity that represents the mother;
- the ninth house ends in the IC and designates the father.

ASCENDANT OR FIRST HOUSE (ABOVE THE HORIZON)

The temperament, the potential vital energy, health, the preferred physical activity, outer appearance, the physical body, hereditary tendencies and predispositions, environment and general conditions of existence, especially during childhood. Character and, notably, reactions to outer circumstances, deep hopes and aspirations that produce behavior patterns.

Note that all of the former reveals itself to be valid only in practice, through the sign or the two signs of the zodiac in question, in the case where this first house is empty of planets. In the opposite case, the presence of luminaries or planets exercise a preponderant influence. The planets are very near to us; the fixed stars, which make up the zodiacal signs, are very far away. Their apparent diameter and their luminosity are both greatly reduced in relation to the planets.

Note, too, that the point of the Ascendant, radical or progressed, assumes considerable importance in matters of health, through aspects and transits, right throughout the life up until death.

SECOND HOUSE

Finance and fortune in general, banking, nourishment, material possessions, wealth, income, salaries and remunerations, real estate, agriculture, goods acquired through the subject's personal labors and initiatives; management as well as the qualifications and circumstances that come together to bring about the acquisition of material goods. The subject's financial position as seen from the outside. Possessions and aptitudes that cause them to fructify. Behavior with regards to material goods. Buying power. Personal gains and, consequently, also loss in the case of affliction due to exaggerated overspending or bad management.

THIRD HOUSE

Intelligence, concrete intellect, common sense, characteristics and preferences of studies, intellectual pursuits and the power of understanding. The desire to be upwardly mobile, the ability to satisfy ambitions, and the professional vocation. Writings, correspondence, paperwork, documents, general meetings and advertising. Transportation, short journeys, and postings. Conferences, exchanges and communications. Blood relatives, brothers, sisters, cousins, as well as neighbors, colleagues and professional associates. Professional and family surroundings. Relationships more of an intellectual than an affectionate nature. Assistance (or lack of) from those who are close.

FOURTH HOUSE

Career, professional activity, the place of employment, the employer, the degree of authority within the professional field; professional occupations but more so, those that are imposed by circumstances and independent events over which one has no control. This can be favorable or unfavorable. The struggle to obtain and keep one's social position, in other words, *le panier de crabes* (the basket of crabs), as Dr. Libert-Chatenay said in *Les cahiers astrologiques* (March 1954), not without humor, as he attached, as we do, this house to the sign of the Crab.

Public life, reputation, popularity, prestige, honors, titles, dignities and public office. The name, the well known and respected brand, the work that will be remembered. Relationships with authority. Glory and celebrity but also total reversal and the fall from power.

The mother and to a lesser degree, family life, but only what is known and visible from the outside.

The MC, radical or progressed, and if the hour of birth is absolutely exact, takes on primordial importance through aspects and transits in order to fix the stations of destiny.

FIFTH HOUSE

Attachments at birth, sentimental relationships, love life, children and relationships we enjoy and cultivate. Vital energy prolonged into the following generation. Pleasures, hobbies, personal creations, artistic, literary and scientific works. Speculation, games of chance, lotteries, strokes of luck, the stock market (securities, commodity exchanges, and so on). Gifts, gains and losses other than those earned through labor. School, university and education.

SIXTH HOUSE

Sickness and disabilities, notably those contracted through work, hygiene, especially nutrition and all that is related to diet. Worries and the wounds inflicted on one's pride during the course of one's professional life. The psychosomatic troubles that follow on from this.

Professional tasks, all that is ungrateful and imposed therein, carried out without one's own initiative and under the constraints of others, the situation of the officer below the rank of captain. Employees, domestic servants, that is to say, being a part of the house, as well the nature of the relations that are maintained with them. The capacity to serve. Harvests, fruits, savings, and things that have been accumulated. Small animals, especially familiar ones and household pets.

The spouse, be it a man or a woman, and the dominant factors concerning him or her. The best friend and confidant.

SEVENTH HOUSE

Alliances, associations, groups, and parties to which one belongs, partnerships, marriage, and the marriage contract if there is one. Contracts of all types, and the possible breach of same. Rivalries, declared adversaries, and competitors. Theft and robberies. Trials, lawsuits, and the adversary's barrister or lawyer. Problems and obstacles. The struggle for survival.

Owing to the fact that this house is in opposition to the Ascendant, it informs us about relationships with others, more especially with regard to those who openly oppose the subject or his course of action. One of two things can happen: either one comes to an agreement, or one begins to do battle, which results either in reconciliation or in a conflict of interests. The magnitude of the conflict will generally depend upon the situation of the subject.

Note: The cusp of the seventh is also known as the "point of death" for obvious reasons, since it is diametrically opposed to the Ascendant, which is the life source. The importance given to it by the astrologer, while conducting research into the periods that are dangerous for the health, will be in direct relation to the degree of exactitude attributed to the hour of birth.

EIGHTH HOUSE

Represents profound changes, the main one being death, the circumstances surrounding death and by extension serious illnesses, injuries, and accidents. The world beyond, life after death, spheres that are invisible to the eyes of mortals, the esoteric sciences, and all that is mysterious. Criminology, inasmuch as it is concerned with these matters.

Regeneration, life, and sexual instincts.

The partner's finances, financial clauses in contracts, the marriage partner's fortune, the state of the patrimony after marriage. Inheritances, legacies, wills. Possible advantages arising out of the deaths of those around the subject. Earnings easily procured, hardly without working; annuities, monopolies, privileges, royalties, exclusive commercial rights, private means of income.

Antiques and, generally speaking, all dead things, archaeology, numismatics, philately, and so on.

NINTH HOUSE

Long-distance travel, foreign lands, and all that the native draws from these. Tools and armaments.

Well-thought-out social action. Apostolate and social works.

Long voyages of thought, abstract superior intellect, intellectual speculations, scholarly works, and scientific research. Philosophy, idealism, and law. High aspirations, possible adhesion to moral principles or moral isolation, religious dispositions. Slumber and dreams, contacts with the beyond, astral projection, spiritual experiences, and spiritual evolution.

Above all, it is the father's house, whatever the sex of the subject, whether one is born during the day or at night; it is also the house of the possible spiritual master, of the Guru.

TENTH HOUSE

Heredity, profound and faraway origins, atavistic tendencies, easy or difficult destiny imposed at birth, and the support or impediments, which could eventuate from this. Heritage, if by this we mean the environment, goods, and chattels available right from the cradle. Ancestors and the influence of a birth into rich or poor circumstances. The many different places of residence commencing with the birth place. Real estate, property, inheritances, mineral wealth, hidden treasures.

Intimate home life, attitudes toward family members living under the same roof. Comfort and the embellishment of the home, as well as the attacks it could sustain either from human beings (burglary, fire, acts of war) or from acts of nature (weather, earthquakes, cataclysms). Shelter and refuge.

Ripe old age and conditions of existence in the latter years of life. Ultimate realizations. The tomb.

Note: Above all in horary astrology, the end of the matter.

Eleventh House

Friendships, including those of a secret or intimate nature. Relationships, masters, protectors, educators, and counselors. Customers, clients, pupils, and disciples. Associations, groups, clubs, cooperatives, and unions that are frequented. People who contribute to development. Conciliators. To sum up, all that is brought to bear on the native from the outside, from surrounding people and the nature of relationships and behavior toward those one encounters.

Hopes, desires, and projects. The profitable use of friends, protectors, and benefactors. The subject's ability to take advantage of favorable circumstances and to lessen, through diplomacy or the intervention of powerful and helpful relations, all that is negative and thus opposed to his objectives.

Twelfth House

Obscurity. The secret and hidden life. Mysterious things and the research that leads to their discovery. Bad habits and vices. Drugs. Worries, hardships, problems, and discontentment. Criminal actions, murder. Despair, self-destructive characteristics that could lead to suicide. However, with the accompanying influence of the spiritual life, there is the courage to react and to surmount the most unfavorable conditions.

Here the two fish of the corresponding twelfth sign are found, one of which lets itself be drawn along by the current, while the other struggles against it and overcomes it.

Detachment from material things, sacrifices and renunciation. Personal evolution, which is acquired either through trials and tribulations or through wisdom, studies, and meditation.

The mystical life, occult sciences, the arts of divination, metaphysics, and their practice.

Obscure occupations, ambushes, snares, and plots. Solitude and exile. Secret enemies. Intrigues, imposters, and treachery. Obstacles and impediments, constraints, and hindrances of all types that could hamper the subject. Lack of liberty, fatality, and free will. People, actions, events, and circumstances that are unfavorable to the subject's destiny. All that is opposed or unknown to one, at least temporarily.

Childbirth. Large animals and ferocious beasts.

The material difficulties of existence, notably unemployment, poverty, restrictions, limitations and deprivations, the reduction of purchasing power, and the string of consequences arising from this, the effects of which are felt within the family circle.

Places where a certain number of people are brought together and where there reigns either a rigid discipline or a sense of the loss of liberty, as in the case of mental asylums, hospitals, clinics, sanctuaries, retreats, boarding schools, certain hostels, convents, and prisons.

Invalidity and accidents. Illnesses that act in an underhanded way and still remain undiagnosed and, consequently, untreated, so that they drain the vital sources. Serious illnesses, which are often chronic and require periods of hospitalization or surgery, thus often leading along the slow path to death, which fully justifies the fact that astrologers call this house "the hell of the horoscope."

Note that there also exists a trap for the interpreter. One has to be extremely skillful, in certain cases, in order to differentiate between the subject who knowingly acts maliciously versus the subject who passively suffers acts of wickedness, which are directed against the person.

Also note that one could find the above list a little long. I do not deny this fact. However, there is not one iota that does not have its basis in the purest tradition as far as the house is concerned. Practice teaches that one of the luminaries or Mercury (the mentality) in a favorable aspect, or one of the benefics placed in this house, brings very great satisfaction and success in the areas that are within its sphere of influence. Men and women of science who have spent their lives in laboratories for the benefit of humankind, great surgeons, and the most gifted sleuths who have saved human lives through their activity, as well as famous esotericists, all owe their success to what they are able to draw from this sector of the horoscope.

QUADRUPLE HARMONY

Let us stop here for a moment to contemplate the harmony that reveals itself before our very eyes.

1. The oriental houses, counting clockwise from the IC to the MC—10, 11, 12, 1, 2, 3—grouped around the Ascendant, have a bearing more particularly on the subject: the temperament, the desire to acquire, thoughts and short journeys, residence, friends, and enemies.

2. The occidental houses, counting clockwise from the MC to the IC—4, 5, 6, 7, 8, 9—which are in opposition to the subject, enlighten us as to the nature of his or her surroundings: mother, children, marriage partner, partners and associates, financial obligations in relation to a third party, and the father.

3. The houses situated above the Horizon, counting clockwise from the Ascendant to the Descendant—1, 2, 3, 4, 5, 6—demonstrate what we are able to see for ourselves from the outside: the physical body, the standard of living one can enjoy because of financial status, professional proceedings, social position, leisure activities, and work.

4. The houses placed under the Horizon, counting clockwise from the Descendant to the Ascendant—7, 8, 9, 10, 11, 12—reveal to us all that is hidden: contracts that are concluded, serious illnesses and testaments that may bring benefit, idealism and spiritual master, family life, plans for the future, and worries and concerns.

What must be abandoned above all is the mental connection that has been established by force of habit between the tenth house, the Midheaven and the professional and social life; likewise, the association of the fourth and the IC. It is not the numerical order that counts; this is secondary, given the importance of the subject being treated. However, it cannot be denied that a certain effort is needed in the beginning to manage this. What really counts is that the most elevated part of the heavens represents what is visible from the outside. Your intimate thoughts are unknown to us, nor is your ideal or even the vote that you cast at the polling booth. However we do know that your professional activity is there for all to see. The MC is the highest point of the ecliptic and the astrological factors found there symbolize and evoke all that is visible and known.

CHAPTER 9

THE TEN PLANETS IN THE HOUSES

ACCIDENTAL EXALTATIONS

In our previous work, *Return to the Stellar Zodiac*, we spent much time on the subject of the exaltations of the seven classical planets. Through the application of the law of analogy, it follows similarly that, even when the Sun is in exaltation in the sign of Aries in the sidereal zodiac, it is also considered to be in accidental exaltation in the Ascendant, the first house of life.

The Moon is in exaltation in the sign of Taurus in the sidereal zodiac. Therefore, it will also be considered to be in accidental exaltation in the second house. This does not mean to imply necessarily that it is more benefic, but merely stronger, which is actually very different. It is obvious that someone who has a favorably aspected Moon in the second house will quite likely be the object of favorable changes in the financial situation. Nevertheless, the proverb, "A rolling stone gathers no moss," ought to be borne in mind here, and one should be wary of changes that occur too frequently because of the Moon's possible influence over the subject's financial situation.

We know that Mercury's domicile is the sixth sign, Virgo, and that its degree of exaltation is found at the fifteenth degree of this same sidereal sign. Thus, when Mercury is in the sixth house it is in accidental exaltation. Likewise, Venus has its real degree of exaltation in the twenty-seventh degree of Pisces, and we consider that it is in accidental exaltation when it is found in the real twelfth house, that of secret things, which reminds us of a saying in French, *"Pour vivre heureux, vivons caches"* ("To live happily, let us live secluded").

The exact degree of exaltation of Mars is at the twenty-eighth degree of Capricorn in the sidereal zodiac. Thus, it is said to be in accidental exaltation when it is found in the tenth house of a chart, the one that leaves from the IC. Let us remember, as Plutarch already used to say, that the planets are not better when they are in exaltation; rather they are stronger. This can have grave consequences in the case of Mars and Saturn; in this instance, Mars could cause us to fear domestic quarrels and struggles, which may not decrease with age, since this use enlightens us on the latter stages of life.

Jupiter, the great benefic, since it is in exaltation in sidereal Cancer, it naturally follows from this that it is in accidental exaltation when it is in the fourth house, which for us, remember, starts clockwise from MC. We have already insisted on the factors of chance that this brings, since it seems to be even stronger when it descends from the MC than when it climbs toward it, that is when it is only in our third house.

Saturn's exact degree of exaltation is at the twenty-first degree of Libra, the seventh sign of the natural zodiac structured on the constellations. It will, thus, be in exaltation when we find it in the seventh house, that is, to the west and under the Horizon. We shall not go any further into the details, but we strongly suggest that you examine these considerations by reviewing some of the charts that go to make up your personal collection.

ACCIDENTAL DIGNITIES AND DEBILITIES

Our concern is to develop the system of planetary rulerships of the signs, otherwise known as the dignities of the planets, which is something different than the planetary exaltations. The same applies to "debilities," which are the positions of the planets in the signs opposite to their dignities.

Let us keep in mind that the signs of the debilities are those that, on the zodiac wheel, are opposed to the dignities' zodiac signs. Thus, for the

Sun, we have just seen that it is in accidental exaltation in the first house, and there you will find all that we have said in the beginning on the subject of what it brings as soon as it rises.

The sign of downfall is the zodiacal sign opposed to that of exaltation. Since the Sun is in exaltation in Aries and in downfall in Libra, the accidental downfall of the Sun will be in the seventh house through the law of analogy. And how! What could possibly cry out more loudly in favor of my way of operating? The Sun has just fallen and disappeared below the Horizon.

The Sun has its domicile in Leo, the fifth sign of the zodiac; it will therefore be in accidental domicile in the fifth house where it pushes precisely toward creativity.

A zodiac sign in exile is the one that is opposed to the domicile. Since the Sun's domicile is in Leo, its exile is in Aquarius. Consequently, by virtue of the law of analogy, it will be in accidental exile in the eleventh house. Indeed, a great king can hardly have true friends.

Meditate upon and thoroughly work upon these questions, as they will assist you considerably in the interpretation of the chart.

DELINEATIONS

Warning: The following delineations must be considered as being only a quick reference to aid students in the difficult task of delineation. These pages cannot be taken literally, since they consider only one factor of the horoscope, and a good interpretation can be the product of a synthesis of influences from only the various configurations in force. The interpretation of a planet in a house will be modified by the presence of other planets or by the nature of the aspects received by the planet under consideration and by its position in the sign.

Many of the old delineations and modern, psychological ones still apply when you apply them to the clockwise houses. For example, if your Pluto is in the clockwise third house, then do not read the delineation of Pluto in the traditional tenth house, but stick to the third house.

THE SUN IN THE HOUSES

The Sun represents individuality, the immortal spirit incarnate, the "I," the superior me, the divine spark in each human being, the individual self, identifiable with the supreme unity, the highest form of expression in the individual. For those who believe in reincarnation, it is the unalterable individual essence throughout successive lifetimes.

In the interpretation it informs us as to the profound side of the native's nature, tendencies, and faculties, the innate gifts that are developed during the course of existence, the native's evolution, will power, and the spirit of synthesis.

Because the Sun is the center of our Solar System, it symbolizes authority, direction, high-ranking jobs, success in career, elevated places, and honors. It is essentially masculine, and in the case of a child it stands for the father. Then, in the case of the adult woman, it becomes an important factor in the study of her love life, as it is the general significator of the husband. However, this is seen mainly from a social perspective; for the intimate and sexual life, preference is given to Mars, another very masculine planet, which informs us about the husband as a lover, so to speak.

Physiologically, the Sun is primordial, for it provides information about the native's vitality—in general, one's state of health and vigor, and in particular the heart. Its position in the houses enlightens us, mainly, as to the domains toward which the subject directs the conscious psyche and how one makes use of the will.

THE SUN IN THE FIRST HOUSE

The Sun is thus very well placed; it is, in a way, in exaltation owing to the analogy between this house and the sign of the Ram (Aries). It gives a strong personality. The native is strong-willed, authoritative and wishes to exercise an influence on surrounding people. The subject is conscious of self-value and has untold self-confidence. One is noble, dignified, truly magnanimous, the foe of paltry things and pettiness, and scornful of those who are unworthy of one's confidence, sometimes displaying a certain arrogance.

The health is fortified as well as one's resistance to fatigue and ill health. One has an accentuated vitality except where the heart, blood circulation, and blood pressure are concerned. If the Sun is afflicted, there will be troubles with eyesight.

It is one of the best configurations for destiny. Generally happy, one's childhood marks a good start in life. Then the will to expand, to succeed, leads toward a high-ranking situation. One likes to shine and to frequent those who walk the corridors of power. Social success is promised, perhaps even a certain renown.

THE SUN IN THE SECOND HOUSE

The Sun so positioned gives financial ambitions, possibly of an unreasonable or extravagant nature; however, these needs are met thanks to the fact that a lucrative profession is practiced. We are prepared to accumulate material possessions to the point that idealistic leanings are lost. But we are also charitable and spend without counting, which gives us a certain credit. We judge people according to their fortune. There is a tendency to live beyond our means.

It bodes of a brilliant financial situation, earnings from important business ventures, sometimes from jewelry or precious metals. We hold positions of importance or responsibility, for example, a government post. Finances depend on social life. They are favored by the protection of men, notably the father, or through associations with high-ranking personalities—a consideration that brings stability to the destiny.

If afflicted, one may have a high income but the costs will also be high. One may indulge in wild spending in order to live in luxury. There is a certain danger of waste or even grave losses.

The subject loves nature and country life.

THE SUN IN THE THIRD HOUSE

Here the Sun grants a good upbringing and solid education. The subject has leanings toward the letters and the sciences. It grants the gift of synthesis. The person has excellent prospects for success in an intellectual occupation as well as in transportation, especially the vehicles of thought, for example the press. One has great self-confidence and an avidity for social success. There is a strong personal influence in the immediate family and professional entourage. Success is probable from middle age on, and honors will also fall upon the native's immediate family. There is not only a strong will to succeed, but also an equally strong desire to make one's success public. Such a person aspires toward repute. One will use intelligence in the professional activity as well as to make a fortune. Marks of favor from the great, professional success, and social prestige are undeniable. One should be wary of dispersing one's energies, especially mental energy. A sudden change in direction or goals will give rise to failures or outright defeat.

THE SUN IN THE FOURTH HOUSE

The Sun, essentially masculine, thus placed, indicates a certain influence from the family, notably from the father. Usually, it accords favorable influences from birth onward. It gives a certain pride, self-confidence, and ambition, with a possible arrogance, owing to the fact that one's privileged position arises from one's origins rather than one's own merits.

This is one of the best positions possible for a post of authority, confidence, and responsibility. It grants favor and protection from people in power, as well as prosperity and independence. At times, luck could be uncertain. There could be fluctuations that would be dependent on the family's influence.

Honors, success, and social achievement are promised from middle age onward. One then becomes freed from the authority of others. Brilliant results are assured, but they will depend most often on the esteem and popularity that one can manage to obtain, as well as on one's relations, entourage, public life, and the prevailing politics—in short, upon the circumstances over which one has little or no real control.

THE SUN IN THE FIFTH HOUSE

The Sun in the fifth house increases vitality, even into the following generation. It promises satisfaction in theaters, concert halls, amusements, social games, toys, leisure activities, and vacations. The same goes for all that touches education, schools, universities, the fine arts, and the publishing business. Furthermore, professional success often incites the native to teach what one has acquired. Success is promised in personal business ventures and initiatives that make this individual stand out, and even put one into the limelight. Sudden windfalls or prosperity through speculation are possible.

A flattering liaison may bring a certain amount of prestige. One is likely to have few children; an only child is likely to be a boy. The birth of children might lead to problems. Children may need careful education. This person has a tendency toward pride and jealousy in love. One should take care that excessive behavior does not harm one's reputation or strike a blow against one's esteem.

THE SUN IN THE SIXTH HOUSE

When the Sun, the source of life, approaches sunset, it loses vitality. This points to a weak heart and possible intestinal problems. In the case of sickness, the native will recuperate slowly and with difficulty. One's poor state of health could harm professional prospects. This person must avoid all types of overwork. However, the Sun so placed, will give an interest in, an aptitude for or even success in professions connected to hygiene and medical affairs. The same goes for everything that touches nutrition, pharmaceutical matters, drugs, health, cosmetics, and the clothing business.

The subject will easily find work and will be practical and ingenious. One's analytical and discerning mind favors an executive career and assures success in positions of minor responsibility. One will find work easily. The person is sensitive in the face of superiors and feels under-appreciated in terms of real worth. One is liable to suffer from the feeling that one's true ambitions are thwarted and being prevented from full self-realization. One could have a proud marriage partner from an elevated social rank. In certain cases, a maternal uncle could provide aid and protection.

THE SUN IN THE SEVENTH HOUSE

Here the Sun is in its accidental fall. The Sun so placed diminishes the subject's resistance to fatigue and sickness, most often because of a cardiac weakness. In the case of sickness, the convalescence will be long and drawn out. In general, such a person should economize on energy and organize the days so as to have enough time to rest fully and keep trim by practicing a sport. One will have an aptitude for meditation.

The subject's integration into society will prove difficult and depend greatly on how well one gets on with others. One's success, therefore, depends on the ability to be diplomatic. Time and time again, one will face naturally authoritative, high-ranking personalities of great prestige, which could assure success and open the doors into high society. Success could give rise to rivalry. As far as possible, it is advisable to avoid lawsuits and clashes with authority.

In the case of a female native, there will probably be a profitable match or marriage that will contribute to her social elevation. In the case of both sexes, union will play a primary role in destiny.

THE SUN IN THE EIGHTH HOUSE

With the Sun in this position, there exists an incitement to create light where there is darkness. This leads to an interest in the beyond, mysteries, and the occult. The subject can be engrossed in a detective story or film to the point of forgetting the everyday worries of surrounding life. Heart problems will lead to decreased vitality.

The role of others' fortunes comes to the fore, particularly those of the marriage partner. Frequently the subject's financial situation will ameliorate after marriage. Partners and associates can profit from large incomes, but also be spendthrifts. There is a possibility of becoming involved in a lawsuit over money matters or of being required to meet the debts of other people.

The female native's love life tends to be gloomy owing to heartbreaks caused by death or loss. Death is often a source of income; important legacies are possible. Possibly, one's vocation involves activities involved with death, such as undertakers, insurance agents, or attorneys. Such a person seems to work for posterity; one's lifelong work continues past death and may lead to posthumous awards.

THE SUN IN THE NINTH HOUSE

This is an excellent configuration for intellectual and scientific pursuits and speculations of the mind. One is self-confident, cultivated, intuitive, generous, and has a high sense of ideals and a sense of prophecy. This person is broad-minded, with an ability to organize and synthesize ideas, giving clarity in judgments and conclusions. There is an interest in law, religion, philosophy, metaphysics, the inaccessible, and the adventurous. Breaches of the law threaten legal problems. This is a good position for teaching or professions such as bureaucrat, counselor, ecclesiastic, or any activity related to exchanges over a long distance, such as embassies, missions, wholesale or freight businesses, or vocations related to the import–export business.

The father's position is highlighted, as is the hereditary paternal influence. There is an aptitude for foreign languages, and numerous voyages over long distances will be advantageous. Success, honors, and prestige are likely in foreign countries.

THE SUN IN THE TENTH HOUSE

This individual has great love for family, parents, and origins, and exemplifies familial love. One can feel a certain pride owing to one's origins at birth. However, this does not exclude possible reversals of fortune. Professionally, one is attracted to real estate, construction, architecture, and mining. The individual is economical and stubborn. A secret ambition is often the real motivation, and one has serious opportunities for achieving it through the help of relationships in the right places, the protection of those in authority, the administration, and the government. This one often encounters impediments in career until an advanced age, but later success and ultimate attainment are certain. The happiest time of life and the greatest respect, even renown, may happen in old age. This position also gives rise to introspection and meditation with an interest in philosophy, mysticism, and esotericism.

THE SUN IN THE ELEVENTH HOUSE

The individual tends to procrastinate, making many plans and building castles in the air. Whenever possible, the subject should take heed of the motto "Here and now" and limit ambitions. Having made this reservation, it is an excellent position for putting wise and measured aspirations into concrete form, while taking into account aptitude, means, and circumstances. Fortunate plans will thus receive a favorable welcome and often reach fruition through the help of friends, elders, and superiors, primarily because they enjoy an elevated social position rather than because of any affection for the subject. This native should, therefore, cultivate relationships. A great deal will depend upon one's ability to maintain links in high places. To ensure success and prosperity, there will be a need to placate the high and mighty and to nurture one's contacts and friendships with those who hold government office. Complete attainment might come after middle age. This native can preserve and conserve things and values, shed light on difficult situations, and has a talent for diffusing explosive situations.

THE SUN IN THE TWELFTH HOUSE

The Sun placed here warns of hindrances and the sapping of vital energy through hostile and sly acts executed in secret. One must be careful where to place trust. This one must guard against careless talk, making statements imprudently, and leaving compromising correspondence unguarded. One could become the victim of calumny. The native will thus be equipped to unmask false friends, employees lacking tact or scruples, and adversaries of all types who oppose one's dynamic energy and exceptional success. The native will, in this way, vanquish secret enemies, while their astonishment at one's perspicacity will provide not the least of one's personal satisfactions.

The native can succeed in an occupation of a withdrawn nature, notably laboratory work, scientific research, law enforcement, information services, intelligence work, or a profession that involves people meeting together in one place, leading to the loss of liberty, including retreats, boarding schools, clinics, hospitals, asylums, and prisons.

There could be an intense interest in the occult sciences to the point where the native could succeed professionally in this area. One may be blessed with occult protection and could come into contact with a spiritual master and acquire knowledge about certain secrets of nature. This native may also reach a certain degree of dignity in a secret society.

THE MOON IN THE HOUSES

The Moon represents the personality, the soul, the visible human being, the emotional life, instinct, or the lower psyche, receptivity, personal character traits, and matter, in contrast to spirit. The Moon is the *Kama Manas* of Hindus. It is associated with the etheric body, which is in close contact with the nervous system and plays an important role in being a medium.

In interpretation, it informs us as to the native's appearance, instincts, emotions, feelings, and sentiments. It is the face that one shows to the world, the mask behind which to hide. In the same way as the Moon (the celestial body) reveals only one side to the Earth, the Moon (in the horoscope) is the human being's visible face.

As Earth's satellite, the Moon acts as a mirror, transmitting to children at birth the influences that it receives from the other celestial bodies in keeping with their respective positions. It also exercises its own influence on the subject's receptivity and it enlightens us as to the person's general behavior, one's way of reacting to the ordinary little events of everyday life and one's organic life.

The Moon, moving twelve to thirteen times more quickly than the Sun, remains only two-and-a-half days in each sign. It is thus a more personal factor. It symbolizes the night, and all the psychological implications thereof, such as dreams and desires.

In the horoscope of a child, the Moon represents the mother. However, in the adult male, it describes his sentimental life, as the Moon is the significator of a woman in the sense of a spouse. For the intimate life, one should instead consult Venus. The Moon provides information about the family, the home, public life, popularity, changes, and trips abroad.

THE MOON IN THE FIRST HOUSE

This native is very sensitive, imaginative, impressionable, capricious and eccentric, at times lacking assurance, often timid or excessively modest. One often drifts off into a dream world. Owing to a lively curiosity, one has a tendency to make frequent changes. Generally, this one should heed intuitions. One should strive to develop the will, perseverance, and the ability to make decisions.

This person is influenced by heredity, especially from the mother more than others. One's outer appearance is pleasant enough, but there is often a tendency toward early corpulence. The human organism, particularly the digestive tract, must be kept under close watch. The native is romantic and would be wise to control the emotions. One is prone to a strong influence from associates in general and from women in particular.

Success will be more sound by avoiding changes that bring no real improvement to the situation. Success will be linked to social life and to the role of family relations. One makes numerous contacts with the public and attracts popularity. The native should not yield too easily to another's authority, as this could lead to servitude.

THE MOON IN THE SECOND HOUSE

In a way, here the Moon is in exaltation because of the analogy that exists between this house and the second sign, Taurus. It creates a sensitivity toward all that concerns money and the interest that the public has in finance; hence activity, ingenuity, and imagination in this domain. One could also hold public office.

There could be gain through contact with the public, as a commercial traveler, salesperson, or through trade in public commodities, especially in relation to water, liquids, foods, or other nutritional products that require a rapid turnover. One could have a career in marketing.

The fortune undergoes fluctuations. Financial instability is such that the native would be wise to give preference to seasonal activities or businesses with variable returns, rather than squarely oppose a particular tendency of one's horoscope. This one should try to roll with the punches of one's horoscope. Financial success will frequently depend on the masses, the public, rather than on a small number of people or an employer. Goods and profits will come from various different sources. One should be cautious about possible dangers or problems and avoid wastage.

In the case of a man, women—initially the mother and then the spouse—will play an important role in finances. Family expenses could weigh heavily on the family budget.

THE MOON IN THE THIRD HOUSE

One is mentally active and curious, but also capricious and disorderly. The imagination is fertile, but the powers of concentration could leave much to be desired. There is a thirst for knowledge in the most varied subjects, and there are numerous, unusual, and whimsical intellectual pursuits. This native is skillful but suffers from instability and flees monotony. One may completely change direction during studies and switch educational institutions during youth.

One could be successful through intellectual occupations, especially through works of the imagination, including reporting and publicity. The native displays an aptitude for becoming interested in a wide range of subjects simultaneously. One will be successful due to popularity, which will always have to be nurtured. One is greatly influenced, for good or bad, by immediate circles in the professional and social life, especially by women, notably those from or distantly related to the family.

Finances will depend on this popularity where the public is concerned, especially the female public. There could be numerous voyages, preferably with the family or as part of a group, and if the rest of the horoscope permits, an attraction to sea cruises.

MOON IN THE FOURTH HOUSE

This is the typical position of changes in situations. The Moon, here, is in the house that corresponds to its sign, Cancer. There is a latent ambition to obtain a favorable job situation, often one in which one is in the public eye or connected to women. There is an aptitude for responding to changing tastes, fashions, and up-to-the-minute trends. Work could involve food and drink, household products, and all that touches the sea. There is a strong desire to realize one's ambitions but once attained, are often difficult to maintain. Changes in occupation have a tendency to be too frequent and should not be considered unless they bring an improvement to the social condition. Women strongly influence the destiny, for better or for worse, particularly the mother in the first part of life—whether she is protective or over-protective—then the wife, in the case of a male nativity. Social success depends on the favor or the hostility of the public. One would be wise to steer clear of all scandal, defamation of character, and treason, which could arise from those in an inferior position or from jealous people. The profession calls for frequent traveling. It will be necessary to keep a watch on the organs, particularly the stomach.

THE MOON IN THE FIFTH HOUSE

Although one's education may have been interrupted or suffered a change in orientation, there is an interest in all that touches schools and universities, as well as theaters and places of entertainment. The native seeks and obtains pleasure through all types of amusements and forms of entertainment, including festivals, celebrations, meetings, and group outings, preferably at the seaside or on the water. There is a lively interest in games or speculation. Business enterprises and personal creations are subject to changes.

There is popularity, especially with women. Many love affairs, pleasant but ephemeral, enjoy a place of importance. At times, the subject will fall victim to a strange attachment, becoming entirely absorbed, all the more bizarre since the object of the said attachment is not always worthy of one's affection. Liberation from slavery to the senses is possible through an exceptional experience, probably related to the sentiments. There is also the possibility of a great many children, particularly daughters. Frequently life is linked in a very particular way to one of the children.

THE MOON IN THE SIXTH HOUSE

The greater part of experience will be psychic. Indecisiveness and hesitation will lead to the loss of certain opportunities.

There may be a weakness of health, especially during childhood, quite possibly inherited from the mother's side. There may be physiological problems, notably affecting the stomach and intestines. The need for hygiene is paramount, especially where food is concerned. Medicines must not be abused, and medical advice must always be heeded. There is a sensitivity to atmospheric changes, while possible psychosomatic conditions may be caused by excessive worry over matters of health. Overwork drains vital energy. It will be necessary to keep in shape by practicing a reasonable amount of sporting activities.

Living conditions could be unstable, owing to the number of different occupations in which the native is engaged. Many staff changes, both domestic and professional, will give satisfaction but also cause worry. Often success will be obtained by remaining the "right hand" of a strong personality or by staying in a company that has a well-defined hierarchy, rather than by going it alone. The Moon in this house favors contacts with the public, or an occupation connected with liquids or with towns near water. The partner's health risks being delicate.

THE MOON IN THE SEVENTH HOUSE

One cannot bear solitude and is irresistibly pushed toward union in one form or another. Life will be inextricably linked with the person the native has chosen as a partner, whether de facto or legally. The partnership will have its joys and its torments, because the two destinies seem to be so strangely tied together. Health will be delicate, especially during one's childhood.

Contacts with the public are favored. Many people will be met, among whom will be those who travel extensively. Success will depend on one's popularity with the public, but because this is a fickle matter by its very nature, doing anything that could lead to being discredited should be avoided. One's social life could be characterized by numerous frequent relationships that are always superficial, changeable, and brief. The degree of success in life will depend greatly on the quality of one's marriage. There could be several propositions and indecision and hesitation in the choice of a partner. Sensitivity and emotional instability could harm domestic life.

Litigations, which could be numerous, will bring varying results. Enemies will not be very powerful, since they lack resolution; however, they could be harmful by leading to one's discredit.

MOON IN THE EIGHTH HOUSE

This position favors suprasensory perception, hypnotism, magnetism, and the study and practice of all that is secret and mysterious, as is the case in the occult sciences. There will be an interest in the "beyond" and in metaphysics, and sometimes a fear of death. There could be many dreams, even nightmares, accompanied by heavy breathing upon awakening. There is the possibility of a certain danger on the water as well as during the course of travels if other factors in the horoscope point in the same direction. There could be posthumous fame or death in the public eye or during a public disaster or collective accident. One should travel only under conditions of maximum security. One's disappearance will be talked about.

Finances are favorable, but they will be influenced strongly by marriage or association. Sometimes there will be financial instability after marriage, caused by the partner's lack of foresight or caution. Civil service could be attractive, as a public servant or administrator.

Inheritances, presents, or important gifts will generally come from women. There could be legal disputes among family members over sharing legacies. Sometimes the early death of the mother or a female associate, with the possibility of one death shortly following another, leads to an inheritance. Such an omen can be confirmed by other factors (see notably, the fourth and sixth houses).

MOON IN THE NINTH HOUSE

A lively imagination favors creativity. There is an aptitude for the study of science, law, philosophy, law, metaphysics, religion or occultism. Ideals are unstable, strange and fickle due to a search for newness. The native studies profoundly and at great length before forming an opinion. One has a prophetic sense, many premonitory dreams, and should follow one's intuition.

Success will depend greatly on all that is outside the immediate environment. On an abstract level, the recognition of one's own talents and efforts in the field of research and discovery is promised. Such an enterprise will bring enrichment, both intellectually and materially. On the material plane, success and popularity are announced far from one's native land. Long voyages overseas are promised. These travels will be all the more interesting if an effort is made to understand the inhabitants, their language, local habits, and customs.

The Moon in this position stresses the importance of heredity and the role that the family-in-law will play in one's destiny.

THE MOON IN THE TENTH HOUSE

The subject will be interested in history, folklore, and one's origins and family tree. The native spends too much time dwelling on the past and worries far too much about living conditions during old age. One needs to learn to live in the present while drawing satisfaction from living one day at a time. The native is sensitive to warm surroundings; the color and intimate conditions of the home are appreciated. A sense of family is developed, but too great a dependence on family members could provoke domestic problems. One cannot easily be free of the influence of one's entourage, especially in the case of the women in one's environment. Real estate will be acquired, notably through an inheritance.

There could be numerous changes in surroundings and place of residence, even toward the end of life. This period will often be the richest in one's entire experience, quite possibly the most unstable but not necessarily unpleasant. Often there is even a certain belated public acclaim.

THE MOON IN THE ELEVENTH HOUSE

Progress and improvement will be realized through relationships and friendships, which will be numerous, varied, and unstable, but continually renewed. The subject has the gift to fraternize, to mix easily with people, and to understand their problems, while looking for and obtaining their friendship and drawing the best from relationships to favor personal goals. One's fertile imagination impels work at many projects. There is an aptitude for all that involves waves, rhythms, vibrations, electricity, and aviation, as well as psychology. The native is very sociable and could play an active and useful role in community groups and collectives such as unions, cooperatives, or friendly societies concerned with community welfare. Among one's relationships will be many women. However, a judicious selection will be warranted. At first, there will be a great deal of satisfaction, but disagreements may be unavoidable. The resulting complications will be detrimental to one's emotional health. This is an excellent configuration for a public career. In the case of a merchant, a feminine clientele is favored. It is a sign of many children and, in certain cases, indicates that one's partner will have a child from a previous union.

THE MOON IN THE TWELFTH HOUSE

Frequently, the native withholds an important personal secret or that of a third party, which cannot be revealed without great cost. One has an inquisitive and curious mind, striving to reveal and understand all that is hidden. The subject will make greater progress through discreet efforts, undertaken in a concealed place rather than through brilliant action in full view. There is a lively interest in mysticism, magic, and channeled messages. There is a love of solitude, contemplation, and surrender to meditation and reverie. Sensitivity makes certain noisy and vulgar places unbearable. One may be exposed to back-biting and secret enmities, especially from women. There is a possibility of participation in a secret society. A sentimental and secret liaison with a person not in good health is also a possibility. It is strongly recommended that excessive drinking be avoided.

MERCURY IN THE HOUSES

Mercury is the planet nearest to the Sun. It completes its orbit around the Sun in only eighty-eight days. Mercury is considered to be the messenger of the gods, and as such it serves as the intermediary between the Sun and the other planets. Its symbol, the caduceus, is a herald's wand surrounded by two serpents, which are intertwined and topped by two wings. The wand represents the current of the vital force, while the two serpents stand for the negative and positive polarities of this force, which runs through the entire body and can be controlled by our thoughts. The two wings carry the caduceus from the Earth to the heavens. Mercury symbolizes the intellect, thought, reason, the word, speed, exchanges, means of communication, and voyages. Its position in the houses shows the direction of the intellect when it wishes to express itself—that is, the direction by means of which the mind works for the greatest benefit.

MERCURY IN THE FIRST HOUSE

This influence is quick to make itself felt and we notice it right from the earliest age onward. The mind is forever alert, lively, subtle, adroit, and ingenious. Such subjects can easily express themselves both through the spoken and written word. Written works show originality and invention. They love public speaking, though sometimes a little nervously. They are gifted with quick wit and easy elocution. Impassioned by studies, these subjects are fascinated by a wide range of topics. With inquisitive minds, they are always eager to acquire new information. They are extremely adaptable and supple. Lively and developed intellectual faculties assist them in drawing the maximum profit from circumstances. They have business and commercial sense and an aptitude to play the role of intermediary.

In the case of affliction, the subject could become the victim of criticism, gossip, and exaggeration, and, above all, be very nervous and high strung. If the weak points are kept under control, one appears younger than his age.

Health depends greatly upon the family and professional surroundings, to which such a one is highly sensitive. The native is always moving and completes a great quantity of short, frequent journeys.

MERCURY IN THE SECOND HOUSE

The intelligence is centered on the means of earning money and making a fortune. Thoughts are absorbed, sometimes excessively, by financial matters and one shows a great deal of skill in this domain. Financial success results from an ability to easily use both written and spoken words. The subject makes many written exchanges and arrangements and travels extensively. Gains are favored by their repetition, by the diversity of their source, and through suppleness and know-how, rather than through their far-reaching quality, consistency, and regularity. Income could come from several different sources simultaneously. Mercury here favors the role of the intermediary, a representative, distributor or commissioned agent, and these subjects could make gains through brokerage, dividends, and various deposits, as well as those obtained through collaboration with brothers or other members of the family. It is often the sign of great fluctuations. If Mercury is afflicted, there exists a certain danger of allowing oneself to be drawn into immoral or illegal practices. Mercury is also the god of thieves; one should take care not to fall victim to thefts or swindles. One must procure the necessary insurance coverage.

MERCURY IN THE THIRD HOUSE

Mercury is well placed here, in view of the rulership it exercises over Gemini, the third zodiac sign. Easy self-expression through the spoken and the written word will contribute to social and professional success. An intellectual foundation permits the subject to take up higher studies, thus acquiring a wide scholarship. The well-known adaptability of these natives allows them to leap from one subject to another, thus embracing several matters at the same time. They possess remarkable powers of penetrative thought, which will bear fruit once they learn to concentrate, which does not always happen.

They can apply their mental capacities to the arts, science, business, the press, publicity, and transportation. They should avoid dissipating their efforts and uselessly spreading out their activities. The subject has an aptitude for sharing ideas with others. One is suited to the role of intermediary, commissioned agent, or representative. There will be a great number of relationships, either through personal contact or through mountainous correspondence. One has an easy success with the opposite sex. Professional activities work through partnerships or close collaboration and require frequent travels. In the case of afflictions, there may be anxieties concerning the family, even family conflicts.

MERCURY IN THE FOURTH HOUSE

Frequently, the native is gifted with a great deal of intelligence and probably owes his or her youthful and joyous character to one's mother. A happy event, which no doubt happened very early in life, will have allowed the subject to acquire a good education or will have awakened a lively interest in activities related to the fields of literature, journalism, publicity, or commerce. One will enjoy success through intellectual occupations, including literary, scientific, or commercial activities in which one demonstrates a great amount of skill, suppleness, and the ability to adapt to any and all circumstances. Such a one may act as intermediary in occupations in which mental capacities are preponderant. It favors a post in an important administrative body. The possibility of success is greater in a subordinate occupation, in which one gravitates toward a more powerful personality. Many relationships involve contact with young people and intellectuals. One should try to stick to the job at hand and to overcome a somewhat latent state of anxiety.

MERCURY IN THE FIFTH HOUSE

The educational domain is put into relief here. Pleasure and amusement will occupy an important place in one's life. The subject will be intellectual more than sensual. There is the possibly of a lively interest in poetry, music, and dramatic art and the probability of acquiring an extensive education of a cultural nature. One prefers the less violent sports and games that demand greater presence of mind, quick gestures, resourcefulness, and finesse.

This one has an aptitude for teaching and could be successful in one of the occupations mentioned or in personal creation. One loves theatrical entertainment and possesses an aptitude for mime. The subject is a skillful speculator and can make significant gains if one is wise and not led astray.

Sentiments are controlled by reason, and the subject loves through curiosity more than anything else. One uses powers of seduction for amusement, but lacks passion. One possesses the ability to combine the demands of the heart with the needs of the wallet. When feelings absorb the thoughts too much, the subject feels a certain anxiety. There is a love of children, but one's offspring will be few in number, though very intelligent. Occasionally, this configuration creates a certain fatality concerning relationships with a child.

MERCURY IN THE SIXTH HOUSE

Here, Mercury is in accidental dignity—domicile and exaltation—by analogy with Virgo. This position frequently denotes an interest in medical matters, even if the profession is not linked directly to the health of sick people. Thoughts are very often directed toward work, in which such natives show themselves to be helpful and efficient. Frequently, they will have greater success working as the right-hand assistant rather than as one's own boss. Chemistry, photography, administration, the military, law enforcement, or secretarial jobs will suit such individuals perfectly. If Mercury is afflicted, conflicts in the work field are to be feared. Subordinates should be watched closely: there is danger of indiscreet employees. This configuration frequently promises great success thanks to intellectual faculties and brilliant scholarship.

It often indicates a certain nervous irritability, along with too much tension and a risk of suffering caused by one's environment. Cares and anxieties harm the health and lead to mental or nervous fatigue. The results are frequent digestive problems. In extreme cases, there is a risk of nervous breakdown. Certain trips can be beneficial to one's state of health. Prevention is better than cure; thus, a pleasure trip for the entertainment it provides could turn out to be an effective remedy.

Frequently, a union takes place with a person close to the family or someone encountered in the course of employment. The loving partner could be of lowly origins, but very intelligent (perhaps too much so).

MERCURY IN THE SEVENTH HOUSE

Thoughts are directed toward one's entourage, contacts and associations. The native can hardly bear solitude, engaging in long conversations and prolific correspondence.

These arrangements reflect on the subject's social life. One entertains many business relationships in the areas of commerce, science, and literature. When Mercury is afflicted, problems, altercations and wrangles are to be feared. This is due largely to a contradictory nature. The native frequently disagrees with people in conversation. One ought to resist descending to a position of lower status just to avoid irritation. Such individuals should be prudent when speaking or writing and during the course of travels.

Friendships are many but unreliable. Partners will be intelligent, at times very young. There is a great deal that indicates the possibility of an unstable married life. Lawsuits are to be feared, either over matters concerning employment or those connected with marriage. As a general rule, litigation should be avoided, as one will often be confronted by skillful and cunning adversaries and a serious danger of losses.

MERCURY IN THE EIGHTH HOUSE

Natives of this house can realize their innermost wishes only by firmly maintaining positive images, thoughts, and statements concerning their desires—that is, by the healthy practice of real mental magic. Sometimes, melancholia will lead to serious thoughts about death and the problems it entails. This position favors studies, research, and investigations deeply into history, metaphysics, occultism, and mysticism.

At times, these individuals may become overly anxious or indulge in excessive mental activity, which could lead to more persistent nervous disorders. There exists the possibility of a serious illness contracted during a journey or toward the end of life while far from home. The mind will remain lucid right to the end. Premature deaths of brothers or sisters are also possible.

Fortune will be fickle; financial difficulties could arise over a partner or employer. There could be slight but repeated money worries after marriage. There are possibilities of a small inheritance, gift, or legacy, as well as revenues obtained through rents.

MERCURY IN THE NINTH HOUSE

This position engenders a great thirst for knowledge and provokes over-whelming mental activity. Natives of this house are capable of advanced studies for the sole pleasure of self-education. I once knew a doctor on welfare who was like this. He continued to study while his children had the responsibility of guaranteeing his upkeep, despite the fact that he was already in his sixties.

These people can learn a great deal on their own. The main areas of interest could be law, the sciences, philosophy, religion, metaphysics, and esotericism. They can be broad-minded, but frequently change their views and maintain contradictory opinions. Constant efforts should be made to concentrate and avoid flittering about aimlessly, whether in thought or deed. The father is often well educated. Ideas are expressed easily and clearly. Normally, they will have a happy disposition and be successful as writers, teachers, or anything in which the mind is heavily involved.

One longs for faraway places, sometimes with no specific aim other than a desire to satisfy one's curiosity or education. One is gifted in the art of learning foreign languages. Further advantages will be obtained when such people take an interest in the culture of the countries they visit. They could be involved in business dealings with foreign lands such as import-ing and exporting.

MERCURY IN THE TENTH HOUSE

Thoughts are directed toward family and residential matters. The subject is far too anxious about domestic life. It is important to one's mental and physical health to have congenial surroundings and that the home be comfortable and pleasant. Thoughts and all that one reads have a great bearing on the subconscious. The native of this house is bound to make many changes in residence, often brought about by one's profes-sional life, even up to a ripe old age. It is simply inherent to the character of these natives that they move about constantly, unless Mercury is heav-ily afflicted. They should take care that their old age is sufficiently pro-vided for, especially where residence is concerned. They will remain lucid throughout life. Late intellectual or literary successes are possible. This configuration also favors an occupation involving the ground (construction or agriculture) and all that is under the Earth's surface, as well as a career in the public service.

MERCURY IN THE ELEVENTH HOUSE

Natives of this house will have numerous and frequent friendly relationships, especially with lively and alert people. These will lead to intellectual affinities rather than strong emotional attachments, often making such connections fickle and short-lived. Friends of both sexes will generally be younger than these subjects. They will attach great importance to these friendships, but reason, indeed calculation, will prevail over the heart. It thus follows that friends should be chosen carefully and trust should not be placed too naively in relationships. If this advice goes unheeded, in the case of the planets being severely afflicted, the subject runs the risk of being greatly deceived by their deeds.

These natives will enter relations with literary or scientific associations and notable results will ensue, whether good or bad. There is a tendency to dream up many different projects, some quite audacious, in which relationships will play an important role.

This configuration strengthens the intellect and increases powers of concentration, allowing ideas to be stated and fixed more clearly. It improves intuition and favors study and the use of psychology with practical goals in sight.

MERCURY IN THE TWELFTH HOUSE

These people give the impression of being discreet, secretive, or mysterious. They are rather like philosophers with a tendency toward introspection. This seems almost to act as a brake on one's mental capacities and prevents self-expression. These subjects could be inclined to underestimate themselves, failing to see their own true worth and, in spite of promising mental attitudes, they sometimes deprive themselves of opportunities to exploit them fully. They must avoid all mental or nervous fatigue, and they must have sufficient rest while being entertained to take the mind off their worries.

There is an aptitude for laboratory work or some sort of undertaking done in a quiet, calm, and isolated situation. In certain cases, one's occupation will involve mysterious investigations such as those carried out in occultism or police inquiries. One often possesses an interest in activities that occur where a great number of people are united in common captivity, such as in the case of hostels, clinics, asylums, mental institutions, boarding schools, convents, or prisons.

No careless words should be spoken, and these subjects should take great care over what they write down, since there could be secret enemies who seek to harm them. Above all, they should observe the golden rule not to misuse their intelligence.

VENUS IN THE HOUSES

Venus is the second closest planet to the Sun. It completes an orbit around the Sun in 225 days. After the Moon, Venus is the brightest celestial body; in fact, she shines so brightly that some people, when seeing it high in the sky in broad daylight, notably through intense heat, have taken it to be a flying saucer. For the Greeks, it was Aphrodite, and it is known as the "Shepherd's Star." In astrology, it is the lesser benefic, which brings a certain element of good fortune. It reigns over beauty in all its forms, as well as over artistic expression, attraction, harmony, and tenderness. Its symbol (♀) represents a woman's breast. Above all, it is the goddess of love. It is the only planet that can go through a year without turning retrograde. Indeed, around the Earth it draws a five-petalled rose as it makes its five retrograde motions in eight years. Love is a force that transforms, raises, and emphasizes the good. Love cannot go backward: it is destined to vanquish. As Christ stated, "Love is the fulfillment of the Law" (Romans 13:10). In the horoscope, Venus provides information on chances in love and the power of sensory solicitations. It represents all that is associated with pleasure, such as ballroom dancing, theaters, concerts, and liaisons. It grants charm, grace, gaiety, elegance, and the protection of influential women. It acts favorably in matters of conciliation, making choices and bringing things to perfection. However, if it is afflicted, it could lean toward slothfulness and a certain depravity.

Of course, all of this is valid for both sexes. However, Venus will be far more explicit in matters of the heart in a man's horoscope, as it represents the spouse or female partner, and above all, in the intimate relations between a man and woman. It also reveals the female partner's prowess as a lover.

VENUS IN THE FIRST HOUSE

Venus rising is greatly favorable from many viewpoints, sentimentally as much as materially. It is characterized by kindness, gentleness, a loving attitude, a warm welcoming personality, good humor, seductive manners, and sexual appeal that invites reciprocal feelings. One's physical appearance is pleasant, often very beautiful or handsome. The person has a magnetic nature. One's health is protected, provided Venus is not afflicted, and the lifespan is prolonged if the person is not pulled into abusing the good things in life. These individuals are attracted to finery, ornaments, and elegant clothing.

There is an aptitude for artistic activities, including fine arts, good literature, music, song, and dance. They love receptions, parties, and all forms of celebration. Their social life is successful and brings the greatest satisfaction.

The Goddess of Love, who has just arisen, promises a peaceful and happy life from birth, as well as protection against violence and conflicts—except, of course, in the case of serious affliction. Relations with the opposite sex are favored and include skill in matters of sexual relationships. There is a promise of great sentimental happiness, provided one does not unduly abuse one's undeniable innate charm.

VENUS IN THE SECOND HOUSE

This position favors finances and undoubtedly brings a factor of good fortune in this domain. Relatively speaking, earnings are gained easily without undue effort. Unless repeated acts of imprudence are committed, this is the sign of financial prosperity and the absence of great worries in this field. Very often, earned income will come from associations, including marriage, as Venus rules Libra, the sign corresponding to the house of marriage. Generally, this indicates a close link between earnings and the subject's love life.

This configuration also favors revenue from activities governed by Venus—that is, the practice of any form of art whatsoever, business involved with luxury items or connected to haute couture, jewelry, decoration, furnishings, fashion, hosiery and clothing, as well as the hotel and restaurant trade—this last owing to the analogy between this house and Taurus, the second sign on which nutrition depends.

These natives know how to make themselves appreciated in their professional life, and they maintain pleasant relationships, especially with those in elegant society and with young women and artists. They easily gain help from friends, above all from female friends.

There is a tendency to spend heavily on items of pleasure and those connected with appearance. They should be careful not to fritter away their fortunes by leading a life of dissipation; all good things are, of course, decreased or removed in the case of the planet being afflicted.

VENUS IN THE THIRD HOUSE

All mental capacities are attracted by everything that is beautiful and uplifting to the soul—fine arts, literature, poetry, music, and painting. The mind is brilliant, harmonious, peaceful, and confident. These subjects express themselves easily. Their education is favored and often accomplished with great care and attention.

The chances for success are increased through the practice of Venusian professions such as luxury trades, businesses connected with aesthetics, care of the body, beauty products, finery, fashion, decoration, clothing, and perfumery. Their social life can be very brilliant—including a noticeable rise, dazzling receptions, choice relationships, above all, where young women and artists are involved.

Frequently, these people follow an artistic vocation. Of course, this will be realized only when circumstances allow. Very often, through their sincere affection, relatives or friends dissuade these individuals from undertakings they consider to be unprofitable or uncertain. In this case, where their impetus has been cut off in midstream, they will possibly take up their original desire as a hobby. This will leave them with a certain sense of frustration.

Family relationships are generally peaceful and favor the career. Journeys for pleasure will have fortunate repercussions on the love life.

VENUS IN THE FOURTH HOUSE

Social success is easily achieved, whether through the practice of a Venusian profession or simply through the charm that the personality exudes, through the excellence of relationships (especially feminine ones) or at the beginning of one's career through the mother's influence. Working conditions will be pleasant, but will not depend necessarily on a Venusian occupation, such as artistic activities, luxury trades, or body care.

Thanks to good fortune, happy events could occur without any effort. These natives benefit from the corroboration of influential women and from beneficial and powerful relationships that will often depend on their love life. They will know how to draw satisfaction from any situation, thanks to the feelings of sympathy that they awake in others.

Often, this configuration brings about an advantageous marriage, from which sentiments will not be absent. It is often the promise of a happy and peaceful family life.

If the planet is afflicted, there is the danger of one's reputation being stained by a scandal or affair.

VENUS IN THE FIFTH HOUSE

Venus, the Goddess of Love, could not be better disposed than here, in this sector of the love life. This stems mainly from the fact that these natives give first place to the family and sentimental life in all that touches their decisions. Above all, they wish to satisfy their amorous longings. Their pleasant disposition draws pleasant people, with whom they enjoy reciprocal and affable relationships. They attract happy living conditions and know how to draw the maximum amount of pleasure from life. They are courteous and diplomatic and are assured of enjoying peaceful relationships free of clashes.

One loves amusement and entertainment of all kinds—shows, theaters, and other artistic and musical performances. Moreover, these individuals sometimes even take an active role in such activities. In any case, they have the necessary creative aptitudes for these various fields.

Finances could depend, if only in part, on such activities. Speculation, teaching, and publishing are favored. Generally, these natives show signs of tenderness, which assures a happy love life. They could have many children, especially girls. Her progeny indicate promise, especially insofar as the eldest child is concerned, and even more so in the case of a girl. If Venus is afflicted, there is the risk of tarnishing one's reputation through sentimental relationships of a dubious nature.

VENUS IN THE SIXTH HOUSE

This configuration generally gives a harmonious constitution and a well-balanced state of health. However, there is likely to be a weakness in the throat and urogenital organs. Health frequently improves after marriage. In the case of sickness, these natives will be well cared for. Somewhat curiously, sickness could bring positive results in many different ways to their destiny. This Venusian configuration protects the health very well indeed. Should the health suffer in any way, this could have been brought about by one's own negligence, either through bad habits, bad diet, lack of hygiene, the abuse of life's pleasures, imprudence, or excessive sexual activity. One should avoid activities that cause long periods of fatigue.

This configuration also favors and harmonizes work conditions and professions. Colleagues, superiors, and subordinates will be likeable, obliging, and loyal, especially in the case of women. It is better not to set up one's own business, unless the rest of the horoscope indicates otherwise. Sometimes work becomes a pleasure, or vice versa.

One's partner is frequently a Venusian type, sometimes of great beauty, elegance, and fortune. One could come from humble origins. It is recommended that these people are careful to select partners who are truly loving. They are devoted to sick people, those in need, nature's outcasts, and small domestic animals.

VENUS IN THE SEVENTH HOUSE

Venus here gives protection against adversity. With the exception of unwise actions and repeated errors, the native should remain sheltered from open hostilities, struggles, and revolts. Even when legal matters do lead to lawsuits, generally they will be settled through arbitration or in a conciliatory spirit.

Social success will depend on associations, agreements with professional associates, and family members, and with the constant role of someone close, usually the spouse. Teamwork or subcontracting is a good idea. These people are understanding, generous, and altruistic. In short, it is one of the best configurations for human contacts.

Obviously, this is experienced most in married life. Provided Venus is not afflicted, it is one of the best indications of a happy marriage and a family life without a cloud, provided the partners bring to their relationship the minimum of demands in the form of wise and sensible behavior. Often the marriage is undertaken in ideal conditions, indicating great domestic happiness. When this is not the case, it is because the native has misused free will. For the most part, destiny will depend on the union.

VENUS IN THE EIGHTH HOUSE

This position gives a gentle, benevolent influence in a domain that is at times greatly dreaded—death. These subjects will not be apprehensive or shrink from death and even view it with serenity. The unknown and its mysteries will hold no terror for them at all. It is often a guarantee against a violent, sudden, or accidental death. Generally, the end of life will be peaceful, calm, happy, and natural. Urinary problems could be feared, as could diabetes and sometimes obesity. Travels for health reasons will be especially happy and could bring pleasant encounters. There is also the possibility of intense dreaming, whether agreeable dreams concerning one's love life or erotic ones that reveal a certain sexual obsession.

Finances are favored, and there is a clear indication that they will generally be dependent on the fortune of associates, notably the marriage partner, and on contracts whose financial clauses should, consequently, be examined with great care. There could be legacies or inheritances, very often from women. Frequently, financial fortune smiles on the subject after marriage or during middle age.

If Venus is afflicted, there is danger of the subject being a spendthrift or sinking into a disorderly lifestyle. Heartbreak, or the heart in mourning, is to be dreaded. There is the risk of an inheritance being dissipated or of a reversal of fortune after the death of someone close.

Venus in the Ninth House

These subjects love poetry, the fine arts, and beauty in all its forms. They draw inspiration from beautiful and good things, loving kindness, the cult of peace, and a certain joie de vivre. The mind is cultivated and they have a philosophical and religious bent. They love all forms of mental improvement and have the ability to make precise, clear-cut judgments. They are interested in psychology. Head and heart are in harmony. They can help their neighbors resolve problems of the heart and can discover the sentimental reasons behind everything. They are protected against real tribulations, and legislation seems to swing in their favor.

Long-distance journeys give great satisfaction. On the one hand, from a professional view, success and good fortune are assured far from one's birth place. On the other hand, in one's love life, happiness will be found in the arms of a foreigner, or far from home. A powerful, loving link seems to attach the subject to the father. If an initiation into secret matters is to take place, it will occur through a love relationship.

Venus in the Tenth House

In very early youth, these natives have frequently had a pleasant, easy, and comfortable life. They display greater affection as they grow older. They appreciate a peaceful, comfortable life in the home and do not scorn luxury. Relationships with the various members of the family are harmonious. Except when the planet is afflicted, and considering the rest of the horoscope, this is the first indication of domestic bliss, and natives of this house should do their utmost to conserve this. They are hospitable and their receptivity is warm and intimate.

They can develop and improve inherited real estate. They may receive family possessions through legacies, and they know how to look after them. These subjects will often inherit artistic aptitudes.

The years spent in the paternal home and the final years will be among the happiest in life, and there will be a certain satisfaction that old projects have come to fruition and that they have lived a full life.

VENUS IN THE ELEVENTH HOUSE

These people will have very many pleasant relationships, certain of which will assume a loving character. They will be very popular, above all in relation to the opposite sex. They will have a brilliant social rise, notably thanks to associations and the loving help of devoted friends. Projects are realized through outside assistance or through those with whom they enjoy loving relationships. There is an indication of winnings and gains, luck and happiness through friendships, especially female ones, and within artistic circles.

Earnings through real estate, including farms, are favored. They would be advised to aim investments in such directions, which will assure economic profit without undue strain. It sometimes indicates a legacy from the mother's side, as the eleventh house is the fourth from the eighth. There could be happy repercussions on one's destiny as the result of a close relation traveling afar.

The subject could meet love in the workplace or during a period of ill health. Very often, a health matter will serve to reinforce a love tie. The only menace to the subject's destiny could come from a relationship with someone of dubious moral character, notably when the planet is afflicted.

VENUS IN THE TWELFTH HOUSE

These are both devoted and compassionate toward the sick, those suffering from an infirmity, and those who are nature's outcasts. They are capable of acts of sacrifice and self-denial. A certain love for large animals is also noticeable. From a career perspective, this could steer one toward the medical profession or professions allied to it.

There is a desire for peace and tranquility that could lead one to choose a reclusive lifestyle. Often one's job is performed in a secluded place or demands the utmost discretion.

This configuration plays a part mainly in the domain of one's love life and predisposes to secret love affairs. Often, a strong attachment to someone will go unnoticed by those who are close. Love affairs are upset by obscure circumstances. If these natives marry too early in life, they risk attraction to others later on. They will then have to choose between sacrifices of the heart or clandestine relationships with all the harmful repercussions that such liaisons involve.

Mars in the Houses

Mars is generally known as the god of war. It is also the first planet whose orbit is outside that of Earth. It completes a revolution around the Sun in twenty-three months. Whereas Mercury and Venus, whose orbits are inside the Earth's, enlighten us on intellectual subjects and matters of tenderness and affection, Mars is the first planet that actually pertains to the material world. Mars is the symbol of the aperture that looks into the outer world and, as such, stands for activity, energy, dynamics, and struggle for survival. It is a planet of aggressiveness and combat, giving enthusiasm, courage, and initiative and encourages undertakings requiring sacrifice. It accords skill and quick action. How else could humankind have survived if people had not displayed this kind of courage and aggressiveness that indeed enabled humankind to combat and conquer a savage world of prehistoric monsters?

Mars is vindictive and leads to impulsiveness, jealousy, and anger. It predisposes to fevers, wounds, and accidents. Its symbol alone surely translates all these things, since it represents both the male genital organs as well as a weapon (♂).

If Mars is too powerful in a woman's horoscope, it is detrimental to her femininity, and we have seen in the introduction to this work that a female astrologer has devoted an entire book to this issue.

The position of Mars in the houses will show just where these subjects direct their activities. It will also serve to enlighten us about the areas in which they risk being combative. The study of Mars is one of the most instructive in mundane astrology; on the one hand, ingressions into the cardinal signs of the zodiac (Aries, Cancer, Libra, and Capricorn) and during New Moons, and on the other hand, by the place it occupies in the horoscopes of the world leaders.

MARS IN THE FIRST HOUSE

Here Mars is in accidental dignity, as it were, because of the analogy between this house and the first sign of the zodiac, Aries, in which Mars is dignified. It reveals persons who are audacious, courageous, ready for a fight, energetic, dynamic, intrepid, reckless, imprudent, and impulsive. Their enterprising spirit and need for activity lead them to launch into a particular venture as soon as the idea comes to mind, without necessarily planning the details, the time needed to realize a project, or even the possible repercussions of the project in question. They love competition, rivalry, and conquest. They display a certain foolhardiness, seeming oblivious to the possible dangers that could be engendered by their actions and gestures. They have an undisputed talent for leadership. They are uncontrollable, even in youth. One's career will be strewn with struggles; problems arise, owing either to rash actions or to disproportionate ambitions.

They should take care to reserve their strength and guard against haste that causes them to act with imprudence that could lead to an accident. There is a danger of wounds from a sharp, cutting, piercing instrument, or from fire, especially when the planet is afflicted. This configuration can give bodily wounds (often facial or to the head), sometimes right from birth or during birth (perhaps through the use of forceps). There is a predisposition to fevers. Although one may have a strong constitution and muscular frame, one should nevertheless guard against wasting energy.

MARS IN THE SECOND HOUSE

Here there is a great deal of financial activity and a strong urge to amass material possessions. These people have an aptitude for huge projects, often daring or dangerous and often in the world of industry, especially involving metallurgy. These natives have a great deal of initiative and capacity to earn money. Their business ventures will bring profits that they will quickly reinvest, leading to cash-flow problems; or they will have to face very heavy expenses in a very short period of time. Their character traits, as well as their circumstances, will bring about burdensome costs in the reimbursement of debts, all of which will make it difficult to save money or increase a ready cash supply.

Thus, there will be a great deal of cash movement, either through unwise financial dealings or through poor management. They will have difficulties holding on to material possessions or creating a nest egg. Even minor afflictions will be severely felt, owing to the accidental exile of Mars caused by the analogy with Taurus, the second sign. If these subjects suffer heavy losses through extravagance, disproportionate generosity, or foolhardy speculations, they will nevertheless always have the courage to begin again from scratch. Most of the profits are accompanied immediately by expenditures of equal value. In the face of this curious inability to amass ready cash, despite their keenness to earn, these people should direct all their efforts toward thrift, even if the amount saved represents only a very small percent of the amount gained, no matter how minimal the profit. Above all, they should then redistribute this investment in various ways, always taking care to do so safely.

MARS IN THE THIRD HOUSE

Mental activity is considerably favored. The mind is lively, alert, ingenious and resourceful, but also critical, sarcastic, and mentally aggressive. These subjects often look for quarrels about nothing, even without realizing it or through lack of self-control. They risk being provocative through cutting remarks or imprudent statements and careless writings. They expresses themselves easily, frankly, and forcefully. Their gift for spontaneous repartee gets them into arguments and verbal battles. They wish to put their concept quickly into practice. They have constructive skill, speedy execution, and initiative in business matters.

Subjects intensely desire to practice the profession that suits their aspirations, and they will develop their activity in this direction. In order not to spoil their image of quality, they need to control their impatience and irritability, thus avoiding conflicts with both professional associates and family members. Indeed, there is a risk of conflict with brothers, sisters, and close relatives.

These people should avoid sudden departures. When driving, they should never be a slave to the clock, but rather always be wary of the dangers of exceeding speed limits.

MARS IN THE FOURTH HOUSE

Mars in the fourth house, analogous to Cancer, is in accidental fall. Natives of this configuration will develop a great deal of energy in the pursuit of their profession. Decisions will be rapid, they will show great initiative, and they will be hard on subordinates, but they will also be examples to others and assume blame. They possess a deep desire to succeed and to scale the social ladder, no matter what the cost, even if they have to put up with incessant quarreling. This configuration does not harm the chances of success, but it does announce a career filled with struggles. These natives will make great efforts to remain in the position they have attained, which no easy task given the amount of jealousy that their rise in station will have caused along the way. They will be the objects of criticism and frequently unjustified backbiting. However, whenever they veer too close to illegal practices, social disgrace and scandal await. They will face rivalry from colleagues and associates and even from the boss; but they will achieve success through the skillful execution of tasks and their tenacious efforts.

In their need for conquest and the desire to obtain freedom, these people should be wary at all times of exhausting their sources of energy by trying to go beyond the realm of possibility. Their audacity and courage are probably inherited directly from the mother, but there is a serious risk of falling out with her or of an accident that involves her.

MARS IN THE FIFTH HOUSE

They have a direct and demonstrative nature. It is likely that their education is based largely on discipline, love of work, and the cult of masculine values such as frankness, audacity, courage, and the practice of physical exercise. They love games, somewhat violent sports, and speed. Natives of this house should guard against needlessly wasting energy in the pursuit of pleasures. They are prone to accidents caused by clumsy gestures during games, competitions, and races.

They take initiative in their professional activities and launch themselves into daring ventures or those that contain an element of risk.

They will be attracted by speculative investments. Chances are doubled in the case of metallurgy. They could be profitable if all the right elements are available. However, rash acts will lead to heavy losses.

They are fond of love affairs that are brought quickly to fruition; their relationships will be mostly sexual, but they will be open and natural. Their appetites are strong, and liaisons will be concluded suddenly and unwisely. However, if Mars is afflicted, notably by Venus, quarrels will be frequent, often caused by jealousy. Their children will be robust and enjoy sports, but their health could be endangered, especially in the case of the eldest child.

MARS IN THE SIXTH HOUSE

These people will display a great amount of get-up-and-go and enthusiasm in the exercise of their professional tasks. They will expend a large amount of energy to improve their living standards and to climb the social ladder. Their professions often concern industry, mechanics, iron, fire, the military, police, medicine, and public service.

Their success will depend mainly on the quality of their relationships with colleagues at work, especially those under their command. There is a high risk of conflicts in the workplace. If such clashes become unbearable for these natives by virtue of their frequency or intensity, and if they give too much of themselves in the service of others, they would be advised to become their own boss. This configuration favors physical prowess and professional sports.

To avoid injuries or burns, these people should be very careful when using tools, instruments, and machines. There is a danger of falling victim to infectious and inflammatory diseases, notably those involving the intestines. However, in the case of sickness, recovery is rapid.

Partners (in marriage) will be energetic and dynamic, but also rather authoritative, seeking to impose their own will. That will either stimulate action or become the source of arguments. The partner's health could also be delicate.

MARS IN THE SEVENTH HOUSE

The planet of activity, as well as aggressiveness, in the sector of relationships indicates that certain associates—particularly those associated either by legal contract or through mutual agreement—will stimulate these subjects to activity. However, to their detriment those partners could overstep the limit by seeking to exercise undue authority over the subject. Thus, success will depend greatly on the affinities (or otherwise) that the subjects enjoy with such people, and the amount of diplomacy they are prepared to display where they are involved.

Indeed, one could achieve a great amount of success through collaboration with others. The subject will instinctively search for contact, assistance, and the additional help of a third party's energy and forcefulness, which could allow the attainment of one's goals. The native could be the brain behind a group project. However, this does not imply necessarily that one's collaborators will provide an essentially docile element in the association. One will have great difficulty in succeeding without the help of a good legal adviser. If the subject agrees to form a partnership, then one should have a contract drawn up by an expert in the field, one whose devotion to duty is assured.

The native of this house will marry early in life, more to satisfy sexual instincts or through the need for an energetic partner than because of any genuine feeling. The partner could show signs of wanting to rule despotically or of being argumentative, thus causing incessant discussions through systematic contradictions. The possible sudden loss of a partner could bring about the turning point in the career.

Here, of course, Mars is in accidental exile, since the seventh house corresponds to Libra, which is opposite Aries, and possible afflictions clearly accentuate the risk of litigations.

MARS IN THE EIGHTH HOUSE

Mars in this house provides a warning that if these subjects are not careful, the organism will wear out prematurely. These people seem to squander their vital forces, especially their sexual energy. However, quite to the contrary, this energy, if properly used, could be converted into a certain psychic force or occult strength. They ought to exercise great caution with metallic objects and instruments, including fire arms. They could have a delicate constitution or be the victims of an acute illness, fevers, or infections. There is also a certain tendency toward accidents or the need for surgery.

Throughout life, these natives should display a great amount of vigilance where personal interests are at stake. They must defend their goods and possessions and constantly stand up for their rights. This is especially true when it comes to matters concerning accounting proce-dures in a partnership, the financial clauses of a contract, or commonly held goods, as well as all that is connected with legacies. They should keep a close watch on all their insurance policies, especially those that cover losses as a result of theft or fire. There is a danger of wrangles over an inheritance, or the need to call on the services of the courts to settle a matter. Financial losses are to be feared after marriage, whether through the marriage partner's extravagance, because of spendthrift habits, or through unusual circumstances that are difficult to avoid. There are possibilities of litigations involving state fiscal services. One's financial situation could be burdened by debts, and the temptation of buying on credit must be resisted, thereby avoiding heavy financial commitments that cannot reasonably be met.

However, because Mars finds itself here in accidental dignity, owing to its rulership over Scorpio, the eighth sign, these subjects will find the energy needed to defend their interests when threatened.

MARS IN THE NINTH HOUSE

They express their opinions frankly, defending them with all the energy they can muster, and seek to share them. When they embrace a cause, they fight enthusiastically for it. They may even overstep reasonable bounds and border on fanaticism, though they are generally skeptical of religion. Their ideals tend to be more material. They admire forceful, audacious, and courageous prowess. It is the astral signature of pioneers and athletic champions.

If their education allows, they can study brilliantly and go far in the field of academics. They will never take on a legal battle without having all the cards stacked completely in their favor, since the eventual legal decision could go against them.

They probably owe the energy and strength that animates them to the father. However, there is a certain amount of danger where the father's health is concerned, and there is the risk of a falling out, even a certain rivalry, between them.

These people are strongly attracted by international travel, and traveling will play an important role in their lives. There is also the possibility of great realizations in this area, but also the danger of encountering a certain degree of hostility.

MARS IN THE TENTH HOUSE

Force and energy will remain with the subject right into old age. One will continue working, even if from home, to improve living standards. However, if these subjects wish to maintain friendly and affectionate links with those around them, they are advised to keep a close watch on their thoughts and to check their moods to avoid becoming unbearable in old age because of critical attitudes. Very often, this configuration points to great achievements later in life and to the fact that old projects will finally come to fruition, despite the hostilities that they have had to face for such a long time. Here, Mars is in accidental exaltation because of its relationship with the tenth sign, Capricorn, whose ruler, Saturn, allows the accomplishment of long-held aspirations.

These subject's birthright in the form of real estate could lead to jealousies in the family circle, and quarrels are to be feared in this way. One's residence is threatened by fire, theft, or burglary. Thus, the subject should be well covered by insurance. The home atmosphere from birth onward, and the hostilities one encounters, could influence the native to go farther afield and seek fortune elsewhere.

Mars in the Eleventh House

Mars, the planet of activity, thus placed in the sector of projects, signifies that these natives will work with energy, confidence, and enthusiasm to realize their ambitions. Sometimes they enter head-first, too quickly, and, consequently, without sufficient reflection. Certain projects could be compromised because they have acted too hastily in the execution of their plans, because their projects are too numerous, because they begin something new without finishing what was already begun, or because they overstep their own possibilities, either because they have been too ambitious or because they simply lacks the necessary means. If they exercises prudence and caution, things will go very differently. These people can count mainly on the assistance of energetic, hard-working friends who will also be chaotic and demanding. They will therefore have to be very diplomatic to avoid clashes with friends and relatives. They should choose helpmates with care, since some may lead them astray and cause them to dissipate energies or, at least, try to do so. True friends will be few and far between. Friendships will be mainly men, including enthusiastic, athletic, courageous, and energetic personalities. However, struggles of rivalry could arise between the friends themselves, or between them and the subject. They will all try to dominate one another.

In a woman's horoscope, this configuration is particularly significant in view of the very friendly relationships that are promised with men. The nature of such friendships will evidently depend on the other planets with which Mars is connected. A good Mars aspect to the ruler of the Ascendant, or to the Ascendant itself, is the most desirable influence.

MARS IN THE TWELFTH HOUSE

This configuration is of great importance and constitutes a serious warning. However, as the old saying goes, "Only a simpleton is ruled by the stars; a wise person rules them." If these subjects act unwisely and impulsively under the influence of passion or anger, grave consequences are to be feared that would provoke hostile feelings, and these would be all the more serious since they would be carried out covertly. One should, therefore, avoid all excessive behavior.

Research that is carried out in isolated places and demands secrecy suits these natives. This is the case for laboratory research workers, the police, doctors, and, in a more general sense, all activities in places where people are united with a certain sense of loss of liberty, such as in hospitals, clinics, asylums, boarding schools, convents, and prisons.

These subjects should make every effort to escape or detach themselves from servitude, freeing themselves from constraints, invisible hindrances and obstacles.

They should be wary of imprudent or clumsy gestures likely to provoke accidents or require a surgery. They have a certain predisposition for fevers and inflammations.

JUPITER IN THE HOUSES

Jupiter is known by the Greeks as Zeus. He is the father of the gods and humankind and, for astrologers, he is the greater benefic.

Jupiter remains in each sign for the average of just under one year. Its glyph, a crescent above a cross ($\u2643$), is the symbol of the conscience that rises above the material world. It reveals secret and hidden things. It is the planet of expansion, and the aura that encircles each human being is mainly subject to Jupiterian vibrations that are in turn modified by those received by the other planets. Jupiter is sociable, charitable, and generous. It gives equilibrium to the organism, great sensitivity, a sense of hierarchy, and awareness of judgment. It is the preserver and giver. It tends to combine acts and circumstances harmoniously; this combination is often more simply and conveniently called "luck," or the element of chance. It loves elevated, professional situations, large business ventures, and wholesale commerce, and it is appreciative of honors and social distinctions.

For the ancients, Jupiter was the largest of the planets. As a result, it has become the synonym for expansion, development, upward mobility, progress, and abundance; however it can, at times, represent the unhealthy conditions of over-indulgence and excessiveness.

In mundane astrology, it acts in favor of peace. Since it provokes optimism and confidence and incites purchasing activity, it becomes a factor in rising values on the stock exchange.

In the horoscope, Jupiter is indicative of the domains in which the subject exercises instinctive judgment. Favorable circumstances therein will bring material assistance. It goes without saying that, since it is benefic by nature, we expect it to be well placed in the descriptions that follow. However, if it exchanges unfavorable aspects, then all the goodness promised will be diminished, indeed, even withdrawn. For this reason, we shall not repeat this factor further on in this exposé.

JUPITER IN THE FIRST HOUSE

It gives a jovial, dynamic, expansive, optimistic, benevolent, and generous nature. These natives display good judgment, but also a little too much self-indulgence. They prove themselves tolerant and good-natured. Their good humor and moral values are infectious; thus their company is greatly sought after, a fact that contributes to their success. They give the impression of being self-confident. Their outer display of self-confidence tends to rub off on others, creating feelings of empathy and mutual understanding. They are magnetic, having a rather sanguine temperament and a strong constitution. They ought to avoid straying too much from healthy eating habits, lest greediness causes them to be afflicted by a "middle-age spread." If they do not keep a careful watch over their diet, there could be a tendency toward an arthritic condition, liver complaints, or high blood pressure.

A happy existence is favored, more often than not right from birth, and this is often seen in the form of a good education. A friendly disposition assures them of good-willed assistance and useful protection from others. Their efforts are generally blessed with success, and if they do not unduly abuse their fundamental good luck, they will enjoy a prosperous existence.

JUPITER IN THE SECOND HOUSE

This configuration offers the chance of huge success in financial matters, as here Jupiter is the great benefactor par excellence. On the one hand, one could amass great wealth through pure chance, for instance if one is born into a family that is wealthy; on the other hand, one could benefit from exceptional opportunities, as well as a great deal of effective support from outside elements. Generally, these people will take advantage of a harmonious combination of their own actions, prevailing circumstances, and the environment in which they evolve. They will earn a large income from Jupiterian occupations—that is, wholesale trading, imports and exports, large business ventures, the grocery trade, law, the teaching profession, the sciences, public office, or government posts.

They will gain the assistance of banks, credit companies, financial institutions, and the like, or they will themselves hold positions in such business concerns or in a large firm. They will, relatively speaking, find it easy to obtain the finance needed to develop their business ventures or purchase items on a large scale, notably in real estate. It could be said that they will earn their living easily, and they will build up their personal assets without much effort, mainly because of a great organizing ability combined with a certain amount of innate good luck, as well as their discernment of the material world. They should endeavor to control any displays of extravagant generosity and avoid legal procedures involving financial matters.

Because Jupiter is the general significator of material possessions, any possible affliction in this house—more than in any other—could point to the removal of hoped-for material gains. Bad aspects exchanged here by Jupiter threaten heavy financial losses, especially to those subjects who are born to wealth.

JUPITER IN THE THIRD HOUSE

The subject is capable of coordinating ideas with actions. A spirit of synthesis allows one to grasp a wide range of matters. One has a sense of hierarchy or natural order—hence, a sense of values. Jupiter bestows good judgment, a broad mind, and an enthusiastic and optimistic character. It is often the sign of high moral values and a careful education. Mental faculties are favored and lead to the pursuit of further studies. Sincerity and courtesy are prevalent, not only in oral expression, but also in written works. One could earn an income through writing; in any case, the heavens promise success through communication.

Success is achieved through the practice of a professional activity corresponding to the chosen vocation. So if natives of this house follow their dreams and aspirations, their work situation will evolve easily. The result of this will be brilliant social success.

Great profit will be gained during travels, notably those undertaken in lands bordering on the place of birth. A member of the family, possibly a brother, could play a fortunate role in one's career.

As though by a miracle, one could escape unharmed from a car, train, or airplane accident.

JUPITER IN THE FOURTH HOUSE

Jupiter here gives an acute sense of justice and accords an optimistic, jovial, honest and generous nature. This configuration is the surest indication of success in life, both professionally and socially. Chance smiles on these subjects through support and assistance, which begins with help coming from family members, sometimes from the mother. A fortunate concatenation of circumstances favors the career and pushes the subjects toward success, which is obtained without a great deal of effort on their part. Indeed, here Jupiter is in accidental exaltation. Placed at the summit of the horoscope, it is a configuration commonly found in the charts of financiers, corporate heads, managing directors, and those in responsible positions in governments and large firms—in short, those in high income brackets.

These subjects enjoy good reputations and earn credit for themselves, literally and figuratively. Honors will be reserved for them; sometimes they will even reach the dizzying heights of celebrity. However, Jupiter is also the final judge, and this explains why those who abuse his benevolent influence will suffer changes in fortune if ever they show signs of acting with a lack of probity.

JUPITER IN THE FIFTH HOUSE

This house position brings good fortune, both in matters of the heart and material wealth. There is a tendency toward excess in the pursuit of pleasure, or possibly in the practice of sporting activities. They are sociable and love community entertainment, amusements, and being out on the town. They smile at life, and life smiles at them in turn. They have the reputation of being lucky. One enjoys being in their company.

They display a lively interest in all sorts of games and are skilled in matters of speculation. There is the possibility of considerable amounts earned through games of chance and in business ventures that involve a certain element of risk. The stock exchange seems to be an area of preference.

These individuals will enjoy loving relationships with good, rich, and honorable people. They are lucky in love. Their children will be essentially good and grateful; the eldest son could attain a position of importance. They are successful in everything that involves children, which could make them suited to teaching posts. One could reach an elevated position and become a leader in one's field.

JUPITER IN THE SIXTH HOUSE

This configuration grants an element of protection from the perspective of health. When ill, one will receive the needed treatment, will recover easily, and may even gain something through the illness. This position does, however, constitute a warning against high living. Excessive behavior could lead to premature obesity, liver complaints, circulatory conditions, or arthritic conditions, to which this constitution is susceptible. One is also prone to carbuncles and abscesses. Sensuality manifests through a highly developed sense of smell. The subject helps the sick and the needy and loves small animals.

These natives could hold positions of responsibility, more likely as subordinates rather than self-employed. This position is absolutely indicative of the executive. They work enthusiastically for a large salary; they will earn the esteem of their superiors and the respect of their subordinates. Whether they are independent or not, they will greatly benefit from the role played by those who are lower in rank. They will exchange confidential information with them; they will be somewhat like partners; in short, a pleasant work environment prevails.

Marriage partners will have a jovial and optimistic character and bring luck, assistance, support, and protection. The natives will benefit in various fields from the presence of their partners.

JUPITER IN THE SEVENTH HOUSE

This position favors contacts, social action, popularity, promises social prestige, and success in legal matters, partnerships, and marriage. These natives will receive interesting business propositions and could become linked through contracts to someone of great value who will contribute strongly to their personal success, either through offered assistance, prestige, and forthrightness, through that person's fortune, or through both of these. These people benefit from a certain protection against hostile actions, conflicts, legal problems, and lawsuits. In the case of a disagreement, they will often come through as winners, probably as the result of an informal agreement. Profit could arise from struggles, adversities, or winning a court case. Staunch adversaries or competitors could turn into friends or associates.

It is one of the best factors for the institution of marriage and announces social success through marriage. Social and financial advantages could come as a direct result of such a marriage because of the marriage partner's comfortable financial situation; if this is not exactly the case, then it naturally means that the career will progress after marital union.

It is quite obvious that these few lines concern only a particular configuration and must therefore be taken with a certain amount of reserve, since there are a number of other factors that come into play. We will simply retain the fact that Jupiter brings his assistance to partnerships and associations.

JUPITER IN THE EIGHTH HOUSE

Jupiter here promotes an interest in the occult sciences and matters of death, life after death, and all the religious implications that are raised as a result of this preoccupation. Sometimes this attraction can go a little too far. Usually, dreams are vivid and remain heavily imprinted on the mind, so that the subject is able to remember and recount them in minute detail. This in itself is impressive.

This configuration greatly favors finances in two main ways. First, through marriage, either because of the partner's fortune or because of an improvement in the financial situation after the union has been concluded. Second, because it is the best position for inheritances, gifts, legacies, and all kinds of donations. Sometimes these inheritances are obtained only after legal processes. Generally, some deaths produce financial gain. It is more than likely that the subject will pass away gently and naturally.

JUPITER IN THE NINTH HOUSE

Frequently these natives inherit from the father a profound and broad mind, tolerance, sincerity, as well as religious and philosophical tendencies. They are attracted to legal matters and academic institutions. Success is facilitated if they are connected to the law or are counselors.

This configuration is in itself an important guide, as it indicates that chances for success will prevail in faraway places. It is often a token of the fact that, the farther one moves away from one's place of birth, the more things improve rapidly on a large scale. In any case, long and distant voyages are profitable. If these subjects remain in the country of birth, they will benefit greatly through commercial transactions of an international nature. Contact with foreigners and international trade will contribute to a growing fortune. Possibly they will have prophetic dreams.

The fact that Jupiter is in accidental dignity (because Jupiter is ruler of Sagittarius, the ninth zodiac sign) accentuates the assured assistance, spiritually as much as materially.

JUPITER IN THE TENTH HOUSE

These natives often come from families that are well off, and they will enjoy a climate of prosperity as long as they remain in the parental home. They adapt with much difficulty to precarious situations, and they love creature comforts. They will receive assistance, either financial or through education, from their forbears and from their families in general.

A successful career is gained under parental influence, or even in their birthplace. Real estate is favored, beginning with the subject's' birthright. Often, the acquisition of property is promised through economizing, through sound real estate management, and through legacies. A fortune could possibly be gained through an agricultural occupation. One will have a comfortable and pleasant life within the home and a peaceful domestic environment.

The happiest period of life will be toward retirement age, and late success is promised.

JUPITER IN THE ELEVENTH HOUSE

This position grants a sociable, jovial, and charitable disposition. Subjects display a cooperative and conciliatory spirit. They could be inclined to show an interest in philanthropic works.

Chance plays a role in the excellence of relationships enjoyed with others, contributing to their rise up the social ladder. The more they cultivate their relationships, the greater their success will be. Among friends, they can count a good number of wealthy, influential, and high-ranking officials, legal professionals, and clergy. In times of difficulty they will call on understanding friends who will help them regain their usual vim and vigor. Such friends will be devoted to them and to their cause.

Their innate good fortune is obvious through the fact that they reach goals, realize projects, bring plans to fruition, and meet with the crown of success in their objectives. Often life takes a turn for the better and destiny improves for the subject after the birth of a child (or even from the moment of conception). This is particularly true in the case of the eldest child.

JUPITER IN THE TWELFTH HOUSE

Here, Jupiter is in accidental dignity by virtue of its classical ruler-ship over the twelfth sign, Pisces. It thus brings to this house an overall protection against life's adversities. Note, this is not the same case for the modern ruler of Pisces, Neptune (See "Neptune in the Twelfth House").

This position grants peaceful, helpful and benevolent dispositions. The subject will participate in charitable and humanitarian works and will benefit from assistance, worthy actions, and covert support. One could be successful in a discreet occupation or in a profession carried out in a remote location or in a quiet and mysterious way out of the public eye. One will be happy in isolation. There is a possibility of distinction in a secret society. Their enemies, if they have any, will be astonished when the subject reveals their existence and overcomes them directly or indirectly, almost without them noticing it. One of these enemies could even become an ally. This native will have strange experiences; for example, one could carry on two simultaneous love affairs. Toward the end of life, one will feel attracted to piety and the ascetic life. The subject may already be a high-ranking member of the clergy.

SATURN IN THE HOUSES

Saturn, known to the Greeks as *Cronos,* was until the seventeenth century the farthest recognized planet from Earth. It completes its orbit around the Sun in a little less than thirty years. Its glyph, a scythe (♄), is the symbol of the harvester and of the reaper. Saturn brings to mind ideas of slowness, stability, tardiness, heaviness, limitation, deprivation, and restriction. It represents old, austere, and solitary people.

Owing to the fact that it is far from the Sun, it acquires a sense of coldness, contraction, restriction, and detachment. It is said to be unde-monstrative. It is, above all, prudent, patient, and economical.

For those who believe in reincarnation, it is karma, the great architect who fashions character and corrects mistakes, sometimes with severity, but when we finally become receptive, it accords secret and profound wisdom.

In mundane astrology, Saturn represents conservative political parties, administration, and real estate holdings. It is symbolic of moral restrictions.

Its position in the houses in the horoscope points to the area in which the subject will suffer deprivations and frustrations. As if to compensate for this, it will frequently denote the sector in which the subject shows an aptitude for undertaking long, drawn-out tasks, in which one will eventually harvest the fruits so patiently awaited and long deserved.

Who could ever really say where superstition ends and science commences? When we say that misfortunes rarely come in ones, it so happens that the known vicissitudes result from the same house that is affected by Saturn; and when we say, "unlucky in cards, lucky in love," does it not really mean there is compensation and a balance between two domains of life that depend on the same house?

Owing to its reputation as a malefic, we suppose it to be, in the following pages, in unfavorable aspect. However, if it is located well, its threats will be less menacing and quite to the contrary, it will bring reliability, constancy and stability to the domains of the house concerned.

Saturn in the First House

Saturn rising gives a methodical, industrious, wary, and vindictive mind. Although the subject is respectful of the rules of decorum and shows signs of politeness and seemliness, first contacts are sometimes difficult, for these natives appear to be more strict than they really are, owing to a prudent reserve, humility, or timidity. They speak little and do not waste energy on meaningless gestures.

Saturnian powers of retention often cause these subjects to be gifted with a remarkable memory. Their proverbial perseverance and exemplary patience will grant them an amazing aptitude to engage in, and to succeed at, long, drawn-out tasks. One could say that the time factor means little to these people. Sometimes they work too slowly, and their exactitude may leave a great deal to be desired. The limitation inherent in Saturn makes them hungry for power and gives them a sense of organization and responsibility. Success will come only after renewed efforts and complete self-reliance.

Their rather melancholic temperament causes them to sink into the depths of exaggerated pessimism. They are sensitive to cold, likely to suffer from rheumatism, and predisposed to falls and fractures.

SATURN IN THE SECOND HOUSE

Restrictions will manifest on the material plane, notably in the sphere of finances. These natives would be well advised to make the necessary arrangements (including adequate insurance if applicable) to avoid unsuccessful lawsuits, heavy financial losses, the decrease or termination of normal sources of revenue, and breaches of financial engagements, even when they have been drawn up in their favor. A profession that assures these natives a regular, stable income should have preference. The best occupations would be those related to agriculture, real estate, property management, construction, the ground, and all that is underground. This configuration does not actually contradict the idea of building up a personal fortune, but success in this area will depend on the subject's ability to save and economize wisely. They cannot hope to expect a sudden windfall to make them rich overnight, but rather they should count on a gradual accumulation through repeated efforts, which requires them to overcome continual difficulties, relying on their own personal merits. Long-term investments are thus favored. Their financial situation could be subject to influence from an elderly person. This could be beneficial as well as detrimental. One could either receive gifts and inheritances or be the object of assistance and subsidies from outside sources.

SATURN IN THE THIRD HOUSE

Saturn in this place warns that certain tribulations in life—at the very least, restrictions—will have an effect on studies or mental capacities, on trips, as well as on relationships with those who are direct associates. It favors all serious pursuits of the mind whereby tact and diplomacy must predominate. Natives of this configuration have an aptitude for methodical reflection.

They seem mature for their actual age, especially when they are young, but they will age slowly, especially in relation to their mental capacities.

Moreover, their sense of humor will surely be a great help in the ageing process. At times, they will have to control their cynicism. They have an aptitude for works requiring time and concentration, discretion and secrecy, especially those of a mental nature. Their education could be impeded during youth, but the taste for studies is nonetheless developed because of it. Quite to the contrary, they become increasingly vivacious with age. This is one of the surest indications of great ambition, especially when it is at the end of the house, close to the MC. Everything depends on the other factors in the horoscope.

These people should be sure to guard against the theft or loss of documents. To protect themselves against possible annoyances through writings, they will have to keep a close watch over the pen and cut down on sarcastic comments. Conflicts and disagreements in the immediate family are to be feared. Losses through death will also afflict them from this aspect. Serious accidents or delays of great consequence during travels are also to be dreaded.

SATURN IN THE FOURTH HOUSE

This position gives pride, great ambition, and a craving for domination. Large administrative bodies and politics will be greatly attractive to these subjects. They have a sense of organization and a desire to assume responsibilities. They carefully prepare for the accomplishment of their mission, and everything indicates that they will eventually reach their goal. They inspire respect and fear rather than sympathy and popularity. Their rise will very likely be slow and painful and strewn with obstacles, delays, and ambushes. But thanks to their undeniable know-how and perseverance, they will attain the highest peaks in their fields of activity. Their passing will leave indelible traces. Their disproportionate ambition calls to mind this passage from the Bible: "Again, the devil took him to a very high mountain and showed him all the kingdoms of the world and their glory" (Matthew 4:8).

The dangers of disgrace and growing unpopularity are among the most serious. Family problems are also to be dreaded. The peak years of forty-two to forty-four and fifty-eight to sixty mark significant stages in the subject's destiny. Napoleon Bonaparte, Adolf Hitler, and Richard Nixon, whose native skies were dominated by Saturn, serve very well to illustrate the warning we wish to impart.

SATURN IN THE FIFTH HOUSE

Here Saturn warns that life's ordeals (or deprivations at least) will have an effect on the love life. Delays, deceptions, and hindrances will mark the sentimental life. Sometimes, right from youth, these subjects love someone older than themselves or one whose character is too serious or austere. The failure to realize this first attempt at a union could cause such future situations to be few and far between, for they no longer allow themselves to get carried away. Pleasures, love games, and games of chance are curbed or envisaged with a certain distrust. They will attach a great deal of seriousness and profundity to sentiments. They withdraw into their shell; they could brood over a love for a long time for the simple reason that they are fearful of making their feelings known.

Sports barely interest these people. In any case, they must be careful of the heart, which is rather fragile. They will prefer serious games such as chess or bridge, which require effort and involve method, memory, calculations, precision, and concentration. This position reduces offspring and causes the subject to be fearful of potential problems, sometimes of a serious nature, arising over children.

Essentially, speculations are hardly recommended, since serious losses could arise from such activities. By contrast, however, investments in the earth—in buildings, property, and mines—are favorable.

SATURN IN THE SIXTH HOUSE

This position warns these natives to keep a close watch on their health throughout life, all the more because of the fact that contracted illnesses could become chronic. Their constitution is rather weak, but if they follow simple rules of hygiene and a recommended diet, they will reach a ripe old age all the more easily for not having exhausted their vital energy too quickly to begin with. They are sensitive to chills and predisposed toward rheumatism and skin problems. They will have to fight against a lazy intestine and, above all, avoid constipation and its deadly and very diverse consequences.

These natives are quite likely to experience difficulties in exercising free will over the choice of professions and over conditions under which they are expected to work. Should they direct their activities toward the service of those in need of medical care, they will improve their own destiny. The medical profession or paramedicine would be good choices. They will give the best of themselves in minor posts that require trustworthiness, responsibility, reliability, patience, concentration, precision, and a methodical mind. It is not advisable to fly from the nest alone. They will be appreciated for their regularity and constant efforts in the execution of meticulous and difficult tasks. They will need to keep a constant watch over subordinates.

Their marriage partners could suffer from weak health and/or be persons whose nature is too serious and austere.

SATURN IN THE SEVENTH HOUSE

Certain stumbling blocks in life, or at the very least restrictions, will affect relationships. Success or failure will depend greatly on the quality of their associations and notably the role, whether a happy one or not, that the marriage partner will play.

Often the marriage takes place later in life, and circumstances would seem to oppose the realization of the union. The partner may display a certain coldness. Both parties will have to make a constant effort to maintain the balance, which is so precarious, as conditions pertaining to the character will stifle sentiments and hinder the vital impulses. Nevertheless Saturn in this position can bring stability to the affections. At times, the death of an associate has a significant bearing on one's destiny.

The worldly life is somewhat constricted, though it is not impossible in strict, reserved circles among elderly people who are both respectable and rich in experience. There is the risk of unpopularity, and even a reversal of fortune. Associations are rarely profitable. It is often difficult to free oneself, owing to the existence of a long-term contract that contains severe clauses.

The difficulties inherent in Saturn do not necessarily impede success, which could be obtained through hard work, perseverance, thrift, and wise economic management.

SATURN IN THE EIGHTH HOUSE

The attraction for the occult is very serious. Before the subjects can progress in this area, however, they must make an effort to remember their dreams. They are predisposed toward catching chills and suffering from rheumatism. They should be wary of slipping and could be susceptible to landslides and falls from high places. Death will come with the simple wearing out of the organism at an advanced age.

Their marriage partners will have an important role to play in their fortune. This could be beneficial or detrimental. More often than not, they will never be wealthy, and owing to circumstances beyond their control, the financial situation will often worsen after marriage.

They should never sign a contract without first consulting a good legal counselor. They should always read the fine print in clauses and contracts. There is the danger that one's inheritance will be stolen, frequently after the early death of the father or another close relative. One should avoid getting too far into debt. In summary, there is a danger of litigations with others over money matters, but this does not prevent the success that can be attained through a sense of thrift and by wise financial management.

SATURN IN THE NINTH HOUSE

Saturn will act slowly but surely in the domains that depend on this house. The mind is deep, rigid and austere. A studious and pensive nature, these subjects are interested in philosophical, metaphysical, and psychological questions rather than religious ones. They will preserve their ideal tirelessly. Their opinions will come to fruition after long periods of reflection, but they will be firmly established. They are certainly quite sincere but lack enthusiasm, perhaps because they are a little too fatalistic. They have a strict sense of justice, but remain severe. They can become impassioned over abstract sciences and advanced mathematics and over long and fastidious research that requires deep knowledge of the discipline under study.

There is danger of financial loss following an unsuccessful lawsuit. The father could be ailing, already very old when these natives are born, or they could lose him prematurely. Disputes and disagreements are to be feared in which the father and in-laws are concerned. Lengthy, distant trips barely attract these people—such travels are not very propitious and may be dangerous. In addition, there could be a certain lack of harmony between them and people of a different race, nationality, or language.

SATURN IN THE TENTH HOUSE

This configuration is often an indication of a severe, austere heredity, a strict, rigid education, a monotonous, melancholic life, or of an unhappy childhood. This is often due to the fact that the parents are too old or too traditional. These natives often suffer from the burden of too much responsibility. They have to make every effort possible to exercise their free will.

This configuration underlines the importance of inherited possessions and the role that these will play in life. There are possible wrangles within the family over inherited property or real estate. They will probably be involved in a profession related to architecture and construction and sideline occupations that may include real estate.

Life could be saddened by the early loss through death of male family members. These natives should take every precaution to ensure their old age by setting aside at least the bare minimum needed to avoid a painful environment or an unpleasant residence.

SATURN IN THE ELEVENTH HOUSE

Relationships will be established with difficulty, and friends will not be easily kept, yet these subjects will get on well with people who are older than they are. Success or defeat in their social and professional life will depend greatly on assistance received from friends and relatives or, by contrast, on the betrayals and perfidious actions of false friends liable to cause great damage. It is therefore superfluous to insist upon the need for these natives to choose their friends carefully. Very often, relationships will have some bearing on the patrimony's real estate. They will have to plan future projects carefully and make certain that they do not aim higher than actual finances and knowledge permit; if they do not, frustrated ambitions are to be feared. Great satisfactions are to be drawn from belonging to companies and groups that are frequented by reliable people whose counsel can be heeded.

This configuration does not suit a seasonal trade; if the clientele disappears quickly, they does not always return in like fashion. These natives should avoid lending money; if they do, they risk losing both their cash and their friends. Although the latter could quite easily be of good faith, the best defence against Saturn in this position is to guard constantly against deliberate betrayal by friends.

SATURN IN THE TWELFTH HOUSE

If they do not suffer from a deliberately self-imposed existence of solitude, then they should make every effort and force themselves to make frequent and repeated contacts with the outer world. This is rather against their nature, however, since they generally prefer a withdrawn life doing meticulous tasks that are performed in secret and alone. The personal satisfaction that will be gained from this, as though they were collecting a secret treasure, is worth far more to them than approval from the outside world. For an elite, this configuration could mark an attraction to alchemy, an important rank in a secret society, or a rare spiritual elevation, sometimes ascetic or highly mystical.

These individuals should be fearful of hidden, sly, and cunning treachery and, above all, false accusations to which one could fall victim. They should be careful to adhere strictly to the rules, moral values, and the law. There is also the possibility of injury from an animal or as a result of an accident, as well as a probable period in hospital to treat a chronic illness.

URANUS IN THE HOUSES

Uranus is the first of the planets to be found beyond Saturn. It was known by the ancients as *Ouranos,* the Heavens. The discovery of Uranus occurred as the result of the telescope by the English native William

Herschel on March 13, 1781, between 10 p.m. and 11 p.m. Local Time in Bath, in the south of England. Its original symbol is in fact composed of the first initial of the discoverer's surname (⛢) [in this publication we will use the European symbol, ♅]. It completes its revolution around the Sun in eighty-four years. From it we receive a very strong light. It is considered by many to be the superior octave to Mercury, the planet of mental capacities. It does, in effect, grant extreme cerebral activity, a sharp psychic sensitivity, a lightning fast rapidity of associations, intuition, and the gift of invention.

Uranus also seems to be related to Saturn, which justifies its shared rulership of Aquarius. It is the great awakener of spirit. On the physical plane, it symbolizes the renewal of tissues, muscular elasticity and internal secretions.

In destiny, it acts through surprise, happily or not so happily. Suddenly, without any warning, it provokes overwhelming modifications and upheavals, more often than not through ruptures. It can show itself to be explosive and violent.

All that is rhythmical, cyclical, undulating, and vibrating is attributed to Uranus, such as electronics, radio, television, aviation, space, and astrology. It exercises its mastery over Aquarius, the zodiac sign of the next astrological age; and we also notice that its Herschel "⛢" symbol is reproduced a million times over on the roofs of buildings in France.

In mundane astrology, its discovery in 1781, shortly after the start of the American Revolution and heralding the French Revolution, would seem to justify the fact that we hold it responsible for revolutionary movements.

URANUS IN THE FIRST HOUSE

Uranus strongly influences mental attributes, feelings, and activities. It gives a certain suppleness, thanks to superior intelligence, great originality and independence, a rather disconcerting frankness, brusque behavior, and an irritable and whimsical character. It grants a creative mind, ultramodern ideas in the realms of the sciences, the arts, politics, and philosophy.

Natives of this configuration attach primordial importance to their freedom, and disagreements they have with those around them usually occur because people close to them fail to realize how important it is for them to feel free. These subjects are not easily influenced. They can be cordial and very human, but they cannot bear constraints and controls. All of this is manifested very early on, right from childhood. They know that they are ahead of their times, but they are also convinced that they are on the correct path and that they are right. They care little about the opinions or the approval of the masses, with whom they are actually in intense disagreement. They are born nonconformists.

On the physiological level, they would be well advised to maintain a sound level of mental hygiene—calm, rest, and, most important, self-control. These qualities can be gained through the practice of yoga, conscious breathing exercises, and meditation. Hydrotherapy and electrotherapy also suit them, as well as all forms of therapeutics, whether ancient, renewed or contemporary.

In destiny, this strong position of Uranus causes subjects to take the road less traveled. They enjoy taking risks and lead adventurous lives, sprinkled with ups and downs and strange events. These natives will stray from those around them and will be familiar with abrupt breaks in social ties. They will be greatly interested in metaphysics, the profound, and the marvelous.

URANUS IN THE SECOND HOUSE

This configuration warns of sudden ups and downs that affect finances. They do not always want to take the time to check their daily spending. If they wish to employ an accountant or cashier, they would be well advised to reject any candidate with this configuration. It is an excellent asset for exercising a profession connected with the sciences, especially those that involve the exploitation of new things and inventions. They possess a remarkable flair for sensing whether a deal is a good one or not. They have an aptitude for grasping opportunities while, at the same time, weighing the possible inherent dangers involved. They are capable of risking a large sum of money to exploit an idea. These people are best suited to the exercise of independent activities.

Destiny is generally marked, for better or for worse, by changes that are very abrupt and have their origins in the sudden leaps and bounds affecting finances. One day, they will be short of money and, the next, freely spend large amounts as the result of sudden cash gains, which are large in amount and fully unexpected. The dominant note is financial instability—sudden vicissitudes and spectacular recoveries. This native should therefore take advantage of lucky situations—which will not be infrequent—in order to replenish their cash supply in readiness for further sudden changes in fortune. They should act wisely in matters concerning their fortune. In order to counteract the hazardous nature of such an influence, they would be well advised to assure themselves of maintaining at least a minimum stable income.

URANUS IN THE THIRD HOUSE

Uranus in this position makes for exceptional intellectual realizations. The inquisitive minds and inventive spirit of these subjects will take them to the forefront in areas of scientific discovery, notably in the domains of aviation, electronics, data processing, and computer science, where they can anticipate and make innovations. They should take advantage of their own talents and exploit their ideas in concrete ways. They may be self-taught, but they will frequent those who are gifted and possess rare intellectual capacity. They should be careful of how they express themselves to avoid attracting troubles. These subjects use and overuse the radio, television, electronic media, mobile phones, and the Internet. They may shine in a discipline of their choosing, in particular psychology and all that touches human relationships.

Owing to their strong personality, their rather bizarre air, and the unorthodox ideas they defend—as well as their relationships, both in the family and professionally—their lives are not always harmonious. They would be far happier if they were to limit their contacts to those who share their opinions. Estrangement with close relatives is a possibility. They will often go on trips, modifying their schedule and itinerary with a suddenness that reflects a certain originality in their manner of traveling.

In their professional career, these subjects find a broad field of action that allows them to apply, develop, and manifest their originality. The rest of the horoscope will tell us whether their ideas show themselves to be feasible, when and where these subjects risk becoming social outcasts owing to their ideas, and whether their inventive spirit will project them to the highest pinnacles of success or not.

URANUS IN THE FOURTH HOUSE

A strange personality, these natives will be subjected to repeated ups and downs. They will suffer but strongly benefit from the environment and all that touches their employer. They will experience problems with superiors and will, sooner or later, aspire to professional independence. Periods of credit will alternate with difficult times, and they will abruptly change their occupation. They will stray very early from their family circle, notably from the mother.

Sudden opportunity could manifest through the exploitation of a scientific invention. Difficulties will arise when dealing with public servants, officials, the established order, and people with narrow minds. It often promises exceptional success in quite an unusual area, notably anything avant-garde. Generally, they climb the social ladder in fits and starts and rather abruptly as the result of unexpected and even extraordinary circumstances. They could reach the pinnacle, but almost always their general destiny and, more particularly their professional career, are sprinkled with abrupt changes and vicissitudes. However, after possible reversals of fortune, Uranus offers the possibility of a chance to pick oneself up and start all over again.

URANUS IN THE FIFTH HOUSE

The joys and pleasures of life are particularly attractive to the native. It would be more suitable to allow one free rein in this domain, rather than attempting to impose shackles, which would be unbearable to this person.

Original creativity is often noticeable here, as well as inclinations toward modern art. Sometimes one is a mime artist or stand-up comedian.

One's love life is greatly affected by this position, often involving episodes that are quite out of the ordinary. From a very early age, we notice extravagant whims, constant changes of loved ones, instances of love at first sight followed by separations, revolts against conventions, breaking off of engagements, and above all, precocity, obstacles, and frustrations in love. One's posterity and succession is somewhat restricted; sometimes there is separation from a child, generally the eldest, even when it is the result of a miscarriage.

As children, these people will be difficult to raise, since they are intensely independent. However, one would be wise not to stifle their activity too much, because these independent children may be budding geniuses and, as such, should be treated as responsible individuals.

This configuration brings a great number of irregularities in international finances involving professional gains. Sudden strokes of good fortune, totally unexpected (such as lotteries and so on) could bring in money; but heavy losses could be equally unexpected and sudden. However, such gains or losses will almost always be as a result of speculation. It is often the astral signature of great gamblers and players in every sense of the word. They are completely aware of the risky games they play and thus call to mind Kipling's well-known poem *"If."*

URANUS IN THE SIXTH HOUSE

They have exceptional psychic faculties and receptivity. These natives could suffer from a certain agitation, nervous problems, and spasms. They are predisposed toward sudden irregularities in the natural functions. Health problems may affect the willpower. These natives should lead healthy lives and exercise regularly to maintain their equilibrium. Sometimes, illness that occurs suddenly is difficult to diagnose. They should avoid living close to or working in atomic energy plants. Treatment through electricity, magnetism, waves, and ultramodern procedures will suit them perfectly.

There is a risk of problems in their field of work, owing to lack of discipline or sudden changes in mood. They must display a minimum amount of suppleness and diplomacy. When these natives work for someone else, they will have difficulties in knuckling under and keeping their job, since they abhor the idea of being in a subordinate position. When they are engaged in independent occupations, they could have problems with their employees and subordinates, who, through mistakes or ill will or even malice, could cause them serious losses, with possible repercussions to their health.

One's marriage partner could be rather eccentric, having lived through unusual experiences. A reciprocal liberty must be accorded her, or at least the partner's need for freedom must be borne in mind. An uncle or aunt on the mother's side could play an important role in one's destiny.

URANUS IN THE SEVENTH HOUSE

Uranus, the planet of liberty and independence in this section of the heavens, which watches over alliances and contracts, acts as an intruder. It warns of the difficulties encountered when trying to gain harmony and lasting agreement in associations. The professional life will be marked by unexpected propositions that produce an abrupt end to alliances. A tendency toward the breach of agreements is noted; or the sudden separation from an associate, sometimes as the result of unexpected death. This configuration bodes ill in matters affecting the public or in relationships with others. The native will have to try and overcome a tendency to systematically and continually go against the opinions of others. In a way, one does this almost in self-defence.

This astral signature is felt strongly in one's conjugal life. Frequently, engagements are broken off or impulsive marriages take place. These kinds of marriages can, through the spouse's personality, provoke a rather uncommon or inexplicable situation. It could mean that the union is out of the ordinary, mainly because the spouse displays an exceptional amount of intelligence. This configuration would be harmful to peace and happiness in the conventional sense of the word—hence the frequency of ruptures. Yet, it can forecast a union with a divorced person or a free union with mutual agreement on each others' rights to freedom. Unions should rest on friendship, comprehension, and cooperation and on a perfect commonality of intellectual interests.

URANUS IN THE EIGHTH HOUSE

Rather curiously, this native is interested in "dead" things—antiques, archeology, Egyptology, stamp collecting, or coin collecting. Without being revolutionary, one's particular way of thinking leads this subject toward making reforms and undergoing transformations. From a physiological perspective, anything that may bring about nervous disorders should be avoided.

This astral signature brings about unexpected gains, as well as sudden losses through contracts that link the subject with others. This often announces ups and downs in financial matters after marriage. Sometimes there is a legacy or increase in personal possessions through an unexpected inheritance. This inheritance could be understood to be on an intellectual or spiritual plane. One often notes sudden gains that do not come from work but by chance, such as by lotteries or gifts. Similarly, sudden losses may also occur. In this case as much as in the other, in these kinds of matters the preponderant influence of the partner is obvious.

The passing of third parties has important repercussions for the destiny of these subjects, either through sudden promotion if the field of work is involved, or through an inheritance if the death involves a member of the family. However, the particularity of this influence is that it offers a certain element of surprise and suddenness in the events it brings.

An interest in the occult is common, as well as a penchant for obscure and secret places. Sometimes there is gain through "digs" or research, as is the case of a water diviner and, as it may happen perhaps in the future, of the deep sea diver who plunges into the depths of the ocean to harvest sources of energy.

URANUS IN THE NINTH HOUSE

Uranus finds itself here in a house to which it is perfectly suited. It grants exceptionally rare intellectual aptitudes, notably, a great amount of subconscious activity. Subjects will get the best from their sensitivity, receptivity, and intuition. They may even feel a few religious inclinations, but they will be highly unconventional. They will be much more interested in the happiness of humankind and their own spiritual elevation—one will enhance the other—than in those ideas that are already formed, or in idle and trifling theological discussions. Such subjects should always have a notebook and pen handy, both night and day. They will awake from slumber and jot down an idea that has come to mind. This practice is imperative; if one does not do this, the idea will flee the mind and be gone forever, just like a dream.

These subjects should take special note of their early-morning dreams. They should, when retiring at night, take the trouble to ask the Spirit to enlighten them. They will frequently receive a reply upon rising, even if the idea that comes at the end of the last dream does not seem to have a direct relationship to the problem with which one was preoccupied the previous night. As the Brazilian proverb goes, "God gives a straight reply through winding paths." Quite possibly, one will have inherited one's faculties from the father; however, one risks a premature separation from him. The more these people speak of their gifts, the more they risk provoking disagreements with those around them. They should take note of the great law of the occult: "To know, to desire, to dare, and to be silent."

There could be problems with one's in-laws. One can foresee numerous trips by air. On the whole, the subject's satisfactions will be more on a spiritual plane than on a material one.

URANUS IN THE TENTH HOUSE

Frequently Uranian qualities develop only much later on in life. The obligations of daily living make it necessary to shelve intellectual pursuits for a certain time, even when they are connected to daily life.

These subjects will not tarry when it comes to leaving the paternal home, which is rarely a pleasant environment for them. An important change will surge up in life as soon as they begin to make their own way—notably, when they reach the majority age of twenty-one (three times seven), since the seven-year cycle is typically Uranian. (Eighteen as the age of reaching majority is rather an artificial custom.)

Very often, plans will not always work out the way they were intended. There will be brutal and frequent changes in residence. The interior will be arranged in an original way; and electricity will play an important role in the home. Eccentricity, a taste for adventure, an attraction for difficult and strange realizations, as well as changes of residence, will not decrease with age; rather, the opposite will occur. This configuration is often found with people who have discovered their vocation late in life, and in doing so, their joie de vivre.

URANUS IN THE ELEVENTH HOUSE

The subjects guard their personal freedom jealously and do not wish to be shackled in any way by their friendships. Impulsive attachments are frank and sincere but usually concern people who have a great intellectual originality, or who are rather extravagant. Friends tend to be eccentric and behave rather strangely toward this native, breaking off relationships unexpectedly and without any apparent reason, only to take them up again later in a way that is equally inexplicable. One will behave in a similar way, at times making and breaking friendships briskly, sometimes inconsiderately, as they will often have come from totally different social and educational backgrounds. Moreover, one will then drop them just as brutally, without explanation. It is precisely the character differences and diverse lifestyles that cause these sudden changes.

These individuals will frequent influential people of high positions in important organizations, notably in scientific circles such as electronics, computer science, aviation, radio, television, and astrology. These same people will contribute to the subject's success, but it will be only temporary and not last long. Indeed, friendship often implies an idea of security and fidelity, which does not correspond to the main characteristics of this planet.

Success will come through ingenious projects associated with exceptional circumstances.

URANUS IN THE TWELFTH HOUSE

Uranus in this part of the heavens warns that the greatest dangers will come from hidden enmities, against which it is difficult to defend oneself, simply because their existence is unknown to these people. Such enmities are generally aroused through their strong personalities, their high position that cause others to be envious, and the often brutal manner in which they express themselves. It is therefore in this last area that these natives will have to be careful in exercising their free will.

We must acknowledge that this is not easy for someone who expresses revolutionary views. It is precisely this lack of conciliation that risks rendering natives of this configuration unpopular. They have the gift of being able to dominate their audience, crowds, and large animals with a single look. There is a danger of injury from animals, a fall from a horse, for instance, or a car accident.

They will engage in unusual activities, all demanding much discretion, very likely in withdrawn places such as hospitals, clinics, asylums, boarding schools, laboratories, or prisons. In extreme cases we note a somewhat voluntary exile.

They have a very lively interest in all that is mysterious, the occult sciences for example, and all areas in which they can exercise their faculties, which extend well beyond the norm.

NEPTUNE IN THE HOUSES

Neptune was first noted by Galileo, who observed the planet at 3:00 a.m. Local Time, December 28, 1612, in Florence. However, he mistakenly thought that this new celestial body was a moon of Jupiter. The first sighting and the recognition that it is a planet was by J. G. Galle on September 23, 1846, at the Berlin Observatory. John Couch Adams had come up with an idea about where the planet might be found in 1845. Urban Le Verrier arrived at the same position.

For the Greeks, Neptune was Poseidon, god of the seas, oceans, and the element of water, and armed with a trident, the symbol we use to represent him (Ψ). The planet Neptune is considered by many to be the superior octave of Venus, planet of attraction and beauty, and as such seems to represent a more delicate and more spiritual love. Generally, it evokes the aesthetic and inspiration as well as a musical, artistic, and poetic genius. It is also related to Jupiter with whom it shares its classical rulership over Sagittarius and Pisces. Neptune completes its solar revolution in 165 years,

The three planets, invisible to the naked eye—Uranus, Neptune, and Pluto—would seem to be very far removed from everyday human life because of their ponderously slow movement, the rarity of their mutual aspects, and their very distance from the Earth, unless they occupy a key position, notably through their presence in or rulership of the angles of the horoscope. However, in the long run, they leave their imprint on the same generation and, in doing so, play an important role in mundane astrology. In any event, intensive and careful study of the subject's life reveals that they are far from negligible, and that they are not limited to playing a role only in the lives of those in the public eye.

Neptune unlocks psychic faculties that transcend the normal, such as mysticism, spiritualism, and channeling. A well-placed Neptune, especially if it is in harmony with intellectual significators, announces the spiritual development and expansion of the human being. We cannot help but notice that Neptune's domicile is Pisces, which is inarguably the sign of the Christian era. The reason for this is that, through the phenomenon of precession of the equinoxes, the vernal point, which marks the beginning of the tropical zodiac, turned retrograde into Pisces in the sidereal zodiac c. 214 C.E. In addition, the early Christians used the sign of the fish as a means of mutual recognition.

Alas, however, Neptune also rules cheating and fraudulent practices, false science, and credulity—too readily believing things. Neptune also rules liquids, drugs, tobacco, poisons, gas, petroleum, rubber, and synthetics.

In mundane astrology some relate it to socialism, and we cannot deny that its discovery coincides with the birth of Marxism.

In Horary astrology, an afflicted Neptune at the Ascendant (in the hourly horoscope, quite evidently) often warns that the consultant is cheating the practitioner, or, at the very least, it means that the problem is not very well exposed.

NEPTUNE IN THE FIRST HOUSE

The subject is sensitive, receptive and intuitive. Artistic inclinations are often noticeable. In the case of affliction, or when the rest of the horoscope is weak, we will notice inconstancy, indecision, indolence, and fearfulness. Sometimes one is a visionary, but somewhat lacking in common sense. One has a lymphatic constitution; one's organism can wear itself out imperceptibly through a disease that defies definition.

These subjects could be attracted by the sea. Their career is rather unstable because they let themselves be tossed around by events rather than attempting to be master of them. These people are unsuited to the struggles of life.

NEPTUNE IN THE SECOND HOUSE

Neptune will act only in succedent houses (second, fifth, eighth, and eleventh) if it is in a strong position. If this is not the case, its influence could go unnoticed. If it plays a role here, it will be only to cause these subjects to forsake the idea of earning money through normal channels—that is, through an ordinary job. These natives will therefore be truly interested only in the exploitation of inspired ideas or in speculative arrangements. There could be gains through navigation, liquids, chemical products, synthetics, laboratories, and the secret service. They ought to be wary of dubious speculations, confidence tricks, and losses through fraud. In the case of affliction, they can be heavily handicapped by incessant debts.

NEPTUNE IN THE THIRD HOUSE

If the rest of the horoscope does not contradict, and if Mercury is well placed, this is one of the best configurations when it comes to psychology. The subjects are highly inspired, have a high ideal, a prophetic sense, and may even have a certain genius. Their imagination is boundless; the important thing is to channel it, to master it, and to make it productive—for example, through literary works that are out of the ordinary, including science fiction or those that may have a strong spiritual impact. There could be a lively interest in the sciences of divination or in phenomena such as astral projection. Their ideal is often very different from that of others around them.

There are tendencies toward rather haphazard dreams, nostalgia, and melancholia. For children born under this configuration, it will be necessary to impose a strict education, thus teaching them above all to master their thoughts.

Professional success is possible in maritime navigation and trade in liquids and, especially (if it is in fact possible), through the exploitation of any evident occult gifts.

NEPTUNE IN THE FOURTH HOUSE

Success is possible through exceptional inspiration, the exploitation of greatly inspired ideas, or by extraordinary combinations of circumstances.

The mother is greatly influential, and it is not certain whether one will always remain on good terms with her or not; there may also be a warning concerning her health.

If the whole house is afflicted, or if the point of the MC receives an unfavorable aspect, there is a danger of social disgrace, even a scandal. In brief, these subjects have a rather chaotic destiny, which does not necessarily exclude the possibilities of dazzling success.

NEPTUNE IN THE FIFTH HOUSE

If Neptune is well aspected here, it can bring luck through fortunate initiatives and artistic inspirations. The subjects may even teach psychology, the occult sciences, mysticism, or spiritualism. More often than not, they mistake their fantasies for realities in the main domain of this house, that of the love life. There are generally a great many unexpected occurrences, illusions, and, consequently, deceptions. Their love affairs are extravagant, entangled, and mixed with strange circumstances; sometimes there will be illegitimate offspring. Much difficulty will come about unless they manage to rid themselves of their bodily desires and satisfy themselves with refined, spiritual, and platonic friendships. We will frequently notice that unconventional tokens of affection manifest.

NEPTUNE IN THE SIXTH HOUSE

This house position favors psychic phenomena. On the other hand, it warns against sicknesses of a diverse and undefinable nature. These natives are not well in themselves; they are *"malade imaginaire"* types, stricken by a myriad of psychosomatic conditions. For example, they could suffer from insidious aches and pains, inexplicable diseases of psychic origin, or those that result from bad habits and poor hygiene, especially when Neptune is in a bad aspect to Mars or Venus.

They should avoid alcohol, tobacco abuse, and hard drugs, and should beware of mistakes in medication. All forms of poisoning are to be dreaded. The life of a naturist is recommended. One often notes whimsical behavior in matters of food and dress.

There are problems with staff members and an irresolute bearing where they are concerned. Difficulties and complications in employment can have an astral origin. Health cures and remedies to their destiny should be sought out through the spiritual life. Caring for others by means of an occupation related to the medical profession can be a good solution.

There may be bizarre elements concerning the health of the (marriage) partner, beginning with the state of health. This choice, as important as it is in the subject's life, may be unfortunate.

NEPTUNE IN THE SEVENTH HOUSE

If Neptune is well disposed through sign and aspects, then collective events can favor the destiny. In the opposite case, it is a warning against serious complications that could arise insidiously from associations. Related aspirations are utopian, thus beyond realization. Joint accounts are to be avoided. Lawsuits risk being badly undertaken. Destiny will be affected by a union that goes against nature. One will live curious experiences in this domain. The marriage partner will not cooperate. One lacks common sense and is not adapted to married life. Conjugal life can become greatly tangled and ruin one's existence.

Neptune in the Eighth House

In this house, as much as in the following one, in the case of superior beings, Neptune can facilitate astral travel, the vision of auras, and other metaphysical gifts. However, *superior* must not be taken to mean those individuals who display exemplary moral conduct. These gifts, whether innate or acquired through appropriate training, have in fact very little to do with the individual's morality, contrary to what most people normally believe.

Death often takes place under rather strange circumstances, which we prefer not to enumerate lest we give negative suggestions, all the more because of the fact that these natives are often fearful and could entertain morbid ideas. They should drink only water of the purest quality; they should steer clear of drugs and be wary of poisons. They should warn their friends and colleagues, and possibly even wear an identity plate, that they are capable of falling into a cataleptic state, which closely resembles death. If they allow themselves to be hypnotized, they should place themselves only in the hands of a highly reputable and expert hypnotist whose morality is entirely above reproach.

If they get married through interests, they will be disappointed. There are risks of financial difficulties after marriage. Losses could occur because of the marriage partner or other associates. There are possible fraudulent activities in a legacy matter or in all that involves the personal possessions and goods of a third party.

Neptune in the Ninth House

This is an excellent combination (unless the planet is really poorly aspected). This is so because of the affinities Neptune has with this house and because of the classical rulership it has over Sagittarius. The subject is interested in all that uplifts the soul—poetry, music, religion, mysticism, metaphysical phenomena, and dreams. One is highly impressionable, and ideals are extremely elevated. One is often involved in bizarre pursuits. The subject can discover and understand nature's secrets. The vulgar public will not understand these people. It is quite likely that they have inherited their gifts, often very subtle, from the father, with whom they enjoy very close ties. During their quest, they will encounter a spiritual master who will set them on a path.

They have a great attraction for long sea voyages.

If Neptune is afflicted, we shall find ourselves involved with an eccentric character who has an unstable ideal, whose ideas are tangled, and whose mental attributes are invaded by superstitions.

NEPTUNE IN THE TENTH HOUSE

If well disposed here, Neptune announces a spiritual atmosphere in the home and a mystical heredity. In the opposite case, it can indicate a certain mystery surrounding the birth.

Prudence is indispensable when property transactions take place. Hidden vice is possible. There could be unfavorable ley lines, underground streams or waves in the house. It might be necessary to consult a good water diviner. There could be discord, indeed even treason, between landlords and tenants. Avoid all possible loopholes when drawing up legal documents.

Complications are to be feared when it comes to successions. If it is in bad aspect with the significators of love life, notably the Sun and Mars in the case of a woman, or the Moon and Venus for a man, one would be justified in fearing certain domestic fatalities.

Frequently, it is the indication of spiritual expansion toward the end of life. However, this can also make one fearful of possible difficulties of all kinds, such as discomfort and solitude on growing older—as much on the mental plane as on the physiological or material plane. Sometimes the two phenomena appear simultaneously, especially for those who, throughout their lives, have nourished their subconscious with the doctrine (false, in my opinion) that one must suffer on the material plane to enrich oneself spiritually.

NEPTUNE IN THE ELEVENTH HOUSE

If Neptune is in a favorable aspect here. It indicates high spiritual aspirations and friendships with artists, spiritual people, occultists, or astrologers. There is a fertile imagination, but utopian projects may end up only as illusions.

An afflicted Neptune here forewarns of whims in relationships and of strange attachments. These subjects should fear errors and betrayal on the part of counselors, entanglements with friends as a result of misunderstandings, disagreements with unions or among society members, clubs, and associations, and at the very worst the treachery of friends. Friends may not be real friends at all.

NEPTUNE IN THE TWELFTH HOUSE

Here, more than anywhere else, all depends on the quality of Neptune, according to its position in the sign, the houses over which it exercises rulership and the aspects exchanged with the other planets. Here Neptune is in accidental dignity because of its mastery over the twelfth sign, Pisces. But furthermore, a great number of astrologers consider an afflicted Neptune in this sector of the heavens (the traditional first house or the clockwise twelfth house) to be the "Hell of the Horoscope."

Neptune at the end of the twelfth, thus close to the Ascendant, weakens willpower and vitality. The subject displays a lively interest in occultism and mysteries, and could become devoted to secret investigations. One may have latent psychic gifts.

One loves living in isolation, communicating with oneself and meditating. Good aspects favor success in the practice of occultism or the medical professions. One could entertain a hidden platonic relationship.

If there are afflictions to Neptune, then there could be secret enmities, betrayals, defamations, and unknown dangers of the most varied kinds. In extreme cases, there is the danger of loss of liberty, this danger being even more accentuated if Neptune is ruler of one of the points of the IC–MC axis (residence, social prestige).

PLUTO IN THE HOUSES

Pluto is the "planet" farthest from the Sun. It takes 248 years to complete its revolution. It was first observed February 18, 1930, at 4 a.m. by Clive Tombaugh in the Lowell Observatory in Flagstaff, Arizona. Its orbit has an extremely elongated ellipse, and this is why it sometimes seems to remain for more than thirty years in one sign, while at other times it may only stay for twelve years. Moreover, its inclination to the ecliptic reaches 17°, which is quite considerable in comparison to the other planets.

Pluto's celestial latitude thus makes it leave what is considered to be the zodiac, since this is a circular band, perpendicular to the ecliptic, and because the astrologers have for centuries agreed that it is 8°30' high from one part of the ecliptic to the other that, thus, occupies its median line. This limit was fixed in this way because the inclinations of the different planetary orbits, including those of the Moon, Uranus, and Neptune, are rather reduced. In this way, Pluto is presently the only "planet" to have crossed, to such an extent, the autumnal equinox, 0° tropical Libra, while remaining all the time in a northern declination. It is thus extraordinary from all points of view.

In mythology, Pluto was the "Giver of Wealth" for the Greeks, but the "God of the Dead and the Underworld" for the Romans. In this way, it already reveals itself to be in complete contradiction. From this point, there is only a very small step to take to reach the idea that it brings inheritances on the material plane and/or spiritual plane.

The influence that we attribute to this planet is subject to caution, since we need another two centuries to pass before we can in fact confirm its influence through extensive research. The authors who have taken an interest in Pluto have taken mainly mythology into account and have operated through analogical reasoning. However, we must admit that our predecessors did exactly the same thing when it came to Uranus and Neptune and their computations have, on the whole, been strangely confirmed through experience.

Pluto exercises rulership over Scorpio and Aries. It is, in our opinion, without any doubt, the superior octave to Mars. This conclusion is reached in two different ways. First, in the order of distance from the Sun, we obtain Mercury, Venus and Mars and the attribution of the superior octaves of Mercury and Venus to Uranus and Neptune respectively, seems to be justifiable. Second, if we treat the subject of the distribution of the rulers for Pluto in the order of the succession of the signs, beginning with the Sun ruling Leo, and in the opposite direction beginning with the Moon ruling Cancer, we fall quite naturally on the signs of Aries and Scorpio. Pluto thus finds its two domiciles in the martial signs. Elsewhere, I have found that in very Martian horoscopes, whether it be mundane horoscopes or the celestial charts of personalities, Mars and Pluto are frequently in mutual aspect. It is thus that on June 28, 1914—the date of the assassination of Archduke Franz Ferdinand of Austria in Sarajevo— they were in exact sextile. That murder set off World War I. According to many historians, this war primed the atmosphere that led into World War II and, in fact, we are not completely out of it to the present day. Yuri Andropov, former KGB chief and, more recently, the new master of the Kremlin (1982–1984), was, in fact, born on that very day. Everywhere, you will read that he was born June 15, 1914, but at that time the Julian calendar was still used in Russia; thus we must remember to add thirteen days before we begin to calculate his celestial birth chart.

The role of Pluto in natal astrology will thus, under these conditions, be rather difficult to calculate precisely. All other configurations aside, it will be rather more benefic than anything else from the material, agricultural, and financial viewpoints, as well as on the spiritual plane. In destiny, however, the god of the underworld seems to provoke certain constraints and inexplicable obstacles, unexpected events that are bizarre, repeated, and surging from the depths and against which the subject may be powerless to react. It would seem to be so when considering the planets invisible to the naked eye, as we have already had occasion to state in the case of Neptune. The less visible the influence on the individual, the more it seems to act with force on the larger population. Thus the action of our free will would seem to be rather limited here.

I must admit that what upsets and unsettles me the most in the practice of astrology is this seeming determination affecting people and nations. Upon reflection, it is normal that crowds exercise their free will less easily than individuals, simply because, to act efficiently, each individual member of the crowd must agree with all the others. Indeed, we are very far from that. However, here we have really put our finger on the key to universal peace. Pluto, being the most exterior planet in our solar system, embraces all, which gives it a vision of the whole, and as such, is a spirit of synthesis.

In mundane astrology, its influence is far more pernicious, because it is imperceptible and reveals itself rather in the signs (clearly sidereal, in our opinion) and through aspects exchanged with the other slow planets, than in the houses. Let us add that it was only in 1982 that it really entered sidereal Libra, the sign of international relations. Its discovery before World War II corresponds with the sudden appearance of a great many dictatorships, mainly military ones, and since then, with the decolonization and, indeed, the independence of former colonies. Our world has never known as many heads of state who were former military leaders.

PLUTO IN THE FIRST HOUSE

Pluto herein is a strong personality of great intelligence. The subjects exercise a very great effulgence on their associates through their magnetism, but they remain very secretive about their objectives. They have an independent spirit and are frequently egoistic and unscrupulous. A leader of those whose sense of domination is recognized, they coldly eliminate, without scruples, all those who oppose their actions.

They tend to remain single. They experience sudden changes in orientation, which could lead to the highest pinnacles, more often than not after having scaled the most unlikely obstacles.

PLUTO IN THE SECOND HOUSE

The desire to acquire can become an obsession, but these subjects exercise such powers of concentration on this question that they reach their ends no matter what the cost, even through illicit means. This is secondary in their eyes and depends on the other factors in the horoscope. They will be both spendthrifts and misers, will have many different sources of income and will experience ups and downs and a great many unexpected events in the area of finances. The most curious phenomena can manifest through severe losses on the eve of the harvest. Relationships and the social life will be geared toward the idea of increasing the patrimony and personal fortune.

Pluto in the Third House

The subject's penetrating and investigating mind favors studies. One can be very direct in one's means of expression and feel the need to convince others. One can be mentally aggressive. These subjects should, therefore, watch their words closely and, above all, be careful of what they write if they wish to avoid clashes with their associates. They lack diplomacy because they fail to understand their interlocutors. Relationships are therefore rarely followed through. The subjects tend to be very secretive about their movements during the course of which they should be very prudent.

Pluto in the Fourth House

They can actualize themselves only if they manage to eliminate all outside constraints such as discipline, authority, and hierarchy. These subjects believe that they should accomplish their mission. They will be the object of envy in their professional situations, which will bristle with unusual circumstances. They will suffer great periods of upset in life—crises and extraordinary turning points. They will emerge unharmed from dangers and adversities, against which they seem to have immunity. They could experience success through the destruction of an inheritance, even a spiritual inheritance.

Pluto in the Fifth House

This position favors an inventive mind, artistic creativity, and a penchant for investments of a speculative nature. If badly aspected (notably by Mars and Uranus), it is a dangerous warning, especially for a woman in her relationships with a man. The woman ought to be under careful observation during her pregnancies. Passionate desires, erotic adventures, and sexual anomalies are to be feared. These subjects will probably have known problems during the course of their education. Relationships with their children will be less than easy.

Pluto in the Sixth House

These natives should avail themselves of complementary insurance policies that offer coverage greater than that normally offered according to the law and common practice when they concern work accidents and professional illnesses. However, they will recuperate rapidly.

They could be tenacious at work, to the point of being fanatical, with an enormous capacity for production. They should avoid becoming workaholics. Clashes with colleagues are possible. Illegal employment or antisocial activities are also temptations. The marriage partners will reveal themselves to be perfect eccentrics and enemies of convention.

PLUTO IN THE SEVENTH HOUSE

Marriage will bring the unexpected into the subject's existence, completely changing one's lifestyle. One seeks contacts with the world's great people, and can be successful through relationships in official circles, with high-ranking personalities and in the diplomatic corps. One could also experience success through violence or after an unfortunate incident or calamity. Destiny will depend on the results, rivalries, and obstacles against which one will continually stand and fight.

PLUTO IN THE EIGHTH HOUSE

Research into the realms of the beyond, death, its meaning, and all the mysteries connected with it are characteristic of Pluto in the eighth house. These natives could have fantastic dreams and their thoughts centered on death could become an obsession. Metaphysical experiences are very dangerous. They are also interested in erotica and occultism.

Death for these people may be premature, strange, tragic, inexplicable, or during a collective accident. They could disappear without a trace—the body missing, buried in the depths, unidentified or undiscovered.

PLUTO IN THE NINTH HOUSE

This seems to be a very good position. They seek the truth; their quest is idealistic, ideals are elevated. Their activities spring from deep faith. During life, they could profoundly change their ideals or religion. This position also favors the study of astrology. These people love adventure and far-off travels and enjoy the exchange of ideas with people from other lands. There could be many ups and downs in far-off lands, even somewhat voluntary exile.

Pluto in the Tenth House

The family circle exercises a strong influence. These subjects can become domestic tyrants. There could be family quarrels and complications concerning the family goods, real estate, and property. There could be separations from family members, often caused by untimely deaths. They will make strange changes of residence. The home might be materially assaulted. Both impoverishment and sudden wealth are possible. The end of life will be solitary.

They have a talent for research and possibly aptitudes for water divining.

Pluto in the Eleventh House

They could receive strange and unexpected benefits through relationships. These subjects' friendships are unorthodox. They may struggle to dominate their friends. Their friends could be decimated through death. They cannot bear criticism and can be stubborn about projects beyond realization. They can show signs of altruism, become popular, and then display themselves to be without pity. This attitude could lead to solitude, from which they will suffer deeply, especially if someone of the opposite sex is involved.

Pluto in the Twelfth House

There is great reserve in all areas. They have an aptitude for unusual studies and the practice of occult sciences. This configuration favors laboratory workers, detectives, the police, and secret agents. Subjects will uncover their secret enemies, dominate them, triumph over them, and, as if by miracle, eliminate them. Circumstances seem to take care of themselves quite naturally at times.

If bad aspects are exchanged with the rulers of the Ascendant, the Descendant, or the MC, then trials, tribulations, and unfortunate adventures are to be feared, notably, acts of treachery.

CHAPTER 10

ILLUSTRATIONS OF THE THEORY

ON BOTH SIDES OF THE ASCENDANT:
THE FIRST AND TWELFTH HOUSES

With **Prince Rainier III of Monaco** (May 31, 1923, rectified to 5:58:24 GMD, in Monte Carlo, Monaco), we find the Sun some 14° above the eastern horizon. It appears evident to us that as the Sun symbolizes the Monarchy, the center of our system seems to be better placed above the horizon, and represents the reigning prince far better if we see it in the first house rather than in the twelfth. His radiance will be more obvious if he is born with the Sun above the horizon. We find the same thing with his elder daughter, Princess Caroline, with the Sun above the eastern horizon.

Mars and Pluto below the horizon in the twelfth house indicates his struggles with his governing council, with France over Monaco being a tax haven for French millionaires, Aristotle Onassis and other forces working in the economy of a small state dependent on gambling, tourism and its favorable taxation system.[1] The trine of the Sun to Saturn somewhat neutralizes the square of Pluto to Saturn.

Juan Perón (October 8, 1895, at 6 a.m., rectified to 5:59:44 Meridian 64°W11, near Lobos in Argentina) was born with a Sun–Mars conjunction, which had risen in the east more than half an hour beforehand. If you count the houses according to the same direction as the signs, you

---

1   Wikipedia.

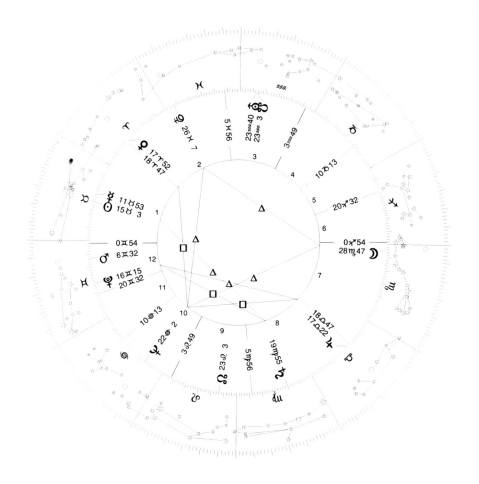

Prince Rainier III
Monte Carlo, Monaco (43°N45, 7°E25)
May 31, 1923
5:58:24 GMD
Vernal Point: 6° Pisces 19'45"

will find this military man in prison, that of the twelfth house, whereas he conquered, came to power and remained in power for many long years. On the contrary, he offers a living example of success obtained through the combination of the Sun (will power) and Mars (action). However, the presence of Chiron in the conjunction provided a warning that his life would not be one without wounds and hurts. We notice that Venus is in sextile and Uranus in trine with the MC. This denotes the role of Evita

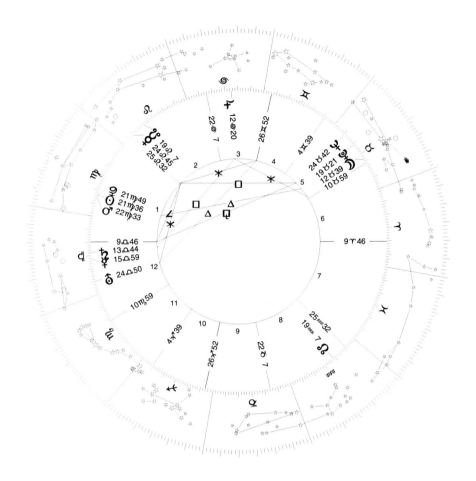

Juan Perón
Lobos, Buenos Aires (35S11, 59W6)
October 8, 1895
5:59:44 Meridian 64W11
Vernal Point: 6° Pisces 42'53"

Perón, who enjoyed untold popularity with the masses. Note that the MC in sidereal Gemini indicates the return to business. Recall that Juan Perón returned from his period of exile in Spain (IC in Sagittarius, the ninth sign indicating foreign countries) in order to return to the leadership in Argentina. His exile is illustrated by Saturn, ruler through sidereal Capricorn of the ninth house of foreign lands, as well as Mercury and Uranus being in the twelfth house. In addition, he has a Royal Yoga, for his Ascendant is

Agatha Christie
Torquay, Devon (50N28, 3W30)
September 15, 1890
4:23:56 GMT
Vernal Point: 6° Pisces 47'8"

Libra, and the rulers of the signs in trine—Gemini and Aquarius—Mercury and Saturn, are in conjunction in the twelfth house, showing that his exile was not difficult. He died in Olivos, Argentina, July 11, 1974.

In the horoscope of **Agatha Christie** (September 15, 1890, at 4:30 a.m., rectified to 4:23:56 GMT, in Torquay, England), the Sun and Saturn are found below the horizon in what we call the twelfth house if we count the houses clockwise; and so, as far as we can see, this champion of detective novels, mysteries and whodunits magnificently illustrates the idea of success obtained through involvement with secret and hidden things. In addition, the Neptune–Pluto conjunction in the third house of writing squares Saturn in the twelfth house and trines Jupiter in the eighth house of death. In addition Saturn rules the eighth house through Capricorn. She died in Wallingford, UK, January 12, 1976.

Jânio da Silva Quadros was born January 25, 1917, in Campo Grande, Mato Grosso, Brazil, at 5:25 a.m., rectified to 5:14:21 AST. This horoscope certainly lacks harmony and is dominated by two groups of planets, one of which is situated astride the Ascendant and the other astride the Descendant; both of them being in square with Jupiter, the second ruler of the Ascendant through Sagittarius. As soon as he was elected Governor of the state of São Paulo, this lawyer came face to face with great difficulties with regard to his administrative entourage; the people who worked for him just could not bear his behavior and his draconian authority, which especially made itself felt in the form of strict orders, written on little notes that he distributed left and right. Well now, he occupied the most prestige-filled position in the government after that of the President of the United States of Brazil himself.

The Sun just below the Ascendant with both Mars and Uranus in the twelfth house warns of hidden enemies plotting against him in secret. Without any shadow of a doubt, this chart shows a man of action, such as is generally the case with the Sun in conjunction with Mars. Anyway, he committed a very serious act of imprudence in a country that is keen on spirituality, steeped in magic and the occult, by engaging in a witch hunt, to such an extent that in 1959 I had occasion to attend a *macumba*, where he was the object of an act of vengeance on the part of powerful sorcerers. His name was never actually mentioned, but after everybody present had chain smoked a number of cigars during many long hours in a very small room, where nobody, not even the nonsmokers, was unduly disturbed by the smoke, and after hours of dancing, chanting and foot-stamping, I pointed out to my uninitiated neighbor that the *macumberos*

Jânio da Silva Quadros
Campo Grande, Brazil (20°S27, 54°W37)
January 25, 1917
5:14:21 AST
Vernal Point: 6° Pisces 25'4"

were in the process of creating an analogy between the objects that they had just thrown to the ground, and the person of the Governor himself. These objects were picture frames that they trampled underfoot without any respite, so breaking the glass with their bare feet, which were in turn cut to shreds, but no blood flowed. The name of the Governor translated from the Portuguese means "frame" in the plural.

The conjunction of Saturn–Neptune in the Descendant signifies a violent hatred on the part of his antagonists and the planets placed slightly below the horizon in the east were not in the first house, but in fact in the twelfth house, that of secret enemies and magic. Without any doubt, I thought, they will obtain his dethronement and downfall. A short time afterward (in the 1960s, actually), Jânio became the President of the Republic. I did not in fact witness what happened with my own eyes, but he was able to show his country very easily and rapidly, the extent of his incapacity. He was overthrown by a military coup and so caused the country to be seized by the military; thus the loss of civil liberties followed; and this situation endures to this very day (1984).

To come back to our personality, the most important Parisian newspapers provided me with information concerning his being taken prisoner by the army and deported by military aircraft into the Amazon. What else could one expect with the animosities, to say the very least, which he engendered everywhere, and Uranus, Mars and the Sun in the twelfth house. The Sun is also in opposition to Neptune in the sixth house and quincunx Pluto in the eighth. It is evident that this points to the loss of liberty, even in the case of a Head of State. He died in São Paulo, Brazil, February 16, 1992.

Marshal Philippe Pétain was born April 24, 1856, at 10:00 p.m., rectified to 22:09:50 LT, in Cauchy-à-la-Tour, near Bethune in the Pas-de-Calais region of France. The twelfth house, that of prisons, counting in the same direction as the signs, is empty of planets; but if you count the houses in the opposite direction you will find the Moon in the twelfth house, in opposition to Saturn and square to Jupiter in the tenth house of residence in Pisces, the corresponding sign of prisons. Jupiter and Neptune are respectively the classical and modern rulers of Pisces. Jupiter is a ruler of the tenth house (later years) through Pisces intercepted and the twelfth house (loss of liberty) through Sagittarius intercepted. If the houses are counted in the same direction as the signs, you would say that you can see Venus in the fourth house that begins in the IC and symbolizes the residence and the end of life, which would surely mean a gentle end to

Philippe Pétain
Bethune, Nord-Pas-de-Calais, France (50N32, 2E38)
April 24, 1856
22:09:50 LT
Vernal Point: 7° Pisces 15'55"

existence, surrounded by affection and a comfort without equal. If he had consulted me, I would have told the venerable old Marshal that, by counting the houses in a clockwise direction, I considered Venus to be in the ninth house, that of foreign countries, and that it would have been better for him to remain in Switzerland, especially with the Moon in Sagittarius, which stands for foreign lands. In addition the rulers of the signs in trine to his Ascendant, Jupiter of Pisces and the Moon of Cancer,

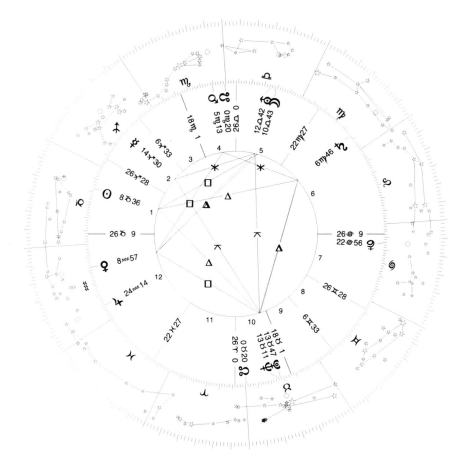

Marcel Dassault
Paris, France
January 22, 1892
8:34:08 Meridian 2°E20
Vernal Point: 6° Pisces 46'0"

were in square, a "negative" Royal Yoga. He died on Île d'Yeu, France, July 23, 1951.

Marcel Dassault first saw the light of day on January 22, 1892, at 8:30 a.m., rectified to 8:34:08 Meridian 2°E20. He was an aircraft industrialist. He refused to collaborate with the Nazi aviation industry, so he was sent to Buchenwald because he was a Jew. Venus, ruler of the house beginning

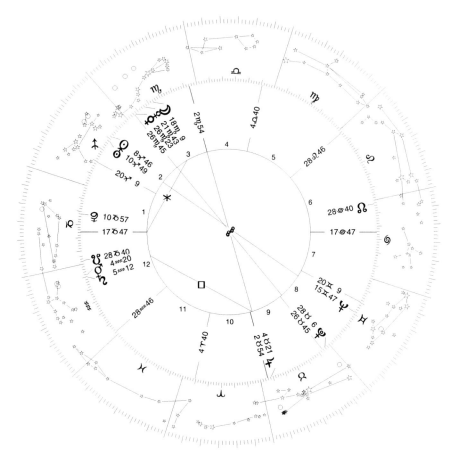

Howard Hughes
Houston, Texas (29°N45'47," 95°W21'47")
December 24, 1905
9:47:29 CST
Vernal Point: 6° Pisces 34'21"

at the IC, thus governs the residence and, for us, it is located in the twelfth house, that of imprisonment. It receives a separating square aspect, of malefic reputation, from Mars, the god of War, very powerful in its own sign of Scorpio, and elevated because it is the planetary body, which is closest to the MC. Nevertheless, we must point out the unbelievable luck that he enjoyed with regard to the conditions of his internment, notably toward the end, and we attribute this, quite obviously, to the two benefics

Jupiter and Venus, situated in this house. Note that Uranus, the planet of aviation, is found in the Air sign Libra, where it receives five planetary aspects—a sextile to Mercury, a square to the Sun, a trine to Venus, and a quincunx to Neptune and Pluto. Finally, and above all, Uranus is in conjunction with the Moon and we remember the preponderant role of a planet so placed in relation to our natural satellite. He survived the war and became the foremost military aircraft manufacturer in France. He died in Neuilly-sur-Seine on April 17 1986.

Howard Hughes (December 24, 1905, alternative times rectified to 9:47:29 a.m. CST, in Houston, Texas) was considered to be one of the world's richest men. This is easily explained by the conjunction in the second house of finance of the Sun and Uranus, the latter being the planet of aviation. In addition, he has a Royal Yoga, formed by a conjunction between Venus, the ruler of Taurus and Mercury, the ruler of Virgo, the earth signs in trine with his Capricorn Ascendant. He was one of the greatest aircraft producers of his generation and he became Chairman and General Director of Trans World Airlines (TWA). He was a butt of the press in that he was the great seducer of some of Hollywood's most beautiful women. All this was due to his triple conjunction of the Moon, Mercury and Venus. Venus is the ruler of his fifth house of the love life through its Libra cusp and Mercury is the sub-ruler through the intercepted sign Virgo. The Moon is the ruler of the seventh house of partnerships, albeit brief.

There is no better astrological explanation for his famous reclusive and secretive nature than the Mars–Saturn conjunction on the South Node in his twelfth house. Jupiter in the ninth house in conjunction with the IC and the Sun–Uranus conjunction in Sagittarius explains his long trips to foreign lands. Howard Hughes was the first man to go round the world in less than four days. He died in an airplane crash near Acapulco, Mexico, April 5, 1976, when transiting Pluto precisely squared his natal Neptune in the eighth house.

Mohandas K. Gandhi was born in Porbandar, near Bombay, October 23, 1869, at 7:45 a.m., rectified to 7:37:45 LT. The rulers of the Ascendant and

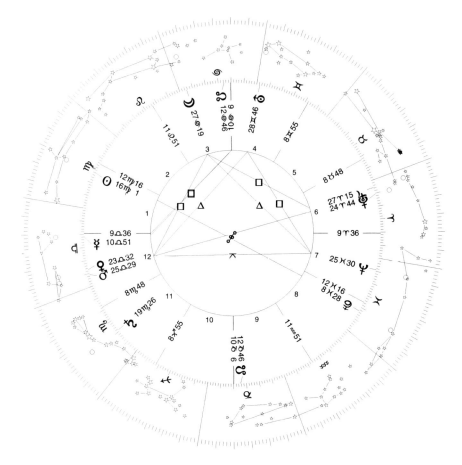

Mohandas K. Gandhi
Porbandar, India (21N38, 69E37)
October 2, 1869
7:37:45 LT
Vernal Point: 7° Pisces 4'40"

the Descendant, which can be considered to be declared enemies, Venus and Mars, are in conjunction in the twelfth house, secret enemies, in opposition to the Jupiter–Pluto conjunction in the sixth house. Moreover, the rulers of the twelfth house cusp (Scorpio) are Pluto (modern) and Mars (traditional). Venus is a ruler of the same house through Libra, and Jupiter is the traditional ruler of Pisces on the eighth house cusp. This points to his period of imprisonment by the British and the threat of death at the

Sede Dedos
São Paulo, Brazil
October 3, 1917
19:57:42 BZT
Vernal Point: 6° Pisces 24'29"

hand of secret enemies, which brought about his assassination January 30, 1948, at 17:13, in New Delhi. We should also note that his Sun was in the first house, which gave him a strong constitution and the strength to fight for rights in both South Africa and India.

Sede Dedos (Seven Fingers) was considered for many years to be Brazil's public enemy number one. He was so nicknamed owing to the fact that,

Timothy Leary
Springfield, Massachusetts (42N6, 72W36)
October 22, 1920
10:42:19 EDT
Vernal Point: 6° Pisces 21'56"

during his unhappy childhood, he was the victim of an accident whereby three of his fingers were severed when he rolled under a tram. He was born October 3, 1917, at 8 p.m., tentatively rectified to 19:57:42 BZT, in the hospital of São Paulo. We know that the Moon, as well as the Quadrant, which goes from the Ascendant to the Midheaven, enlightens us as to the subject's childhood. We have a Moon opposed to Venus and above all, in square to Uranus near the MC. Mars (ruler of the Ascendant through

Aries, and consequently of the entire first Quadrant) is in a wide opposition to Uranus and in conjunction with Saturn. Pluto in Gemini forms a sesquiquadrate with both Venus in Libra and Uranus in Capricorn in the third house, which is analogous to Gemini, the third sign, and Uranus and Venus square each other, all of which gives a logical explanation for his amputation.

The traditional eighth house (death) and twelfth house (prisons) are empty of planets. However, in the clockwise system the Moon is in the twelfth house trine Mercury in the eighth house, which Mercury also rules in this horoscope. The Moon is also the ruler of the IC, the end of life, which is in tight conjunction with Neptune and the malefics, Saturn, and Mars. Thus, toward the end of life his residence was a prison, where he was eventually to die. With Aries rising, the Sun, ruler of Leo, and Jupiter, ruler of Sagittarius, are in trine. If Vedic astrologers consider this to be a Royal Yoga, then it was responsible for his becoming public enemy number one.

Timothy Leary was born in Springfield, Massachusetts, October 22, 1920, at 10:40 a.m., rectified to 10:42:19 EDT. Along with Richard Alpert, Leary founded the "League for Spiritual Discovery," which he described as a religion, declaring LSD as its holy sacrament. We will focus on the twelfth house because he was a psychologist whose primary interest was the influence of interpersonal forces on mental health. Note that Chiron, the shamanic healer, is in the ninth house in T-square with Mars in the twelfth and Pluto in the sixth. The star Antares at 15:01 Scorpio is just 31' above the Ascendant in the first house. He was imprisoned for possession of drugs in California. By his innate charm (Mercury conjunction Venus in the first house) the court decided that he would be safe in a low security prison. However, he escaped and fled the country to Algeria. He escaped once again when they attempted to hold him hostage. He was imprisoned again in Switzerland for a month but escaped again. Mars, the ruler of the ninth house (foreign lands) is in the twelfth house (prisons). He was caught by the FBI when his plane put

Charles Darwin
Shrewsbury, UK (52N42, 2W45)
February 12, 1809
5:59:37 LT
Vernal Point: 7° Pisces55'25"

down in Afghanistan without him stepping onto Afghan soil, where he would have been safe from extradition. This time he was put into solitary confinement where he wrote books. He was released April 21, 1996, and died of prostate cancer May 31, 1996.[2]

---

2   Wikipedia.

Charles Darwin was born in Shrewbury, England, February 12, 1809, at 6 a.m., rectified to 5:59:37 Local Time. He developed an interest in natural history while studying medicine and then theology at two universities. When he made a five-year voyage on the Beagle, he established himself as a geologist. Puzzled by the geographical distribution of wildlife and fossils he collected on the voyage, he investigated the transmutation of species and conceived his theory of natural selection. His book *On the Origin of Species* established evolution by common descent.[3]

He has four planets in the twelfth house, the Moon, Sun, Mercury and Pluto, which highlight his preference for research. His idea of "survival of the fittest" is ruled by the warrior Mars, in exile in Libra, square the Moon and trine the Sun. As Mars is the ruler of Aries and the Sun is the ruler of Leo, signs which are in trine to the Ascendant, then we have a Royal Yoga. He made a long sea voyage to the Galapagos. Even though there are no planets in the ninth house of long journeys, its ruler Venus is in Pisces, ruled by Neptune, and moreover trines Neptune (the sea) and Saturn in the third house. Even though there are no planets in the eighth house, which rules things dead, like fossils and extinct species of plants and animals, its primary ruler Mercury is in the twelfth house in conjunction with Pluto, in square to Neptune and in trine with Uranus. Venus, its secondary ruler through Taurus, which covers over half of the sector, gave him the opportunity to make his famous discoveries through his voyages, as described above.

Abraham Lincoln was born in Hodgenville, Kentucky, February 12, 1809, at sunrise. I have rectified Marc Edmund Jones's chart set for 7:10 a.m. to 7:05:13 Local Time. As a young man he was a good wrestler (Mars in the fifth house). Neptune in line with the star Antares, and in conjunction with Saturn in the fourth house shows that it was inevitable that he would suffer a fall. He was assassinated in the Ford Theater in Washington, DC on April 15, 1865. According to traditional astrology his Sun and Moon would be in the twelfth house and Mercury, Pluto, Jupiter and Venus in the first house. As a practicing lawyer and eventually a politician, I would

---

3   Wikipedia.

Abraham Lincoln
Hodgenville, Kentucky (37N35, 85W44)
February 12, 1809
7:05:13 LT
Vernal Point: 7° Pisces 55'25"

place the Sun and Moon in the clockwise first house. Marc Edmund Jones writes: "Here the myth figure is perhaps most significantly presaged for Abraham Lincoln in the remarkable extent to which he was the loner and kept his thinking process to himself"[4] (Mercury conjunction Pluto in the twelfth house) "or achieved his stature strictly on his own" (Jupiter in the twelfth house) "while yet almost universally accepted into the hearts of

---

4   Jones. *Scope of Astrological Prediction*, pp. 11–178.

Pierre Elliott Trudeau
Montréal, Québec (45°N33, 73°W35)
October 18, 1919
7:06:24 EDT
Vernal Point: 6° Pisces 22'47"

those with whom he had daily association" (Sun in the first house trine Mars in the fifth house; Sun semisquare Venus; Venus trine Neptune). Mars and Uranus are in the house, which rules entertainment, for example the theater, where he died. Uranus trined Mercury and quincunxed Venus in the twelfth house of secret enemies.

Have you noticed that Darwin and Lincoln are birthday twins?

Pierre Elliott Trudeau was born in Montréal, Québec, October 18, 1919, at 7:03 a.m., rectified to 7:06:24 EDT. He was Prime Minister of Canada from April 20, 1968 to June 4, 1979, and again from March 3, 1980 to June 30, 1984. The position of the Sun and Mercury in the clockwise twelfth house and no planets in the first house seems to contradict our house system, as one would expect him to be involved with hospitals, prisons or research laboratories. But here the twelfth house connection points to his enemies whom he overcame. He became Prime Minister when his predecessor, Lester Pearson, stepped down and he won the leadership contest for the Liberal Party. On June 24, 1968, the eve of his first election, rioting Québec separatists threw rocks and bottles at the grandstand where he was seated. He stayed in his seat, facing the rioters, without any sign of fear. On October 5, 1970, the Front de Libération du Québec kidnapped British Trade Consul James Cross, and on the tenth kidnapped and murdered Québec Labor Minister Pierre Laporte. Trudeau invoked the War Measures Act, which gave the government sweeping powers of arrest and detention without trial. He espoused a Just Society (Sun and Mercury in sidereal Libra) and officially made Canada a bilingual country. He was criticized for poor administrative practices that affected the economy (Mars–Saturn conjunction in the second house, but Venus as well) and for his arrogance and lack of understanding of Canada outside Quebec. However, he was considered to be the most charismatic leader that Canada had ever had. His Sun in the twelfth house, 3° below the Ascendant, trines Uranus in the ninth house (international relations); and Mercury in the twelfth house trines Pluto in the fourth house—both of which confirm his charisma. Moreover, Jupiter and Neptune in the third house (literary ability and inspiring speeches) were in conjunction. Venus, the ruler of Taurus, and Saturn the ruler of Capricorn, two earth signs in trine with the Ascendant, are in conjunction, thereby giving Trudeau a Royal Yoga. He died September 28, 2000, in Montréal.

On Both Sides of the Midheaven

There is a fundamental difference between the position of the planets climbing toward the MC and those that have just passed the meridian and are beginning their downward journey toward the Descendant. Planets climbing toward the MC symbolize the aspirations and the vocation, whereas planets beginning their downward journey reveal the role of the environment and circumstances. The planets and/or the luminaries, which are found on one or the other side of the MC have a role to play in the professional activity, the destiny and social life of the native. Those that climb toward the MC seem to allow him more free will whereas, very often, those that have just passed it seem in a way to crush and bear down on him. Inevitably, these latter ones can bring good fortune or bad fortune.

The Sun or Jupiter, which is about to reach the MC, announces success due to the ambition and personal efforts of the subject. It shows hopes, the desire for material success, the need to enhance oneself, whereas when the Sun and/or Jupiter descends from the MC, it seems to be more benefic and often announces the fact that circumstances will intervene strongly in order to favor destiny. I think that when Saturn climbs toward the MC it indicates very great ambition. However, this same Saturn if it has just passed MC, above all if it is afflicted, will be very hard to bear and will almost always provoke a fall. This position is fatal in the case of statesmen. We now begin to understand why certain astrologers, certainly the Hindus, examine what you call the ninth house rather than the tenth house when it comes to studying the profession. What I call the third house, the one that corresponds to Gemini, the sign of mentality, is the representative of the vocation or the profession, whereas the planets that are found on the other side of MC in what I call the fourth house, a cardinal house, enlightens us as to the professional activity influenced by outside factors or the necessities of the moment. Therefore, Jupiter will be considered as being more benefic in the fourth house, which corresponds to its exaltation in Cancer, the fourth sign. For these same reasons, Saturn seems more difficult to bear in this same fourth house when it begins to descend from

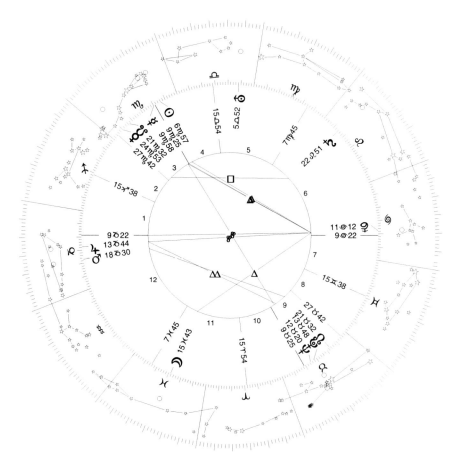

Charles de Gaulle
Lille, France (50°N38, 3°E0)
November 22, 1890
11:56:38 LT
Vernal Point: 6° Pisces 46'58"

MC by virtue of the fact that this place offers an analogy with its sign of exile, i.e. Cancer.

General Charles de Gaulle, born on November 22, 1890, in Lille, has several possible birth times according to astrologers. In the end I came to 11:56:38 Local Time. His Sun, therefore, is in the fourth house and Mercury is in the third house, both in close conjunction with the

Aristide Briand
Nantes, France (47°N13, 1°W33)
March 28, 1862
10:17:19 LT
Vernal Point 6° Pisces 10'58"

Midheaven. De Gaulle also wrote books, thus confirming the Mercury
position. The Sun is in opposition with a Neptune–Pluto conjunction in
the ninth house. This describes his connections to foreign countries and
coupled with the trine of Mars–Jupiter in the twelfth house to Neptune–
Pluto in the ninth house, explains his fall from grace and exile first to
London and later to Algeria, when he was actually sentenced to death
in absentia by Pétain. However, de Gaulle was vindicated after the War

and it was Pétain who had a sticky end. De Gaulle died November 9, 1970, in Colombey-les-deux-Église.

Aristide Briand (March 28, 1862, in Nantes, at 10:30 a.m., rectified to 10:17:19 LT) has Mercury, the Moon, Neptune and the Sun in the third clockwise house. The Sun–Neptune conjunction shows the ideal that animated this statesman. Mercury, ruler of the Ascendant through sidereal Gemini, is in conjunction with the MC, indicating the journalist that he was early in his career and the orator he later became. The triple conjunction Moon–Mercury–MC in sidereal Aquarius explains the fact that he was minister twenty-one times and Président du Conseil (i.e. Prime Minister) eleven times. For Aquarius and the eleventh house represent government ministers in mundane astrology.

A diplomat and fervent peacemaker, with Mars trine Jupiter–Saturn (across triplicities in the sidereal zodiac) and quintile the Sun, three planets in Aquarius and two in Pisces, he was awarded the Nobel Prize in 1926 precisely when Jupiter, the planet of Peace, which confers honors, was approaching his natal MC. While at the height of his influence within the League of Nations, he attended a dinner in Geneva where the guests were given menu cards on which was printed a cartoon depicting the statesmen of the world smashing a statue of Mars while Briand was talking to the god of war trying to convince him to commit suicide. He died in Paris, March 7, 1932.

Pierre Laval (June 28, 1883, Châteldon, Puy-de-Dome, at 10:00 a.m. LT, rectified to 10:00:52) also has Sun–Jupiter rising toward his MC, and in addition Venus and Mercury. With the Ascendant in sidereal Leo, the Sun and Jupiter are respectively rulers of the first house and the ninth house, that of the ideal. This configuration indicates numerous contacts and arrangements. It is essentially a most attractive combination.

However, on the other side of the MC, a stellium (collection of planets) begins to descend, composed of Saturn–Chiron–Pluto–Mars–Neptune; these crush the native and impose on him his implacable destiny. Can one possibly imagine a worse finish to one's life after having attained such dizzy heights? The IC, the end of existence, falls exactly on the

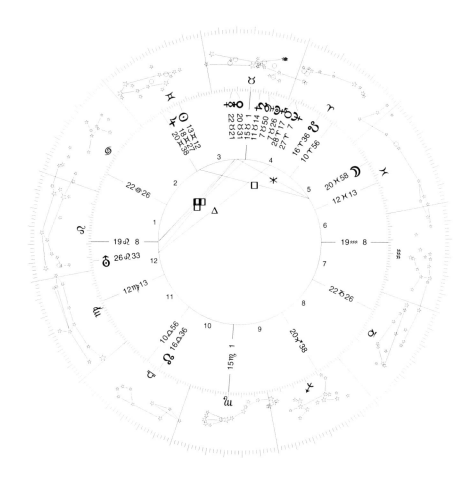

Pierre Laval
Chatledon, France (45°N59, 3°E31)
June 28, 1883
10:00:52 LT
Vernal Point: 6° Pisces 53'10"

star Antares in sidereal Scorpio, the sign of poison. Laval was several times Minister, under the third Republic, and even Président du Conseil. However, he became Minister of State under Marshal Pétain during the Occupation, and by dint of this, was condemned to death shortly after the Liberation. He attempted to poison himself in order to escape the firing squad. However, he was revived and finally shot October 15, 1945, in Paris under truly exceptional and dramatic circumstances.

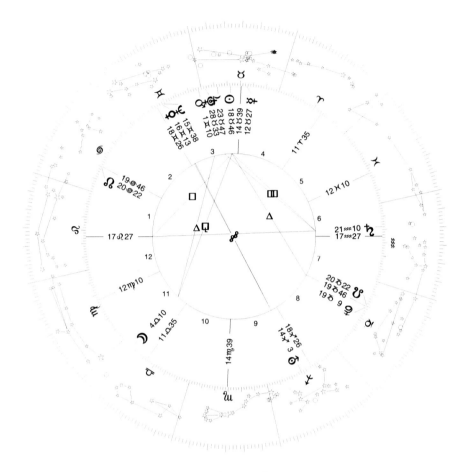

Josephine Baker
St. Louis, Missouri (38°N37'38," 90°W11'52"
June 3, 1906
11:41:02 CST
Vernal Point 6° Pisces 33'58"

We have another case of the Sun–Jupiter conjunction in the third house with **Josephine Baker** (June 3, 1906, St. Louis, Missouri, at 11:30 a.m., rectified to 11:41:02 CST). She was the first woman of African descent to star in a major motion picture. The Sun–Jupiter conjunction placed in the third house indicates not only great ambition, but the chance of being able to realize it, notably through relationships with men; this is valid especially in a female horoscope, as the Sun represents the male element in the chart of a woman.

In this same way we note that Lady Bird, wife of President Lyndon Johnson, was born under this same Sun–Jupiter conjunction.

To come back to Josephine Baker, we find here indications of great personal ambition since the Ascendant in sidereal Leo is governed by the Sun. Six planets are found in the third house, which reveals the disproportionate ambition of this young, black American woman and her subsequent vertiginous climb to the dizzy heights of fame. Mercury, the ruler of the twelfth house through Virgo on the cusp, the house that corresponds to Pisces, which in turn rules the feet, is in conjunction with the MC. Here we find the astrological explanation for her professional success obtained by dancing as well as her involvement with the French underground during the War. Neptune, ruler of Pisces, yet again the feet, is in Gemini in conjunction with Venus, the Arts, in this case, the Art of Dancing. The Sun, framed by Mercury and Jupiter, reveals the generosity of this woman who, after having terminated her acting career, dedicated her later years to the education of a dozen or so adopted children of different ethnic origins. Uranus in the ninth house, that of the ideal, and in sidereal Sagittarius (the ninth sign) in opposition with Neptune, the second ruler of the fifth house of children through Pisces, offers an explanation as to why she was adamant about grouping together children of different nationalities and colors. In addition, Mars, the primary ruler of the fifth house, is in trine with the Moon in the eleventh house of hopes and friendships. In addition, she has a Royal Yoga, from a conjunction of Jupiter, the ruler of Sagittarius and Mars, the ruler of Aries, both trine the Leo Ascendant. She died in Paris, April 12, 1975.

Willy Brandt, the former Federal German Chancellor, was born December 18, 1913, in Lübeck, Germany, at 12:45 noon, rectified to 12:40:22 CET. The Sun, having just passed the MC, is at the beginning of the fourth house, which constitutes a promising rise in life. The Moon, a very important factor in politics as it is the symbol of popularity, is in sidereal and tropical Leo and has the Sun, the ruler of Leo, at its command; moreover, it is in

Willy Brandt
Lubeck, Germany (53°N52, 10°E40)
December 18, 1913
12:40:22 CET
Vernal Point 6° Pisces 27'40"

trine with the Sun. This benefic aspect of the two luminaries, one placed at the MC, having the second at its command, indicates social success on a very large scale, whatever the field of activity. We notice that the MC, Sun and Jupiter are found in Sagittarius, the sign of foreign lands. So it follows, Willy Brandt, a known anti-Nazi, went in exile to Norway where he even took the nationality of the country he had adopted. When he was in power in Germany after the war, he carried out a very European policy while

Pope John XXIII
Sotto-Il-Monte, Italy (45°N42, 9°E40)
November 25, 1881
10:15:50 Meridian 9°E40
Vernal Point: 6° Pisces 54'30"

making overtures to the Eastern Bloc nations. In the astrologer's eyes, this shows the extent of the effect, which we attribute to the influence of Sagittarius. Moreover, the Sun was close to the Galactic Center. He died in Unkel, Germany, October 1982.

We have another splendid example of great social success and personal elevation in the person of **Pope John XXIII**, born November 25, 1881,

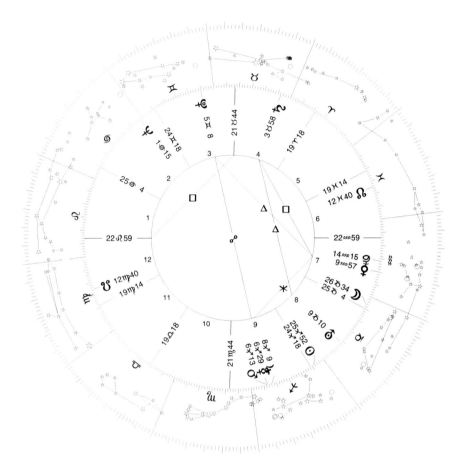

Richard Nixon
Yorba Linda, California (33°N53, 117°W49)
January 9, 1913
21:30:42 PST
Vernal Point: 6° Pisces 28'27"

in Sotto-il-Monte, Bergamo, Lombardy, Italy, at 10:15 a.m., rectified to
10:15:50 Meridian 9E40. His case provides us with an interesting study if
we compare the degree of elevation with the absence of ambition, this latter factor being notably evident when the ruler of the Ascendant is near the
MC. Here, the ruler of the sidereal Sagittarius Ascendant, Jupiter, tends
strongly toward religion and is found below the horizon in the ninth house.
Venus and Mercury, the two rulers of the fourth house, due to Libra being

on the cusp followed by Virgo, are found in conjunction with the MC. He died June 3, 1963, in Rome.

I have already written elsewhere that this particular pope elevated to the nobility that ecclesiastical dignitary whom we nicknamed the "Vatican's Astrologer." I cannot help emphasizing that Uranus, the planet of astrology, makes six aspects, all of them benefic, trines with the Moon, Jupiter, Chiron and Neptune, and weak sextiles with Mars, Mercury and Venus. Here was a Pontiff who sympathized with our art. I think he was also the first pope to travel by airplane, the domain of Uranus.

The following are a few other examples of men involved in the political field (Americans this time), who will serve to illustrate my line of thinking. Former President **Richard Nixon** was magnificently reelected in 1972. He was born January 9, 1913, in Yorba Linda, in California, at 9:30 p.m., rectified to 21:30:42 PST. Here, we find Saturn, which has just descended from the Midheaven in square to Venus, in the seventh house of partnerships and associations. During the Watergate affair, he had to deal with ruthless enemies. The journalists in question did not let go of their prey until they had fully completed their regicide right to the bitter end. Saturn crashes the native and drags him down in its own fall. Pluto in Gemini, the sign of journalism, is in opposition to the triple conjunction of Mars, Mercury and Saturn. Mercury, the ruler of the twelfth house of secret enemies is in conjunction with Mars. Yet according to Vedic astrology he had a Royal Yoga because Mars, ruler of Aries, was in conjunction with Jupiter, ruler of Sagittarius, both signs in trine to the Leo Ascendant. He died April 22, 1994, at 21:08 EDT, in New York City.

By contrast, the former vice-president, **Gerald Ford** (July 14, 1913, in Omaha, Nebraska, at 1:21 p.m., rectified to 13:16:15 CST), who became President after the resignation of Nixon, has the Sun situated where Nixon's Saturn is placed, as far as the position within the houses is concerned. In one case, Saturn placed here provokes a fall, whereas the Sun, in the other case, in the same position and in accordance with the traditional influences we attribute to it, brought the highest honors. His sudden rise from vice-president to president is indicated by Venus, the

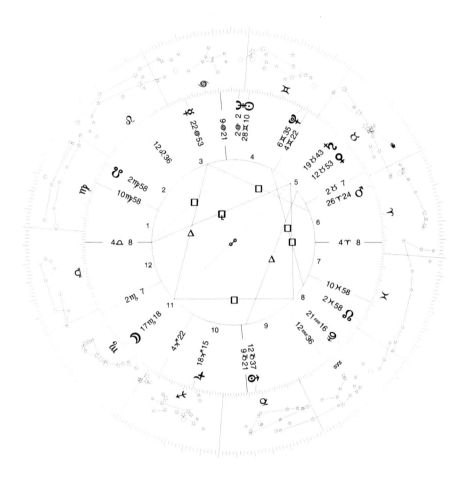

Gerald Ford
Omaha, Nebraska (41°N15'31," 95°W56'15")
July 14, 1913
13:16:15 CST
Vernal Point: 6° Pisces 28'1"

ruler of his Ascendant, in the fifth house, being in trine to Uranus in the ninth house close to the IC. He died in Riverside, California, December 26, 2006.

Nelson Rockefeller, who was born July 8, 1908, at noon, rectified to 11:45:51 EST, in Bar Harbor, Maine, had the stellium Sun–Neptune–Venus–Mercury–Pluto descending from the MC. Consequently, it

Nelson Rockefeller
Bar Harbor, Maine (44°N20, 68°W14)
July 5, 1908
11:45:51 EST
Vernal Point: 6°W32'13"

crushes the native, but this time in a benefic way. The two rulers of this
fourth house, Mercury and Venus, through Gemini on the cusp and
Taurus intercepted, are themselves only a few degrees from the MC,
which they have just passed. Here we find the heritage right from the
cradle. For he was born into one of the country's richest families. The
Sun, ruler of the second house of finances, is in opposition to Uranus
in the tenth house of home. In addition, there is a kind of Royal Yoga

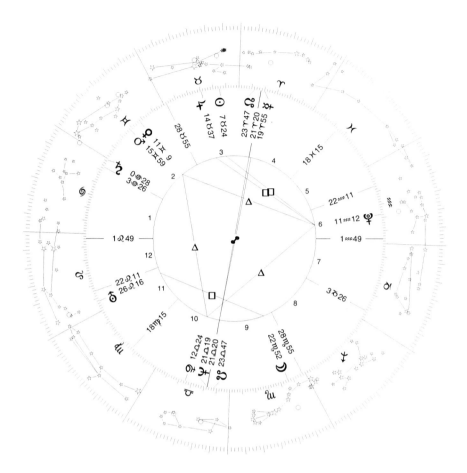

Honoré de Balzac
Tours, France (47N23, 0E40)
May 20, 1799
10:50:56 LT
Vernal Point 8° Pisces 3'34"

through Venus ruler of Taurus, and Saturn ruler of Capricorn, being in square. He died January 26, 1979, in New York City.

Honoré de Balzac, born in Tours, Indre-et-Loire, France, May 20, 1799, at 11 a.m., rectified to 10:50:56 LT, provides a perfect example of someone who succeeded through his own personal efforts with a Sun–Jupiter conjunction, which climbs toward the MC.

THE SECOND AND ELEVENTH HOUSES

The second house is the house of material gains, owing to its correspondence to the second sign of the zodiac, Taurus. We have already seen that if the houses are counted in the same direction as the signs, the part of the Heavens on which finances depend would be that part where the Sun passes, summarily, between 2 a.m. and 4 a.m., that is to say, rather paradoxically, the very twelfth section within the twenty-four-hour cycle when we are the least active. However, totally in contradiction to this, if the houses are counted clockwise, the second house is the one of mid-morning, that is, the one that corresponds with the moment when we are wide awake, at the beginning of our working day and therefore suits quite naturally our remunerative labors.

With **Honoré de Balzac** we find the two malefic planets, Mars and Saturn, in the second house, that of material gains, if you count the houses in a clockwise direction, that is, in the opposite direction to that of the signs. For us, this illustrates perfectly the continual financial worries that plagued the great novelist and playwright (Sun and Jupiter in the third house of literature). Nevertheless, he did make money from his literary masterpieces with Venus, ruler of the third house in his second house. Uranus in his eleventh house well describes his interpersonal problems with his friends. He died in Paris, August 18, 1850.

Paul Bonhoure (September 6, 1883, at 5 a.m., rectified to 4:59:48 Local Time, in the Herault region of France) was the first person to win the major prize in France's National Lottery, five million francs. It is certain that the triple conjunction of Sun–Venus–Uranus just below the Ascendant is already a factor of luck in itself, all the more given that the Sun is the ruler of the sidereal Leo Ascendant and Venus is the ruler of the Taurus Midheaven. Moreover, the fifth house, that of gains through gambling, has for its classical rulers Mars, through the Aries cusp, and Jupiter, through Pisces, which occupies the rest of the house. Mars is in square with the Moon in the fifth house and Mercury in the eleventh house. What interests us even more is the fact that Jupiter, the classical sub-ruler of the fifth

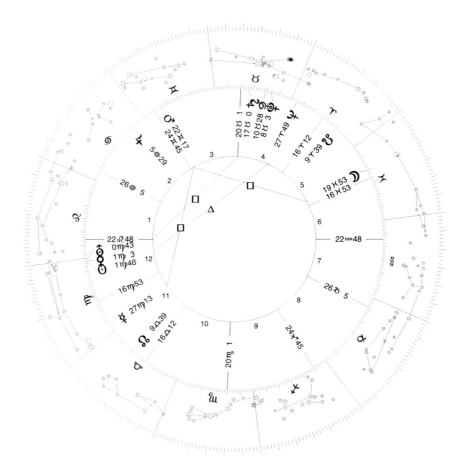

Paul Bonhoure
In the Herrault Region of France (43°N36, 3°E53)
September 6, 1883
4:59:58 LT
Vernal Point 6° Pisces 53'1"

house through Pisces, is found in the second house, that of good fortune, which is very powerful because it is in exaltation in Cancer. On the other hand, the tropical astrologers who count the houses in the same direction as the signs, will find that the fifth house, that of gambling, is ruled in this case through Capricorn by restrictive Saturn in square with Venus.

Now, let us look at the horoscope of **Mohammad Reza Shah Pahlavi**, the former Shah of Iran, born in Tehran on October 26, 1919, at 11:30 p.m.,

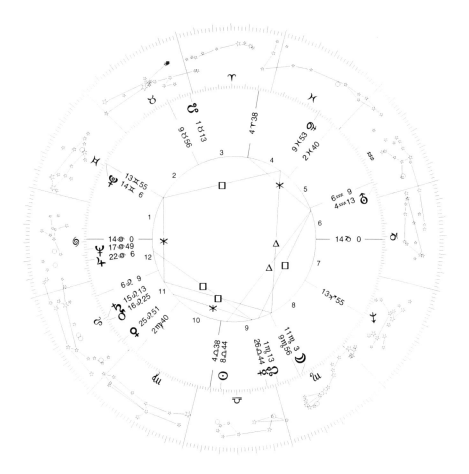

Mohammad Reza Shah Pahlavi
Tehran, Iran (35N40, 51E26)
October 26, 1919
23:28:25 ST Meridian 51°E26
Vernal Point: 6° Pisces 22'45"

rectified to 23:28:25. Meridian 51°E26. If we count the houses in the same direction as the signs we find in the second house the two malignant planets Mars and Saturn in conjunction, a combination that offers us the portrait of a man affected by the greatest poverty, whereas we know that, thanks to petroleum, he was one of the richest men in the world and that his avowed aim was to take advantage of the underground riches of his country in order to bring it in line with the world's industrial nations. It was exactly that, which was the cause of his downfall. By counting the houses in a clockwise direction, we see this terrible affliction in his eleventh house, that of friends and projects. The opposition to his grandiose projects arose among his own people. Where else could you find a better example of the betrayal of friends and of dashed hopes? Ah! Petroleum. Petroleum. How many of the great persons of this world have not sinned in your name? Let us begin with the Shah himself, a man who was the severest of the severe, still more uncompromising than the King of Saudi Arabia in his efforts to obtain the highest rates for petroleum during the discussions between the oil-producing nations and the consumer nations. One can explain his tremendous wealth by his Pluto in the first house within minutes of arc of being in the second house, in a grand trine with the Sun and Uranus (using wide orbs), as well as quintile to Venus, and the joint rulers of the second house of finance in sextile—Mercury through sidereal Gemini on the cusp and Venus through sidereal Taurus inside the house.

Now, when the Shah was overthrown—after October 2, 1978, partial eclipse of the Sun (the King), which took place very shortly before his birthday—he became very seriously ill. He wandered from country to country vainly seeking asylum and shelter from the repeated extradition orders and threats of assassination, which came from Tehran. He was rejected by all and sundry with the exception of President Anwar Sadat of Egypt, a fervent Muslim, who gave more than one Christian head of State a good lesson in courage. The Sun and Mercury in the ninth house indicate that he would eventually live outside his country. Pahlevi died in Cairo, July 27, 1980.

Dag Hammarskjöld was born July 29, 1905, at 11:30 a.m., rectified to 11:37:51 CET, in Jönköping, Sweden. On a diplomatic mission in Africa, his plane was shot down near Ndola, Zambia, September 18, 1961, a little after midnight. If we count the houses in the traditional way, then Mars is in the second house, which would imply that he put his energies into earning money. However, he came from a well-off family and his vocation was in politics. If we count the houses clockwise, then Mars is placed in the eleventh house. Mars in Libra, the sign of diplomacy, Saturn in Pisces and the Sun in Leo form a Grand Septile, made up of a

Dag Hammarskjöld
Jönköping, Sweden (57°N47, 14°E10)
July 29, 1905
11:37:51 CET
Vernal Point: 6° Pisces 34′41″

triangle formed by angles, which are multiples of one-seventh of a circle or 51°25′43″ in the ratio of 2/7:3/7:2/7. The mystical number seven gave him the ability to make perfect order out of a chaotic situation.[5] Mars is also in sidereal Libra, the seventh sign, indicating considerable energy in the realm of relationships. The rulers of the eleventh house, Pluto

5   Heline. *Sacred Science of Numbers*, p. 55.

John B. Adams
Lisburn, Northern Ireland (54°N31, 6°W3)
January 21, 1899
1:04:01 ST, Meridian 5°W55
Vernal Point 6° Pisces 40'8"

through Scorpio and Venus through Libra, are in conjunction in the fourth house of the profession.

John B. Adams, M.D., was born close to Lisburn, Northern Ireland, January 21, 1899, at 1:15 a.m. GMT, rectified to 1:04:01 ST. He was very much in the news in the fifties after having been accused of poisoning his rich clients, who had included him in their wills; but he was acquitted April 9,

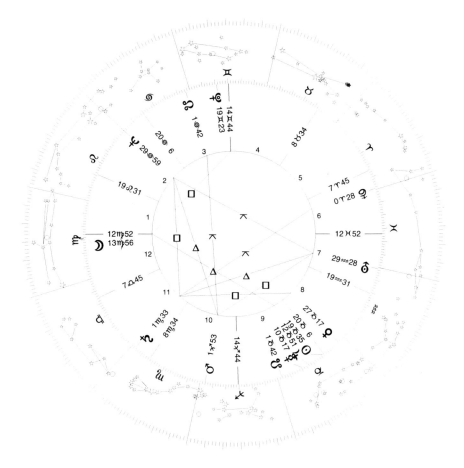

Valéry Giscard d'Estaing
Koblenz, Germany (50°N21, 7°E35)
February 2, 1926
21:17:13 GMT
Vernal Point: 6° Pisces 17'30"

1957, owing to the lack of sufficient proof. But what we would really like to point out in order to provide credibility to our thesis is the important element of premeditation that existed in the case of this criminal. Indeed, the eleventh house is the one of projects and if it is considered in accordance with our suggestion, it is here that you will find within the house the sign of sidereal Scorpio, that of death, Venus, Goddess of Love, closely framed by Saturn and Uranus/Chiron. We shall read "Projects, hopes for deaths, notably through poison." If the houses are counted according to the succession of the signs, these three planets would be found in the second house and the great majority of practitioners and manuals would cause you to say, "Poverty caused by deranged morals, exaggerated expenditure in the pursuit of worldly pleasure." This is far from being the case, as this man grew wealthier thanks to the last wills and testaments from which he benefitted. The editor has not succeeded in finding his date of death.

Valéry Giscard d'Estaing was born February 2, 1926, in Koblenz, Germany, at 9:20 p.m., rectified to 21:17:13 GMT. I would like to point out the role of Saturn as the planet of restriction, frustration and death, by considering it as being either in the second house, that of material gains (according to the same direction as the signs), or in the eleventh house, that of ministers in mundane astrology (if we see the houses as following a clockwise direction, opposite to that of the signs). Thus, Saturn is strongly afflicted; it is first of all both in 25°15' tropical Scorpio and in 1°33' sidereal Scorpio. Thus the planet of death is in the sign of death. Moreover, it is in a T-square with Neptune (in the second house of finances) and Venus (in the eighth house of death). We know that the President's seven years of office were marked not only by the death of several of his ministers (some of them through suicide), but also by a number of resignations, some of which took place shortly after nomination. In the latter case it was a question of the loss of ministers; here death is purely symbolic. Should the houses be counted in the same direction as the signs, the Saturnian restrictions would have had an effect upon the fortune, because the Great Malefic would have been found in the second house. However, we do not believe that the former President of France was greatly troubled by financial problems. (Editor: Jacques Dorsan obviously overlooked Neptune in the second house but it may have behaved more subtly in the realm of money.)

THE FOURTH AND NINTH HOUSES

In the previous pages, we have been anxious to point out the differences that exist between the third and fourth houses, as we have named them according to our system. By these we mean the sectors, which are on either side of the Midheaven. What traditional astrologers consider to be in the tenth house, the domain of professional life, describes for us nothing less than the desires, which have a bearing on the career (the vocation), while more often than not, the professional life, which is imposed by circumstances or present needs, is brought out through a close study of what you consider to be the ninth house, which for us is the fourth house, the one that starts with the MC if we count these houses in a clockwise direction. Employing the procedure, which we recommend, brings about a more significant difference between the houses with a common boundary in the depths of the sky.

If we count the houses in the same direction as that of the signs, the fourth starts from the IC. We generally attribute to this house one of the parents, in accordance with the authors that we have looked at in detail, as well as the residence. For us, the ninth house terminates at the IC. We have already talked about this in our introduction. Through its analogy, it corresponds to Sagittarius. It informs us about long voyages and stays in foreign countries; it also tells us about travels of thought, idealism, religion and metaphysics. The one that leaves from IC, for us the tenth house, is what corresponds to Capricorn, an earth sign, and that, quite logically, enlightens us on matters of real estate in general and the place of residence in particular.

We have already examined former President Giscard d'Estaing's horoscope when comparing the second and eleventh houses. He became President May 19, 1974, and lost the Presidency May 19, 1981. Mercury, ruler of the Ascendant through Virgo, is in conjunction with Jupiter in the ninth house where a stellium of excellent quality is found since it is made up of Sun–Jupiter–Mercury. Well, just like former President Nixon, child of Sagittarius who manifested an obvious interest in foreign affairs, going notably to Moscow and Peking, none can deny that Valéry Giscard d'Estaing was, since the time of the First Republic (1792), the first French president to have had so many contacts with foreign heads of State.

Paul Choisnard (February 13, 1867, Saint-Genis-de-Saintonge in the Charente Maritime region of France, at 10:55 p.m., rectified to 22:51:30 LT), the great French creator of scientific astrology, was a graduate of the famous

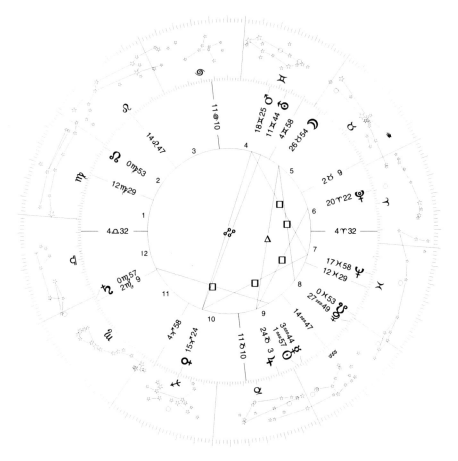

Paul Choisnard
Saint-Genis-de-Saintonge, France (45°N29, 0°W34)
February 13, 1867
22:51:30 LT
Vernal Point 7° Pisces6'52"

Polytechnic High School in Paris [an academic institution of an extremely high caliber, which is a great honor to attend and from which to graduate]. If the houses are counted in the same direction as the signs, then he has a Mars–Uranus conjunction (6:41 orb) in the ninth house, the one of idealism and philosophy, burdened by Mars in the ninth house square Neptune in the sixth house. However, there certainly is a remarkably different interpretation if the houses are counted clockwise. Instead, you will find a splendid

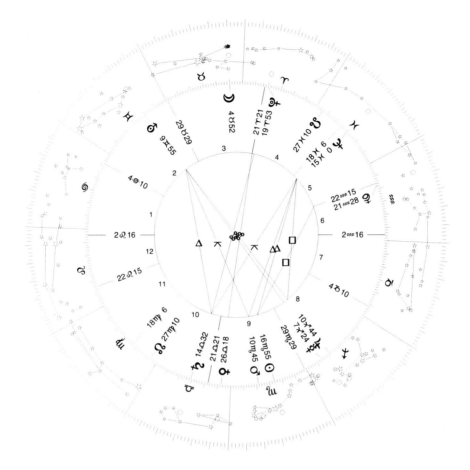

Colonel Ernest Caslant
Nanteuil-le-Haudoin, France (49°N8, 2°E48)
December 1, 1865
22:03:59 LT
Vernal Point 7° Pisces 7'53"

ninth house with a Mercury–Sun–Jupiter conjunction. This is even set off by a no less splendid trine with the Moon, most closely with Jupiter but within orb of the Sun. We do not deem it necessary to enter into details concerning the actual interpretation but, as far as we can see, it is certain that the ninth house, the one of prophecy and intellectual speculation, is represented in a totally different way if our theory is adopted. In addition, Saturn in the twelfth house is able to concentrate on astrological research.

Mercury, ruler of Gemini, and Saturn, ruler of Aquarius, were in square, thereby forming a kind of Royal Yoga. He died February 9, 1930, in Tours.

Colonel Eugene Caslant, also a well-known astrologer, offers something of a somewhat similar nature. He was born December 1, 1865, in Nanteuil-le-Haudoin (Seine and Oise), at 10:00 p.m., rectified to 22:03:59 LT. Indeed, we find the Sun, Mars and Venus in the ninth house. Here it certainly is a question of a truly extraordinary horosocope with the exceptional presence of seven planets in positions of dignity: Venus in Libra, Mars in Scorpio, Jupiter in Sagittarius and Neptune in Pisces, all in their respective ruling sidereal zodiac signs; the Moon in Taurus, Saturn in Libra and Pluto in Aries, all in the sidereal zodiac signs in which they are exalted. We know that Scorpio and Sagittarius lean toward the occult. Mercury and Jupiter are also in conjunction in the eighth house in Sagittarius in opposition to Uranus in the second house in Gemini. There is an analogy between the eighth house and Scorpio. Caslant could not help but be attracted by the realms "beyond." Although trained as an engineer, he was to devote his life to metaphysics. All the editor has been able to discover is that he died in 1940.

Aleister Crowley, the great English occultist, astrologer and magician, was born October 12, 1875, in Leamington, Warwich, between 10:00 p.m. and 11:00 p.m., rectified to 22:41:46 GMT. He died in London, December 1, 1947. If the houses are counted in the way I recommend, a Sun–Venus conjunction as well as Jupiter are found in the ninth house. The Sun receives a sextile from Uranus and a trine from Saturn. Let us note, in passing, that if it is true that astrologers are strongly influenced by Uranus, we could only be aware of this phenomenon shortly before the end of the eighteenth century, when it was discovered. We shall notice this and not only in the case of our distant forbears, Saturn's dominance (abstract studies, studies connected with time and mathematics) in relation to astrology's practitioners. Yet again, we find here as a dominant house, the one that crosses the Sun between 10 p.m. and midnight. This one describes the subject so much better, as well as the main activities of his existence (think of those faraway voyages to foreign lands) if we

Aleister Crowley
Leamington Spa, England (52°N18, 1°W31)
October 12, 1875
22:41:46 GMT
Vernal Point: 6° Pisces 59'37"

attribute to it the sense we normally give to the ninth house, rather than that given to the fourth one.

If the houses unfold in the same direction as the signs, then Uranus is in the second house and Pluto is in the eleventh house whereas if the houses unfold clockwise, then Uranus is in the eleventh and Pluto is the second. Dorsan also considered Pluto to be a ruler of Aries, which is in the second house. Uranus in opposition with Saturn in the fifth house explains the vehement

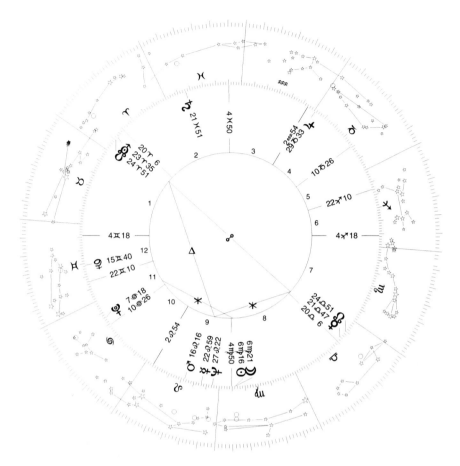

Romy Schneider
Vienna, Austria
September 23, 1938
21:42:36 CET
Vernal Point: 6° Pisces 6'55"

criticism and the secret, hostile feelings of which he was often the object as well as his sexual relationships both with women and men. However, this magician was to meet a sticky end. Mercury, ruler of the IC, thus the end of life, is found in the eighth house in a T-square with Saturn and Uranus.

Romy Schneider's horoscope (September 23, 1938, in Vienna, Austria, at 9:45 p.m., rectified to 21:42:36 CET) has Mars, Mercury and Neptune, in

Erich von Stroheim
Vienna, Austria (48°N13, 16°E20)
September 22, 1885
8:58:42 LT
Vernal Point: 6° Pisces 51'18"

the ninth house in sidereal Leo. Both Mercury and Neptune trine Uranus in the first house and Mercury sextiles Venus in the seventh house. The fifth house, which governs acting, is ruled by Saturn through the Capricorn cusp and by Jupiter through Sagittarius. Jupiter could not be better placed for success than close to the midheaven in the fourth house. Moreover, Saturn in the second house made her work all the harder, which was rewarded by many awards. Saturn quincunx Venus in the seventh house explains her

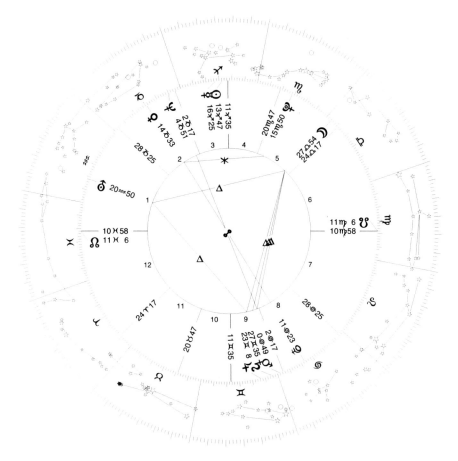

Michel de Nostradamus
St. Reny, France (43°N48, 4°E50)
December 14, 1503
11:50:37 LT
12° Pisces 10'37"

broken marriages, though she remained on friendly terms with many of her partners. Well, we know that Leo exercises its influence over France. This shows just how necessary it was for this actress to pursue her career outside the country of her birth. She died in Paris, May 29, 1982.

Erich von Stroheim, a rather unapproachable *"monstre sacré,"* was kind enough to grant me an audience in São Paulo, Brazil, in February 1954.

During the course of this brief interview he declared to me that he was born shortly before 9 a.m. in Vienna, Austria, September 22, 1885. I have rectified it to 8:58:42 Local Time. He died in Paris, May 12, 1957. Practically all the planets are above the horizon.

According to the habitual order of the houses, the two malefics, Saturn and Mars, would be found in the ninth house, the one of foreign lands. One could hardly imagine a more (words fail me) monstrous error in interpretation. Von Stroheim was to become one of the giants of cinema in Hollywood (Pluto in the fifth house trine Uranus and the Sun in the second house). He owed his success to the fact that he was well outside of Austria. When his acting career in Hollywood drew to an end, he came back to France to retire, where he lived the latter part of his life in the lap of luxury. If the houses are considered in the way I am advocating, the Moon, symbol of popularity, is found in the ninth house in grand trine with Venus, which is just below the horizon, thereby confirming voyages across the seas and artistic expression, and Saturn, thereby protecting him from any great fall, usually associated with Saturn in the fourth house.

Nostradamus was born December 14, 1503, "on the hour of noon," rectified to 11:50:37 LT, in Saint-Rémy-en Crau and died in Salon, France, July 2, 1566 (Julian), at 3:00 a.m. If the houses are counted in the same direction as the signs, then the ninth house is empty. However, quite to the contrary, if the houses are seen to unfold in the opposite direction to that of the signs, then we find Mars, Saturn and Jupiter united in this house, that is to say, all the planets that are outside of the Earth's orbit and that were known at the time. One can hardly deny that the house of Prophecy is well to the fore. These planets are also in trine with Uranus in the first house and the Moon in the fifth house of speculations. That is the very least that can be said. The Sun and Mercury are found in sidereal Sagittarius, the sign of prophecy as well. Pluto is also in the fifth house within a degree of the star Antares, which introduces a sinister and dark element into his prognostications. The rulers of the signs in trine with the Pisces Ascendant, the Moon and Mars are in trine, thereby forming a Royal Yoga.

Pope Paul VI
Brescia, Italy (45°N32, 10°E13)
September 26, 1897
22:51:53 CET
Vernal Point: 6° Pisces 41'15"

Giovanni Montini (Pope Paul VI) was born in Concesio near Brescia, September 26, 1897, at 11 p.m., rectified to 22:51:53 CET, and died August 6, 1978, in Castel Gandolfo, Italy. In his chart Mercury, ruler of the Ascendant through Gemini, is in conjunction with Jupiter, which gives religious feelings. The Sun and Moon as well are in the ninth house, the one of religion and philosophy. Up until his time, no other Pope had traveled so much. He was known as "the Pilgrim Pope." He was the first

208

Pope in centuries to meet heads of the various Eastern Orthodox faiths and the second Pope to meet the Archbishop of Canterbury. Once again, the location of the stellium pleads for a case in our favor. Before he was Pope, during the War, some of his work remains shrouded in mystery. He procured large sums of money to help many Jews to escape and is alleged to have enabled leading Nazi officers to escape the collapse of the Third Reich. Uranus conjunction Saturn in the eighth house can mean unexpected gains and Pluto in the first house is a singular, secretive and strong personality. One of his most famous deeds as Pope was the Encyclical Humanae Vitae, which reaffirmed condemnation of artificial birth control in opposition to the majority of theologians who argued that contraception was morally acceptable. The fifth house of children is totally in sidereal Capricorn, ruled by Saturn, which is in conjunction with Uranus and square Venus, showing perhaps a certain deprivation or lack of consideration of people's feelings. The square of Venus, ruler of Libra, and Saturn, ruler of Aquarius, form a Royal Yoga.

THE FIFTH AND EIGHTH HOUSES

The fifth house is mainly the house of love affairs, of children and of creativity; the sixth is the one of sickness and the eighth is the house of death.

Charles P. Baudelaire was born in Paris, April 9, 1821, at 3 p.m., rectified to 14:59:45 LT. He was a poet, most famous for his collection *Les fleurs du mal* ("The Flowers of Evil"), as well as a translator and a literary and art critic. Here we can see a gathering of planets, seven in all, astride the fifth and sixth houses. Since this group is in sidereal Pisces, it shows us creativity, voyages by sea, solitude, the use of drugs, sickness, mystical and thwarted loves. He refused to be restricted in his choice of theme or his manner of living. His stepfather put him on a ship to India in an attempt to save him from his corrupt life but he jumped ship in Mauritius and returned (Uranus and Neptune in the ninth house of voyages). His mistress, a mulatto woman, inspired his most anguished and sensual poetry (fifth and sixth house emphasis). This horoscope

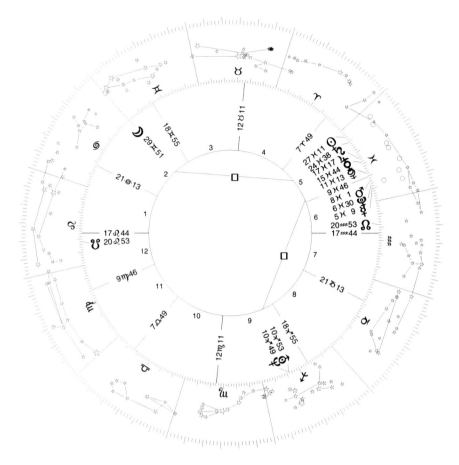

Charles Baudelaire
Paris, France (48°N52, 2°E20)
April 9, 1821
14:59:45 LT
Vernal Point 7° Pisces 45'15"

very well illustrates the trap that exists in the event of the rejection of my proposition, under the pretext that by counting the houses according to the direction of the signs, the stellium in the eighth house would fit perfectly his haunting fear of death, which I quite willingly admit. But the Sun is the ruler of the Ascendant, thus of life, and it is in conjunction with Saturn, the planet of death and both of them are in a square with the Moon. However, the luminaries are placed above the horizon

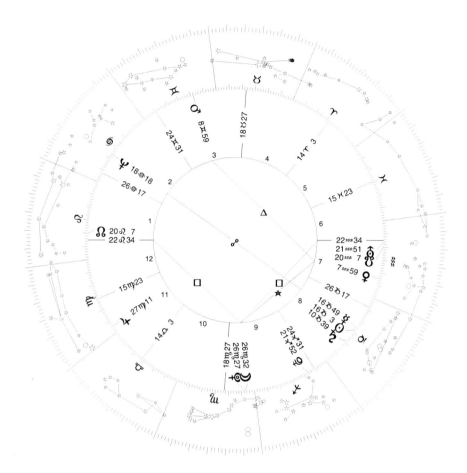

Wolfgang Amadeus Mozart
Salzburg, Austria (47°N48, 13°E1)
January 27, 1756
20:06:35 LT
Vernal Point: 8° Pisces 39'48"

and, by dint of this, they can both be considered to be *hyleg,* givers of life. Their common affliction with the scythe explains perfectly his dread of death and premature death. For in his twenties, he squandered an inheritance within two years, accumulated debt, experimented with hashish and opium, and contracted syphilis, which later brought about his death, at the age of forty-six, in Paris, August 31, 1867, at 11:00 LT.[6]

---

6   Wikipedia.

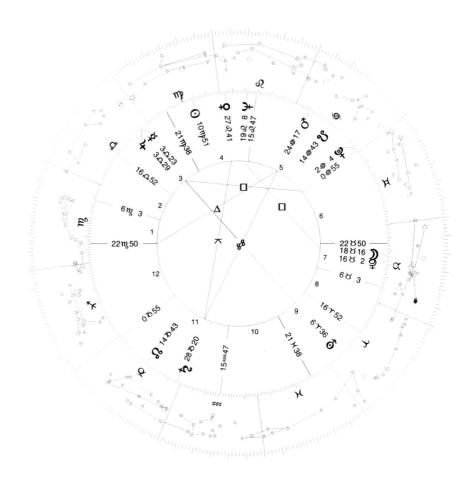

Brigitte Bardot
Paris, France (48°N52, 2°E20)
September 28, 1934
13:21:18 GMD
Vernal Point 6° Pisces 10'16"

Nevertheless, these factors do not detract from his genius, which was helped by a conjunction of Mars and Jupiter, respective rulers of Aries and Sagittarius, signs in trine with the Leo Ascendant, and so forming a Royal Yoga.

Wolfgang Amadeus Mozart was born January 27, 1756, in Salzburg, Austria, at 8 pm, rectified to 20:06:35 Local Time. If you take the houses in the same direction as the signs, Saturn and a superior conjunction of the Sun and Mercury fall in the fifth house. This would stress his romantic and sexual life or suggest that he was an actor or entertainer, which you might be led to believe by the American film *Amadeus*. However, if we count the houses clockwise then these same planets fall into the eighth house. Mozart had a preoccupation with death. He labored for a long time on his great work, "The Requiem," and it is said that every night, when he lay down to sleep, he was conscious that this might be his last night on earth and so he prayed fervently. The eighth house also has to do with the financial situation after marriage, which was certainly a major issue when he left home. Pluto, the Moon and Chiron in the ninth house chimes with his father's strong influence from childhood onward and his begrudging acceptance of his marriage to Constanza. He died December 5, 1797, at 0:55 LT, in Vienna, Austria.

Brigitte Bardot was born in Paris, September 28, 1934, at 1:30 p.m., rectified to 13:21:18 GMD. She was one of the first European actresses to be popular in the United States. Mars and Pluto are in the traditional eighth house or the clockwise fifth house; the traditional fifth house and clockwise eighth house is empty. According to Bill Herbst,[7] a modern authority on the houses, the eighth house relates to issues of power and trust in partnership, the mysteries of ego, death, and rebirth through intense relationships, and the experience of true sexual union; the fifth house relates to creative self-expression, sex, romance, love affairs, sports, games and amusements. According to our clockwise system, the fifth house describes education, love life, sentimental relationships, amusements, theaters and artistic works; the eighth house represents profound changes, death, regeneration, sexual instincts, the partner's instincts and antiques. I consider the clockwise description to have an edge. Her Midheaven and Descendant are in trine. This configuration facilitates the conclusion of professional (MC) contracts (Descendant). We also note that the Moon is in sidereal Taurus, its sign of exaltation, and that Saturn is in its domicile, Capricorn—two Earth signs, which reveal an undeniable practical sense.

---

7   Herbst. *Houses of the Horoscope.*

Martha Rocha
Salvador, Bahia, Brazil (12°S59, 38W31)
September 19, 1932
19:31:00 BZT
Vernal Point: 6° Pisces 11'57"

Martha Rocha, to whom I became very close when I was living in Brazil, was elected Miss Brazil in 1954. She was born in Salvador, Bahia, September 19, 1932, at 7.30 p.m., rectified to 19:31:00 BZT. The Mars–Pluto opposition to Saturn on the line of the meridian, warned of a serious threat, all the more because of the fact that it was square the Ascendant and Uranus—consequently, an affliction that touches the four angles of the horoscope. The Dragon's Tail in conjunction with Mercury and at

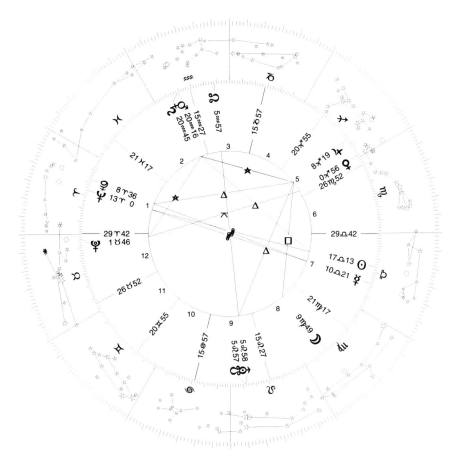

Aga Khan III
Karachi, Pakistan (24°N52, 67°E03)
November 2, 1877
17:58:0 LT
Vernal Point: 6° Pisces 57'54"

the midpoint of the Sun and the Jupiter–Neptune conjunction in what is the fifth house according to the same order as the signs, would lead us to believe in tumultuous love affairs. This certainly was far from being the case. Martha represented her country with great dignity during international competitions, and when she was in Brazil she refused to frequent night clubs, which did not prohibit entry to minors. It is worth pointing out that there were two ages of majority, one at the age

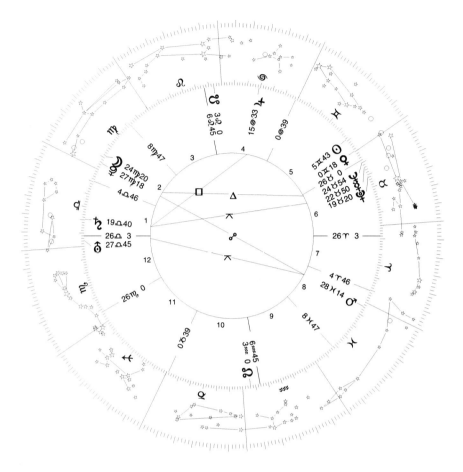

Wallis Simpson
Blue Ridge Summit, Pennsylvania (39°N43'27," 77°W28'18")
June 19, 1896
16:24:05 EST
Vernal Point: 6° Pisces 42'18"

of eighteen, which gave the right to vote, while the other, applied in the case of night clubs, was twenty-one.

To get back to our houses, if they are counted in a clockwise direction, the previously mentioned stellium of planets is found in the eighth house, the house of Death. So this beauty queen married an Argentinian in 1956. The two rulers of the sixth, the husband, Mars (ruler of the Scorpio house cusp) and Venus (ruler of Libra in the rest of the house), were indeed found in the ninth house, foreign lands. Martha was very quickly a widow. The cluster of planets proves to be so much more eloquent if we consider it to be in the eighth house rather than in the fifth.

The **Aga Khan III** (November 2, 1877, at 6 p.m., rectified to 17:58:00 LT, in Karachi, Pakistan) was born with Venus in the fifth house, if counting clockwise; and it is found at the beginning of Sagittarius, the sign of foreign lands. Nothing could better explain the fact that he would marry a beauty queen from a foreign country (Miss France). If we count in the same way as the signs, then Venus, in the eighth house, the house of Death, would have announced his becoming a widower. This was not at all the case. I point out that the Aga Khan was, in fact, born in 1877 and not 1887 as we sometimes read. This is confirmed by the Aga Khan himself on the chart I drew up for him as it bears the autograph he gave me. He died July 11, 1957, in Visoix, Switzerland.

Wallis Simpson (June 19, 1896, at 4:30 p.m., rectified to 16:24:05 EST, in Blue Ridge Summit, Pennsylvania) became the Duchess of Windsor by marrying the abdicated king of England, Edward VIII. Yet again, a stellium of five planets, all within 16½°, astride the fifth house (love) and the sixth house (marriage partner). The Sun and Venus are in conjunction in the fifth house; this symbolizes the royal spouse. It will be noted that Venus is the ruler of the Ascendant, while the Sun is ruler of the MC. If the houses are counted in the same direction as the signs, this Sun–Venus conjunction would be seen at the beginning of the eighth house, which, once again, announces early widowhood. It was not so. Edward died May 28, 1972, and she died in London, April 24, 1986.

Grace Kelly was born November 12, 1929, in Philadelphia, Pennsylvania, at 5:30 a.m, rectified to 5:30:13 EST. Her Jupiter was certainly in the fifth house, which corresponds to Leo, the royal sign of the Lion, and royalty. Her daughter's Sun in Capricorn falls in her tenth house, which in mundane astrology corresponds to government and royalty. She died in an automobile accident. The Sun, ruler of her third house of short journeys,

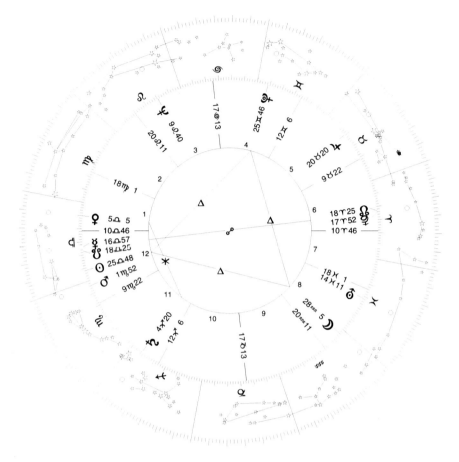

Grace Kelly
Philadelphia, Pennsylvania (39°N57,' 75°W11)
November 12, 1929
5:30:13 EST
Vernal Point: 6° Pisces 14'21")

is in grand trine with Pluto, the ruler of her twelfth house, and the Moon, sub-ruler of the third house, in the eighth house of death.

Herman Göring was born January 12, 1893, in Rosenheim, Germany, at 3:45 a.m., rectified back to 3:16:13 CET. With this Nazi Air Force Field Marshal, we also find the eighth house empty of planets if the houses are counted in the same way as the signs. However, if we count the houses clockwise, we

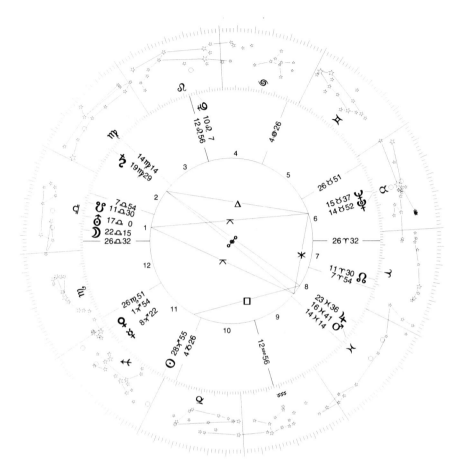

Hermann Göring
Rosenheim, Germany (47°N51, 12°E6)
March 18, 1893
3:16:13 CET
Vernal Point: 6° Pisces 45'11"

find Mars and Jupiter in the eighth, and indeed he was condemned to death. Jupiter, justice, is in square with the Sun, ruler of the MC and in opposition to Saturn, classical ruler of the IC (Aquarius), and modern sub-ruler of the tenth house through Capricorn, which occupies the end of the house going clockwise, and signifies the end of life. Indeed, for a long time he thought about taking his own life. There is premeditation since the twelfth house of confinement and death, containing the sign Scorpio, reflects on death.

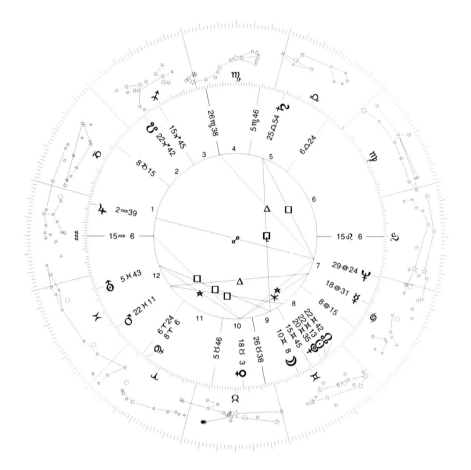

Elisabeth Kübler-Ross
Zürich, Switzerland (47°N21, 8°E31)
July 8, 1926
22:39:37 CET
Vernal Point: 6° Pisces 17'9"

Mars, the traditional ruler of Scorpio is opposed to Saturn and sextile to both Pluto, the modern ruler of Scorpio, and Neptune, the modern ruler of Pisces, which spans the end of the eighth house. In addition, Neptune and Pluto are in conjunction with the Royal Star Aldebaran. In fact, Göring committed suicide by poisoning himself May 1, 1945, in Berlin on the day before he was due to be hanged. He had kept this capsule of poison hidden, right through his period of captivity and during his trial. When the Moon is

Mary Stuart
Linlithgow Palace (55°N59, 3W37)
December 8, 1542
0:35:52 LT
Vernal Point: 11°Pisces 38'02"

in conjunction with a planet, the said planet becomes a dominant part of the theme. So, here we find the Moon in conjunction with Uranus in the degrees, which have just risen from the east, and which is, for us, the first house. Well now, Uranus is the planet of aviation.

Elisabeth Kübler-Ross was an identical triplet born July 8, 1926, in Zürich, Switzerland, at 10:45 p.m., rectified to 22:39:37 CET. Whether we count the houses counterclockwise or clockwise, both the fifth and eighth houses are tenanted. She brought about a tremendous metamorphosis in the attitudes to dying, which I think is more likely to be due to the contrast of Pluto and the Sun on the Moon Node in the clockwise eighth rather than Saturn in the traditional eighth. Mercury, ruler of Gemini and Venus, ruler of Libra, signs that are in trine with the Aquarius Ascendant, are in sextile, thereby forming a Royal Yoga. She died August 24, 2004, in Scottsdale, Arizona.

Mary Stuart, Queen of Scotland, was born December 8, 1542, in Linlithgow Palace, sometime just after midnight, rectified to 0:35:52 Local Time. She had Mars and Pluto in the eighth house. Moreover, Pluto formed an exact square with Chiron in the fifth house, which correlates with Leo and royalty. The royal house, however, is the tenth house (see King Carol's horoscope), in this case ruled by Jupiter, which is in the twelfth house of confinement. As Jupiter was sextile the Sun, she was confined to her house rather than a dungeon. Hence, she was unlikely to ever become a recognized queen. During many years, she became increasingly under the shadow of death until her beheading in Fotheringay, Scotland, February 8, 1587. If the houses are counted the traditional way, then Mars trine Jupiter would suggest several open love affairs but there was only one true love, which happened when she was for a time in Spain.[8]

Doctor **Alexis Carrel** was born in Sainte-Foy-les-Lyon, in the Rhône, June 28, 1873, at 11 p.m., rectified to 22:54:49 LT. In 1912, he received the Nobel Prize for Medicine for his physiological research. He moved to the United States where he was quite a success. The Sun in sidereal Gemini in the ninth house of foreign lands trines Mars in sidereal Libra in the sixth house of health. In fact, the United States is a Gemini nation as July 4, 1776, is in sidereal Gemini. His interest in mysticism and metaphysics is also reflected in the ninth house Sun. However, the dominating factor of his horoscope is a Grand Cross of Mars in the sixth house opposite Neptune in the twelfth house, which explains his work in medical research,

---

8   Wikipedia.

Alexis Carrel
Sainte Foy les Lyon, France (45N44, 4E48)
June 28, 1873
22:54:49 LT
Vernal Point 7° Pisces 1'32"

square to Saturn in the second house opposite Mercury and Uranus in the eighth house. In October 1935, his book *Man the Unknown* was published. Eugen Kolisko[9] makes the point about Carrel's book that "present-day science has no real knowledge of one important field—knowledge of the human being"; moreover, in spite of all our progress in technology, we have not been able to understand what man really is; on the contrary he

---

9   Kolisko. *Reincarnation and Other Essays.*

is a stranger in the world that he has created. Carrel described two great classes of diseases: infectious diseases caused by viruses and bacteria and degenerative diseases due to toxic substances issuing from the organism itself. Unfortunately, his brilliant achievement is spoiled by his theory of natural selection and the description of the superiority of the white race. While Dorsan puts natural selection in the seventh house, I would put this down to his natal Mercury–Uranus conjunction in the eighth house of death as part of the Grand Cross. For if one race is selected then another race dies. The survival of the fittest is definitely ruled by the planet Mars, which is part of this Grand Cross.

Upon his return to Paris from New York in 1944, his brilliant career was not one of the most fortunate, due to his theories on natural selection, which were considered to be closely aligned to those put forward by the Nazis. During 1944, transiting Uranus squared his Ascendant, transiting Saturn conjoined first his IC and then his Sun. He died in Paris, November 5, 1944.

THE SIXTH AND SEVENTH HOUSES

Owing to its analogy with Virgo, the only sign of the zodiac where a woman is pictured, the section of the spouse, together with a notion of service, is attached to the sixth house. Virgo is the sign of servitude and the sixth house is that of servants, work and professional tasks, which are more or less imposed. In antiquity, astrologers were almost always asked to draw up horoscopes only for the great personalities of this world, and more particularly, for men. Thus, quite naturally, the sixth house, because of its correspondence with the sixth sign, represented by a female form, stands for the wife, whereas Libra, the seventh sign, with its two platform scales, stands for justice, equilibrium, all that is complementary and the idea of union, above all, in its legality.

I do hope the members of the women's liberation movement will not accuse me of behaving like a male chauvinist and misogynist because I have given the woman a position of inferiority. I assure you that this is not so. I am only following the information and data supplied by traditional astrology. Anyway, serving people is a very noble task and we are all in one another's service; and I shall add that in the case of a feminine horoscope study, the sixth house is the husband. Besides, we have never seen men help their spouses with household tasks as much as they do now. In Japan, there has recently been an extensive enquiry into the subject of a woman's duty to serve her husband. Those in charge of this investigation were astounded to discover that thousands of Japanese women still went along with the idea of servitude. When France Inter (French Broadcasting Station) reported this fact, their switchboard was flooded with calls from listeners who not only approved of their Japanese sisters, but also stated that they preferred performing household chores to attending to affairs in the outside world. However, we really must get back to our original subject.

We thus establish a very clear distinction between the sixth house, which represents the spouse, and the seventh house, which bears a relation to marriage. The astrological factors representing the spouse can very well announce a person of quality through the presence of benefics in this part of the horoscope. Nevertheless, the marital union could be a very unhappy one. This is clearly the case when the seventh house, corresponding to Libra, is afflicted. It is indeed what happens when the loved one is rapidly lost as a result of death by accident, or following a serious illness. This differentiation between the houses that represent the spouse and union will help us to avoid making any grave errors.

Princess Caroline of Monaco (January 23, 1957, Monaco, 9:27 a.m., rectified to 9:31:00 CET) illustrates our theory magnificently. Indeed, Jupiter in the sixth house very well represents the financier that her husband Philippe Junot was. In the seventh house, we find Uranus, which is opposite the Sun (ruler of the seventh house through sidereal Leo), while Pluto (ruler of the fourth house through Scorpio) squares the Moon Nodes; there you can quite clearly read divorce with a financier. If Jupiter were considered to be in the seventh house (which would indeed be the case if we were to count the houses in the same way as the signs) this would mean a legal union (Jupiter being the law) of a happy and durable nature. Which technician could contradict me? All the more reason to say this as Jupiter makes a superb trine with the Sun, the first factor concerned and which is

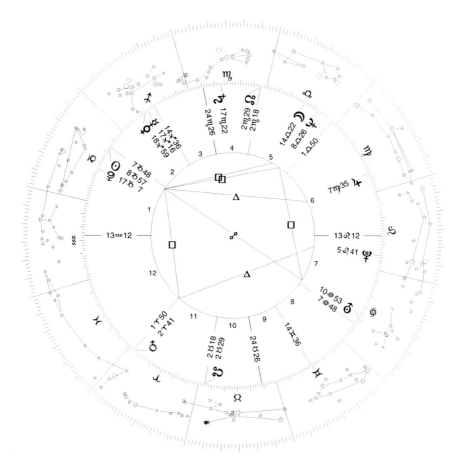

Princess Caroline of Monaco
Monte Carlo, Monaco (43°N42, 7°E24)
January 23, 1957
9:31:00 CET
Vernal Point 5Pisces51'34"

of paramount importance when consulting a feminine nativity, since the Sun is the general significator of the husband. Mercury, ruler of Gemini, and Venus, ruler of Libra, both signs in trine to the Ascendant, form a conjunction and therefore a Royal Yoga.

With **Anne-Aymone Giscard d'Estaing** (April 10, 1933, in Paris, at 5:30 p.m., rectified to 17:26:10 GMD/CET), the husband is represented by the rulers of the sixth house through Pisces—Neptune (modern ruler) and

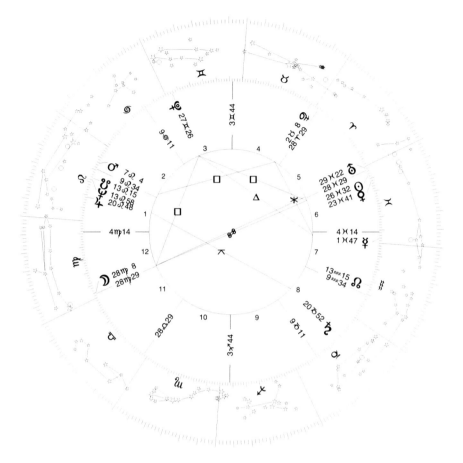

Anne-Aymone Giscard d'Estaing
Paris, France (48°N52, 2°E20)
April 10, 1933
17:26:10 GMD/CET
Vernal Point: 6° Pisces 17'30"

Jupiter (classical ruler). Both Jupiter and Neptune are placed in the royal
sign of Leo in the sidereal zodiac, while their dispositor, the Sun, the king
or the head of state, is in conjunction with Venus in the sixth house, that
of the marriage partner. Mercury in the seventh house makes a wide separating trine aspect with Pluto and a sextile to Chiron, neither of which
aspects seems to have adversely affected her marriage.

Charles Boyer
Figeac, France (44°N37, 2°E2)
August 28, 1899
17:14:54 S.T. Meridian 2E20, Dst=0
Vernal Point 6° Pisces 39'38"

The movie actor **Charles Boyer** was born August 28, 1899, in Figeac in the Lot region of France, at 5:15 p.m., rectified to 17:14:54 Meridian 2°E20. Sun and Venus are both found in sidereal Leo, that of the theater, which allowed this actor to realize such a brilliant career. This success was mainly due to his activities in Hollywood, so he has the second house, material gains, in Sagittarius, the sign of foreign lands, and Scorpio. The Moon, which is itself the ruler of the seventh house, that

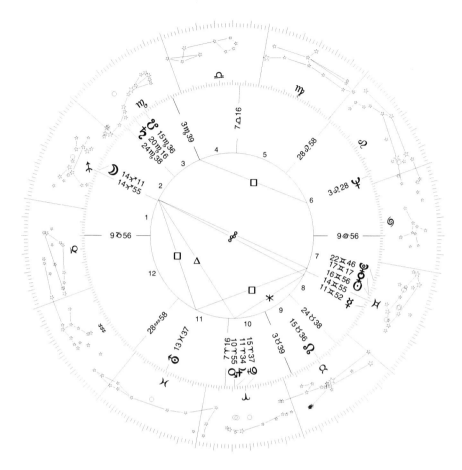

Jacques Chancel
Ayzac-Ost (Hautes-Pyrénées), France (43°N1'29," 0°W5'43")
July 2, 1928
20:57:51 CET
Vernal Point 6° Pisces 15'29"

of contracts, is found in the ninth house, lands abroad. The Sun, Venus
and Mercury are all found in the sixth house, that of work. However,
with Sun and Venus in the royal sign of Leo, sextile Jupiter in the fourth
house and square Uranus in the third house, the professional task could
not have been that of a supporting actor. He died in Phoenix, Arizona,
August 26, 1978.

Jacques Chancel, the well-known French journalist of *Radioscopie* (July 2, 1928, at 9:00 p.m., rectified to 20:57:51 CET, in Ayzac-Ost (Hautes-Pyrénées), France, was born a few hours before the full Moon. This case well illustrates my thesis. The Sun, giving light to the full moon, is in conjunction with Venus and Pluto in the seventh house, that of the interlocutor, rather over two thousand people in dialogue. We also consider them together with Mercury to be in sidereal Gemini, the sign of journalism; and in astrological tradition, the sign, which alone contains these three bodies, without a break, without any other planet in between them, automatically becomes part of the dominant theme. Let us add that the exact Mars–Jupiter conjunction, which is found in the tenth house, is in exact sextile with Mercury, journalism, and in trine with the Moon, which represents crowds and popularity. In other words, there is a "transmission of light" by the Moon onto the sextile, which links on the one side, Mars–Jupiter and on the other, Mercury–Sun–Venus. These configurations, including the Mars–Jupiter conjunction in the tenth house, are all the stronger owing to the fact that they are found in angular houses. There we find the phenomenon that clearly comes out in the statistics established by Michel Gauquelin and about which we have already spoken. The horoscope shows a person who interacts easily with the public and adapts himself to each person being interviewed without losing his own personality. Relationships with other people (seventh house) are easy, harmonious and pleasant. It promised social success, a rapid rise in the profession practiced, and prosperity through a foreground activity (Aries) in journalism (Gemini). Moreover, he had a Royal Yoga formed by the conjunction of Mercury, ruler of Virgo, and Venus, ruler of Taurus, signs in trine with the Capricorn Ascendant. He died December 12, 2003.

CORRESPONDENCE BETWEEN SIGNS AND HOUSES

Right throughout these pages in the footsteps of our predecessors, we have insisted upon the correspondence and the analogy between the twelve houses and the twelve signs. But the converse is true, and this is very easily verified when the two duodecimal divisions of the horoscope are

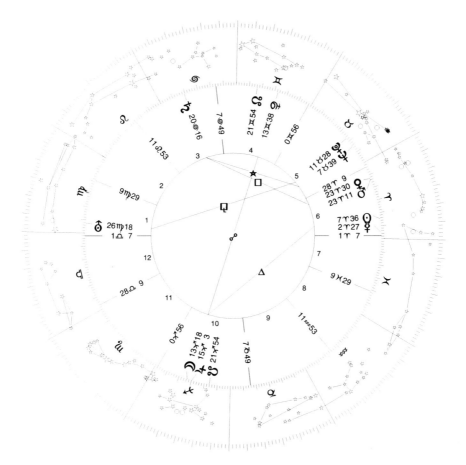

Adolf Hitler

Braunau, Austria (48°N16, 13°E03)

April 20, 1889

18:17:01 LT

Vernal Point: 6° Pisces 48'18"

considered in the opposite direction. Practice will show that this gives an
appreciably wider scope in the interpretation.

Maurice Prevat, in his article "The Origins of the Houses," [10] had
insisted on the connection between the different parts of the human body
and the twelve signs, which is very well known through the expression
"the zodiac man," but he applied it to the twelve houses.

---

10 In *Cahiers astrologiques*. March 1946.

In **Adolf Hitler**'s horoscope (April 20, 1889, in Braunau, Upper Austria, at a rectified time of 18:17:01 LT), we find Saturn strongly afflicted by a square to the conjunction of Venus and Mars, the god of War. Saturn is in the third house and in exile in sidereal Cancer. This configuration offers a certain analogy with an afflicted Gemini, the sign pertaining to mental capacities, especially when Mercury, second ruler of the Ascendant through Virgo, is found in conjunction with the Descendant or the Point of Death. In addition, we have a stellium of four planets: Mercury–Sun–Mars–Venus in the sixth house, which well explains the sick man described to us by certain historians. But as for what interests us at the present time, we point out that the sixth house sends us back to the sixth sign, Virgo, which traditionally exercises its influence over the army. Hitler showed himself to be an incompetent military leader, and the Mars–Saturn square, which precisely links the third and sixth houses explains that it was his very own generals who turned against him, notably on the occasion of an attempted assassination, which led to the repressions with which we are familiar.

THE TENTH HOUSE LEAVING FROM THE IMUM COELI

The tenth house leaves from the IC according to our direction of rotation, and offers analogies with the Earth sign, Capricorn. In any case, no matter what direction is followed, the IC, by its very position, symbolizes the birth place, real estate in general and the personal residence in particular. However, when the houses are seen to unfold in the way we advocate, the approximate 30° of this sector leave from the IC in order to travel toward the Ascendant. Since the quadrant that goes from the IC to the Ascendant represents the latter years of life, this tenth house, starting from the IC, thus constituting the first third of this quadrant, expresses to an even greater extent, the end of things in general and the end of life in particular. Capricorn signifies the Administration and all the elevated posts within it. It also symbolizes the elderly. This house, therefore, provides information about residences, real estate and the end of the career.

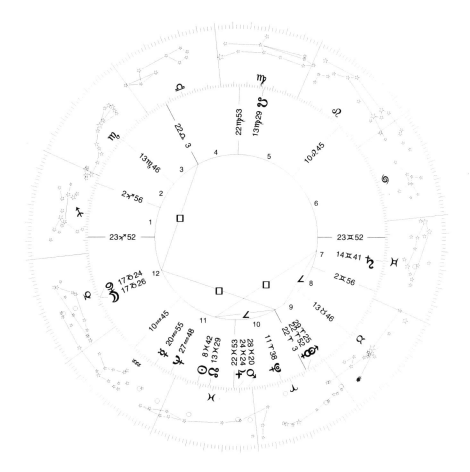

Paul Doumer
Aurillac, France (44°N56, 2°E26)
March 22, 1857
2:51:06 LT
Vernal Point: 7° Pisces 15'10"

Paul Doumer was born March 22, 1857, in Aurillac (Cantal), France, at
3:00 a.m., rectified to 2:51:06 LT. We have Jupiter, Mars and Pluto in the
tenth house. As governor-general of Indochina (1896), Paul Doumer was
a great builder, the domain of Capricorn, therefore the tenth house. He
was elected President of the Republic in 1931 but was assassinated the following year in Paris, May 7, 1932, at 4:37 a.m. The structure of this horoscope clearly indicates his significant rise up the social ladder, gradually

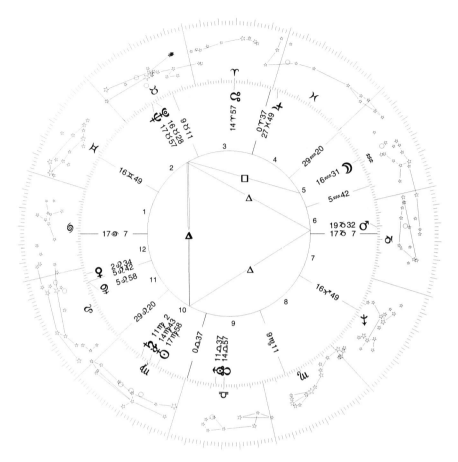

Engelbert Dollfuss
Texing, Austria (48°N2, 15°E19)
October 4, 1892
0:35:51 LT
Vernal Point: 6° Pisces 45'25"

reaching the highest point and the greatest of honors, as he grew older. We notice that the classical ruler of the twelfth house, secret enemies, is Saturn and that it is found in the seventh house in square with the Sun and Moon Nodes, and semi-square Uranus, the modern ruler of the twelfth house. In other words, secret adversaries were gradually coming into the light of day and becoming open enemies, the domain of the seventh house. The position of the North Node of the Moon, a few degrees from the Sun provides a warning for us (if it is noted that the Moon is found at about 50° from the Sun), that there will be an eclipse of the Sun in the days that follow birth; and quite so on March 25, 1857, the eclipse of the Sun took place, in square with Saturn.

Chancellor Engelbert Dollfuss was born in Texing, Austria, October 4, 1892, at 12:30 a.m., rectified to 0:35:51 Local Time. The triple conjunction of Saturn–Mercury–Sun situated after the IC, if the houses are counted in a clockwise direction, sustained by a powerful grand trine with Mars in the sixth house and Neptune/Pluto in the house of finances, reveals a great amount of activity and a high government post toward the end of life. But Mars is found very near the cusp of the Descendant, also called the Point of Death, and the Chancellor was assassinated July 25, 1934, in Vienna for not having shared Hitler's views on the *Anschluâ*—that is, the annexation of Austria by Germany.

King Carol II of Romania was born on October 16 (Julian Calendar)— that is, October 28 (Gregorian Calendar), 1893 in Bucharest, with an MC at 18° tropical Taurus and an Ascendant at 26° tropical Leo, according to Maurice Privat, in his *Astrologie scientifique à la portée de tous.* I have rectified his chart to 0:34:44 ST Meridian 26°E6. He saw his hopes dashed with a conjunction of the two malefics, Mars and Saturn, in the tenth house, which can be interpreted as attacks upon the Royal House (or houses). Note that this cruel conjunction falls on his son's Jupiter (c. 22° Virgo 50), King Michael of Romania, born December 25, 1921. Here we can see an astrological configuration that shows us, as the proverb says, that one person's meat is another's poison. Indeed, we know that Jupiter is the significator of honors, legality and authority; and we take note that in the same place in the Heavens there appears the origins (as seen from an astrological viewpoint), of the loss of a kingdom by one and the subsequent gain by another. We know that in 1940, King Carol was forced to abdicate in favor of his son, Michael. King Carol's Jupiter is the traditional ruler of Pisces, the sign that is on the cusp of the fifth house of children. Neptune, the modern ruler of Pisces is in conjunction with the Moon and Pluto and trines the Mars–Saturn conjunction. King Carol went into exile and died

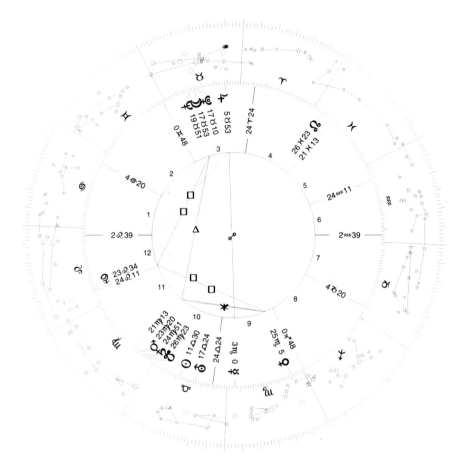

King Carol II of Romania
Bucharest, Romania (44°N26, 26°E6)
October 28, 1893
0:34:44 ST Meridian 26°E6
Vernal Point 6° Pisces 44'31"

in Estoril, Portugal, April 4, 1953, and his son, Michael, eventually had to yield to the Nazis and the Communists.

Carl Gustav Jung, Freud's most famous disciple, was born July 26, 1875, in Kesswil near Romanshorn, Switzerland, at 7:25 p.m., rectified to 19:21:38 LT. It was he who once wrote to the American Federation of Astrologers, to explain that when he was faced with a difficult case, he

Carl Gustav Jung
Kesswill, Switzerland (47°N36, 9°E19)
July 26, 1875
19:21:38 LT
Vernal Point: 6°Pisces 59'48"

had a horoscope made for the case in question, as very often this helped him to discover things, which he could not otherwise have understood. His heavenly chart is a splendid illustration of research into the subconscious and collective unconsciousness.

Starting from the IC, Pluto, the Moon and Neptune are all in the tenth house. Pluto, which is close to the IC squares Saturn in Aquarius in the twelfth house of secret and hidden enemies as well as the subconsious.

William Henry (Bill) Gates III
Seattle, Washington (47°N36'23," 122°W19'51"
October 28, 1955
21:09:06 PST
Vernal Point: 5° Pisces 52'36"

Aquarius is the sign of psychology. Saturn makes a harmonious trine to
Jupiter, ruler of the second house of finances and Mars is approximately
midway between them in the second house. This confirms that Jung could
earn a living through Saturn. Back to the tenth house, the second planet
in a clockwise direction from the IC is the Moon, the psyche, which
squares Uranus in the sixth house of employment and sextiles Mercury
and Venus in the seventh house of encounters with others, that is, clients

and consultants. Finally, Neptune, the third planet in a clockwise direction from the tenth house cusp, squares the Sun, also in the sixth house of employment. However, Jung was not an employee for long. Initially he was a disciple of Freud but broke away to found his own School of Psychology. Moreover, the Mercury–Venus conjunction in the seventh house form a Royal Yoga, due to their being rulers of signs trine the Ascendant. He died in Kusnacht, Switzerland, June 6, 1961.

Bill (William Henry) Gates was born in Seattle, Washington, October 28, 1955, at 9:15 p.m., rectified to 21:09:06 PST. He was born into a fairly wealthy family, which gave him the initial venture capital to make $20,000 by the age of fourteen. The tenth house represents one's destiny at birth and Jupiter and Pluto in the tenth house are in close alignment with the royal star Regulus. Everything that he has earned since then has been dependent on the silicon chip, which with a little imagination can also be assigned to the tenth house as silicon comes from the earth. Venus, the ruler of the second house, which is unoccupied, is in conjunction with Saturn in the eighth house, indicating the various legal problems he has faced owing to his supposed anti-competitive business tactics. However, Venus and Saturn form a Royal Yoga, as they are rulers of Libra and Aquarius, which are in trine with the Gemini Ascendant. Mercury is in the ninth house as well as Mars (the sub-ruler of the second house), which is in opposition with the Moon in the third house. The third and ninth houses govern communication, including the internet. The Sun, ruler of the eleventh house, being in conjunction with Neptune in the eighth house, indicates his charitable work.

A New Way of Looking at the Four Quadrants

Wain Farrants

I began with the hypothesis that the four quadrants correspond to the fourfold human being—the physical body, the etheric body, the astral body and the ego or conscious "I."

At night, when we are asleep, the connection between the ego and the astral body on the one hand and the physical and etheric bodies on the other hand is different from the connection that exists when we are awake. In the daytime, physical body, etheric body, astral body, and "I" may be said to be coupled together in the normal way. During sleep, the connection is loosened, with the astral body and the ego outside the sphere of the senses and of thinking—in other words, the whole sphere of the instruments of consciousness.[11]

It made sense to me that the upper hemisphere should represent the astral body and "I" and the lower hemisphere the physical body and etheric body. However, which two should be east (Ascendant side), and which two should be west (Descendant side)?

Robert Powell reminded me of Rudolf Steiner's comments on the Michelangelo's sculptures *Day, Night, Dawn,* and *Dusk* in the Medici Chapel in Florence.[12]

The figure "Night" can be made the object of a fine artistic study. The gesture, the position of the resting body with the head supported by the hand, the arm placed on the leg—in fact the whole arrangement of the figure can be studied artistically. We can sum it up by saying that if one wished to portray the human etheric body in its full activity, then one could only represent it in the form of this figure. That is the outer gesture expressing a human being at rest. When man sleeps, the etheric body is most active. In the figure of "Night," Michelangelo has created the corresponding position. This reclining figure represents the most expressive portrayal of the active etheric or life body. Now let us go over to "Day." This is no barren allegory. Picture the lower members of the human being more passive, and the "I" predominantly active. We have this expressed in the figure of "Day." If we were now to express in the posture the action of the astral body working freely when the other members are reduced to inactivity, then we should find this in the so-called allegory of "Dawn." And if we sought to express the conditions where the physical body is not altogether falling to

---

11 Steiner. *The Inner Nature of Man and Our Life Between Death and Rebirth,* p. 64.

12 Steiner. *Life between Death and Rebirth,* pp. 103–4.

pieces, but becomes limp as a result of the withdrawal of the ego and astral body, this is wonderfully portrayed in the figure of "Dusk." In these figures we have living portrayals of the four human "sheaths."

At dusk the sun is below the horizon at sunset—hence dusk (the physical body) corresponds to the quadrant commencing at the Descendant and ending at the Imum Coeli. Dawn is the first appearance of light in the sky before sunrise—hence dawn (the astral body) corresponds to the quadrant beginning at the Ascendant and ending at the Midheaven. For the purpose of the other two quadrants, therefore, night (etheric body) begins at the Imum Coeli and ends at the Ascendant and day (ego) begins at the Midheaven and ends at the Descendant.

Sensory Perceptions, Thinking, Feeling, and Willing

Rudolf Steiner states:

> If you take an abstract view of the inner life, you will find that it has three distinct aspects—thinking, feeling, and our will impulses. However, a fourth element has to be added, which consists of our inner reactions to sensory experiences. You see, we do not merely let colors and sounds, the experience of different temperatures, and so on dart past the conscious mind, but we lay hold of them and take note of them. We are able to remember them and keep them in mind, and we are thus able to know that a rose is red not just when we see it. We can carry the red color of the rose around with us and store it and other colors in memory. This serves to show that our inner reactions, the things we note and through which we relate to the outer world, are also part of the inner life. Anything we notice in the outside world is also part of the inner life because we make it so.
>
> Through the world of thought, we acquire knowledge of our immediate surroundings and, in science, knowledge of objects that are more remote. We use thought to make the outside world part of our inner world in a much broader sense than through sensory perception. We do not merely take note of things, but also think about them, and we are aware that this uncovers some of the secrets of the things we perceive.

Emotions and feelings are another part of our inner life. Our feelings are part of our inner life through which we are in touch with the outside world in a way that is in accord with human dignity....

The will is something that makes us of value to the world. It makes us part of the world, so that we do not merely live in our own perceptions and feelings, but are also able to leave our mark on the world. All the will impulses of which human beings are capable represent our true value to the world when they progress from will intent to action. In the realm of the will, therefore, the human being is part of the world, and it is our inner life that streams into the world and becomes part of it.[13]

Concerning thinking, Steiner says,

Thinking is an activity of the etheric body.... You are thinking all night long while lying in bed; since your "I" is away, however,

13 Steiner. *The Inner Nature of Man*, pp. 59–60 (trans. revised).

you do not know that you think.... Generally, our thoughts are much keener when our "I" is away at night.... If the etheric body, which is in harmony with the laws of the universe, thinks by itself and one does not ruin these thoughts, then human thinking, no longer muddled up by the "I" (as happens so often in the daytime) becomes much sounder.[14]

It does not take much effort now to connect sensory perceptions to the physical body, thinking to the etheric body, feeling to the astral body and willing to the "I."

And we can go one step further and connect the element of earth to the physical body, water to the etheric body, air and light to the astral body and warmth and fire to the "I."

In addition, according to Rudolf Steiner, we can connect justice to the physical body, truth and temperance to the etheric body, beauty to the astral body, and morality to the "I."[15]

PHYSICAL/SENSORY PERCEPTIONS/EARTH QUADRANT

Hector Berlioz was born at La Côte-St-André in southeastern France, December 11, 1803, at 5:00 p.m. LT, rectified to 17:01:45. He was "an untalented genius"[16] because he did not show any particular talent for music as a child. He found it difficult to learn to play a musical instrument though he had the talent to attempt to play different ones, attributable to his Gemini Ascendant. But he understood how they all played together and taught himself composition and ultimately created the modern orchestra. Mercury, ruler of the Ascendant, is in conjunction with Mars and the Sun, sextile the North Node and quintile Saturn. The seventh house is highlighted by five planets being there, all working together in the grand partnership of a symphony orchestra. He revolutionized music and many compositions, such as the "Symphonie Fantastique," expressed his passions and life story. Such compositions are

---

14   Steiner. *Man's Being, His Destiny, and World-Evolution*, pp. 67–68 (trans. revised).

15   Steiner. *The Riddle of Humanity*.

16   Schonberg. *The Lives of the Great Composers*, pp. 122–137.

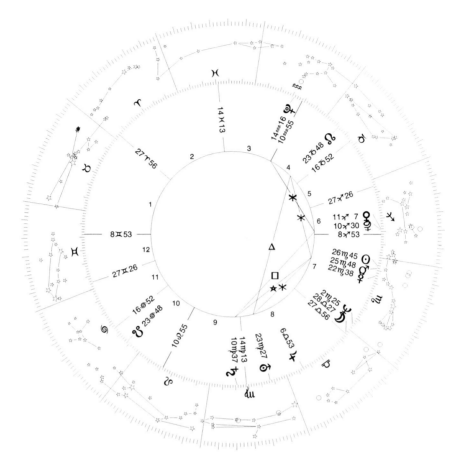

Hector Berlioz
La Côte-St André, France (45°N23, 5°E15)
December 11, 1803
17:01:45 LT
Vernal Poinr 7° Pisces 59'45"

outstanding examples of "our inner reactions to sensory experiences,"[17] highlighted by his stellium of planets in the third quadrant. Venus, ruler of Libra, and Saturn, ruler of Aquarius, form a Royal Yoga by square.

Thomas Carlyle was born in Ecclefechan, Scotland, December 4, 1795, at 5:00 p.m., rectified to 16:49:48 LT. He has seven planets plus Chiron

---

17 Wikipedia.

Thomas Carlyle
Ecclefechan, Scotland (55°N4, 3°W15)
December 4, 1795
16:49:48 LT
Vernal Point 8° Pisces 6'28"

between Descendant and Imum Coeli. He was an essayist, satirist and historian. His three volume set on the French Revolution was filled with a passionate intensity, hitherto unknown in historical writing. Pluto in the third house of writing squared Mercury in the seventh house. He translated many works of Goethe and other German writers. His faith was not from the Church but in Mankind (Uranus and Chiron in the ninth house). But he always retained Calvinist values (Saturn rising opposed

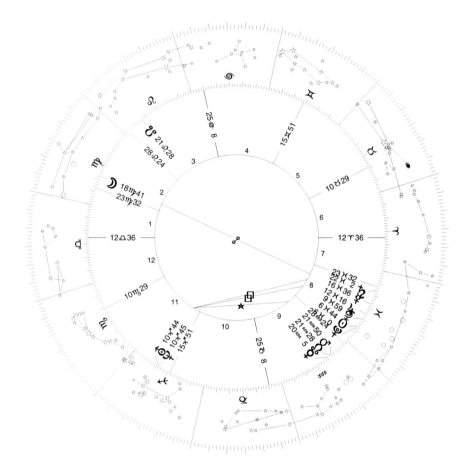

Sir Richard Francis Burton
Hertford, England (51°N48, 0°W5)
March 19, 1821
21:30:56 LT
Vernal Point: 7° Pisces 45'18"

to the Sun). Uranus in the ninth house of philosophy formed a T-square with this Sun–Saturn opposition. He had a distinct distaste for democracy and a belief in charismatic leadership. Only dynamic individuals can master events and direct their spiritual energies effectively. Although he was an intellectual there was a strong emphasis on down-to-earth events by human beings of flesh and bones (the earthly, physical quadrant). His book *Sartor Resartus* is a novel about himself, the clothes we wear and

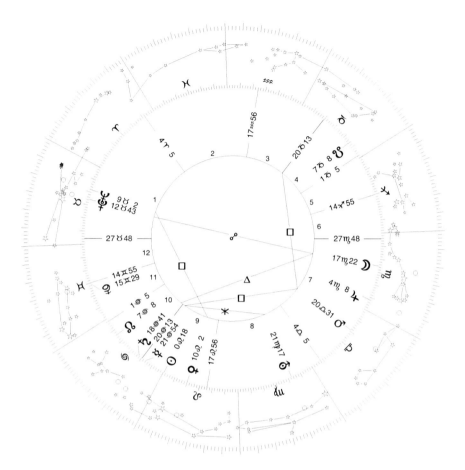

Thomas Edward Lawrence (of Arabia)
Tremadog, Wales (52°N50, 4°W15)
August 15, 1888
23:41:15 GMT
Vernal Point: 6° Pisces 48'52"

what we believe in. He stressed the immediacy of the action of historical events. As soon as ideological formulas replace heroic human action,
society becomes dehumanized. The flaws of heroes should be openly dis-
cussed, without dehumanizing their achievements.

Sir Richard Francis Burton was born March 19, 1821, in Hertford, UK, at
9:30 p.m., rectified to 21:30:56 LT. Seven planets and Chiron are in the third
quadrant (sense perceptions), most appropriate to an explorer. His astonishing

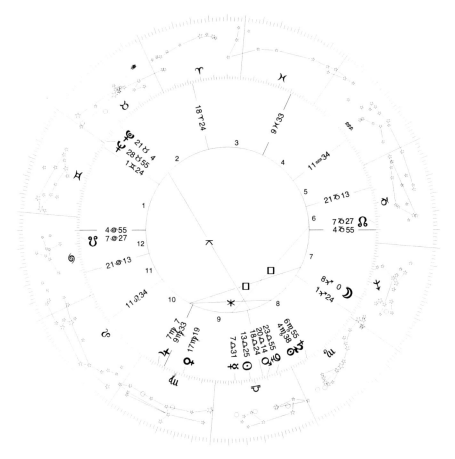

Joseph Göbbels
Reydt, Germany (51°N10, 6°E27)
October 29, 1897
22:10:53 CET
Vernal Point: 6° Pisces 41'10"

aptitude for acquiring languages can be attributed to the conjunction of Venus, the Moon Node and Mars in the ninth house of long distance journeys and foreign lands. Venus and Mars ruling the sixth and seventh houses, assured him of marriage, after leading a rowdy life. In addition he played simultaneous games of chess and won.[18] Mercury, ruler of Gemini, and Saturn, ruler of Aquarius are also in conjunction, thereby forming a Royal Yoga.

---

18 Wikipedia.

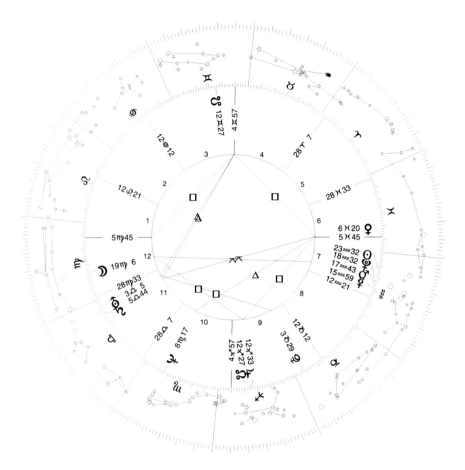

Elizabeth Barrett Browning
Durham, England (54°N45, 1°W40)
March 6, 1806
18:51:36 LT
Vernal Point 7° Pisces 57'53"

Thomas Edward Lawrence of Arabia was born in Tremadog, Wales, August 15, 1888, at 11:20 p.m., rectified to 23:41:15 GMT. In his earliest years he showed the greatest interest in archaeological matters ... but his greatest interest of all was in the study of medieval castles and fortifications. Later when he visited the Holy Land, he came to know Syria, much of north Mesopotamia, Asia Minor, Egypt and Greece like a book. During World War I the British forces under Allenby and the Arabs under Lawrence worked together to capture Jerusalem and Damascus, and later he created Arabia.[19] Seven planets fall into the third quadrant, which no doubt granted him the ability to take in and remember geographical details. Saturn conjunction Mercury across the IC forms a Royal Yoga.

In the case of **Joseph Göbbels** (October 29, 1897, in Reydt, Germany, at 10:30 p.m., rectified to 22:10:53 CET), seven planets and Chiron are found in the third quadrant. There is a strong emphasis on death in his chart with the Uranus–Saturn conjunction in Scorpio as well as Mars and Chiron in Libra all in the eighth house. He committed suicide prior to his arrest. Moreover, he dragged his spouse (Saturn rules sixth and seventh houses of spouse and partnership) and children (Uranus and Saturn rule the fifth house) into dying with him, as well. With Neptune and Pluto in the first quadrant and none in the second quadrant, one cannot help thinking that this man was devoid of feelings and goodwill.

Elizabeth Barrett Browning, one of the great English poets, was born in Durham, England, March 6, 1806, at 7 p.m., rectified to 18:51:36 LT. All of her planets except for Venus are below the horizon—five planets and Chiron in the third quadrant and four in the fourth quadrant. Elizabeth had fragile health as a child and rarely left her bedroom. She met Robert Browning in 1845. Her father, represented by the ruler of the ninth house, Saturn (which was in conjunction with Uranus and square Chiron), objected to the marriage of any of his many children. So Elizabeth and Robert eloped (four planets in seventh house of marriage) and moved to Italy, where her health improved (Jupiter and Chiron in the ninth house squared and sextiled Venus in the sixth house) and she even gave birth to a son at the age of forty-three (Mars, ruler of fifth house in conjunction with Mercury and Pluto). She had the gift of raising her perceptions into great poetry.[20]

---

19 Kolisko. *Reincarnation and Other Essays.*

20 Wikipedia.

Maître Philippe, de Lyon
Loiseux, Savoie, France (45°N33, 6°E20)
April 25, 1849
3:00:21 LT
Vernal Point: 7°Pisces 21'47"

ETHERIC/THINKING/WATER QUADRANT

In the case of **Maître Philippe de Lyon** (April 25, 1849, in Loisieux, Savoie, at 3:00 a.m., rectified to 3:00:21 LT), the most important and richest quadrant is undoubtedly the fourth since it contains all the planets except Jupiter and Neptune. It is obviously the most obscure and mysterious of the quadrants. When this one is strongly dominant, one is often deeply attracted to occultism and the invisible world. The etheric (or life) body is also prominent in this quadrant. Maître Philippe was a healer (Venus ruler of the sixth house of health conjoined the Moon and opposed Chiron, the wounded healer), a magnetist, a thaumaturgist (miracle worker), and the leader of a spiritual movement, which related itself successively to the Martinists (Papus) and Paul Sedir's group *Les amitiés spirituelles* (The Spiritual Friends). We see in his horoscope that Neptune is in conjunction with the Ascendant. The preponderance of the eleventh and twelfth houses for example, the Sun conjunction Pluto in the eleventh house and Pluto conjunction Mercury across the cusp of the eleventh and twelfth houses, explains the fervor and number of his disciples, as well as his profound knowledge of the world of esotericism and the subsequent demonstrations he made with these particular skills.

René Descartes was born in Le Haye, France, March 31, 1596, at 2 a.m., rectified to 1:55:19 LT. He was a student of geometry, science and philosophy. He believed in God but thought of man as a machine. During the twenty-two years that he lived in the Netherlands to escape from the religious intolerance in France, he lived a secluded life in eighteen different places. This is shown by seven planets in the tenth house. One would have thought that the founder of modern philosophy would have been born about two hours earlier so as to have such a stellium of planets in the ninth house rather than the tenth. However, "The fifteenth and sixteenth centuries introduces a new impulse...slowly prepared and slowly absorbed in the life of the soul. A transformation takes place in the organization of the human soul. In the field of philosophical life, this transformation becomes manifest through the fact that thought cannot now be felt as a perception, but as a *product of self-consciousness*."[21] Singleton Mars in the third quadrant represents the old way of sense perceptions and the stellium in the fourth quadrant represents the transformed type of thinking.

Descartes was the first to describe the idea of a unitary universal science that would link all possible human knowledge together into an

---

21 Steiner. *The Riddles of Philosophy.*

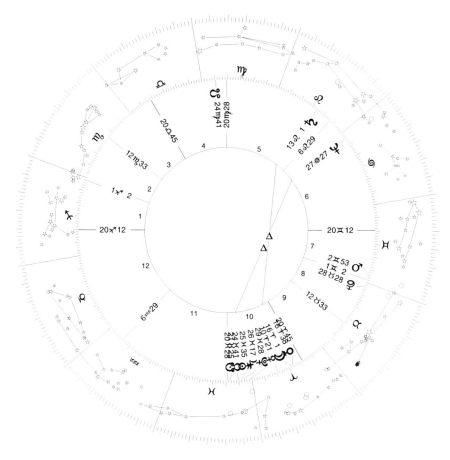

René Descartes
Le Haye, France (46°N59, 0°E42)
March 31, 1596
1:55:19 LT
Vernal Point: 10° Pisces 53'29"

all-embracing wisdom.[22] The resulting unity is reflected in his chart by the multiple conjunction of Sun–Uranus–Jupiter–Pluto and Moon–Venus. The idea first came to him in March 1619. In fact, transiting Pluto opposed his Midheaven March 24 (in the sidereal zodiac). On November 10, 1619, he had a dream that revealed the nature of his science more clearly. Transiting Neptune then opposed his natal Sun and transiting Mercury opposed his

---

22 Wikipedia.

Emmanuel Swedenborg
Uppsala, Sweden (59N53, 17E35)
January 29, 1688
6:12:48 LT
Vernal Point: 9° Pisces 36'40"

natal Mercury. He died in Stockholm, February 11, 1650, at about 4:00 in the morning.

Emmanuel Swedenborg was born in Uppsala, Sweden, January 29, 1688, at 6:15 a.m., rectified to 6:12:48 LT and died in London, March 29, 1772, at 2 a.m. Local Time. He had eight planets and Chiron in the fourth quadrant. His original vocation was inventor and scientist. The Moon

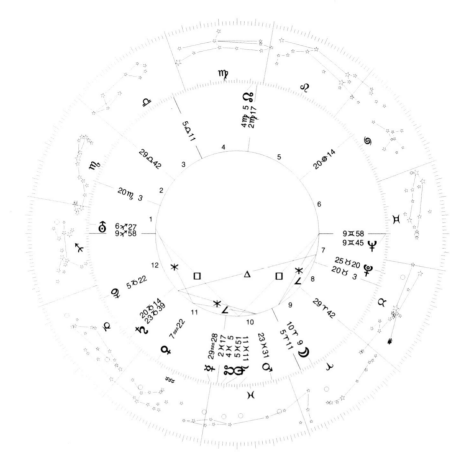

B. F. Skinner

Susquehanna, Pennsylvania (41°N57, 75°W37)

March 20, 1904

1:59:11 EST

Vernal Point: 6° Pisces 35'49"

and Uranus in the tenth house reflect his job on the mining board. Five planets in the twelfth house testify to his secrecy and anonymity about his spiritual leanings in the early days of his awakening. He never did any proselytizing. His ideas spread through his writings and by word of mouth. His greatest desire was to understand the order and purpose of creation and to investigate the structure of matter and the process of

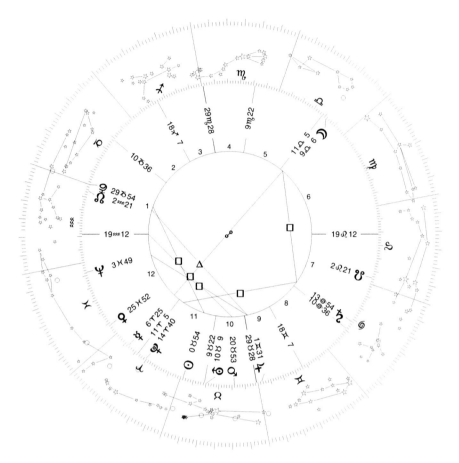

Pierre Curie
Paris, France (48°N52, 2°E20)
May 15, 1859
1:57:09 LT
Vernal Point: 7Pisces13'22"

creation itself.[23] In the Book of Genesis, the earth was without form and void; and darkness was on the face of the deep (third quadrant), but the first real stage of creation was when the Spirit of God moved upon the face of the water (fourth quadrant).

B. F. (Burrhus Frederic) Skinner was born in Susquehanna, Pennsylvania, March 20, 1904, at 2:00 a.m., rectified to 1:59:11 EST. With the

23 Williams-Hogan (Internet).

exception of Uranus just above the eastern horizon, all of the planets are below the horizon—the Moon, Pluto and Neptune in the third quadrant and Mars, Jupiter, the Sun, Venus and Saturn (as well as Chiron) in the fourth quadrant. His Psychological School of Radical Behaviorism taught behavior to be a function of environmental histories of reinforcing consequences. This fits the inner life of the third quadrant, "reacting to sense experiences." The etheric body, connected to the fourth quadrant, is also known as the habit body. Once a pleasure (astral body) becomes a habit (etheric body) it is more difficult to change. Skinner demonstrated this with animals and applied his idea to human beings—teaching children and proposing a utopian society (*Walden Two*). He died August 18, 1990, in Cambridge, Massachusetts.

Pierre Curie was born in Paris, May 15, 1859, at 2:00 a.m., rectified to 1:57:09 LT. He has seven planets in the fourth quadrant. Pierre and his older brother Jacques demonstrated that an electrical potential was generated when crystals were compressed and that crystals could be made to deform when subject to an electric field.[24] Today, most digital electronic circuits rely on this phenomenon in the form of crystal oscillators. He also studied different forms of magnetism. Pierre and his wife Marie, were pioneers in the study of radioactivity, the fallen life ether.[25] All three of the planets after which radioactive elements have been named, Uranus–Uranium, Neptune–Neptunian and Pluto–Plutonium, are in the fourth quadrant. All radioactive elements decay down to lead: thus, Saturn, which appropriately is in the third physical quadrant. He died in a carriage accident in Paris, April 19, 1906, at about 3 p.m., thereby escaping probable death by radiation exposure that later killed his wife.

Samuel Hahnemann was born in Meizen, Germany, April 10, 1755, at 11:55 p.m., rectified to 23:45:26 LT and died in Paris, July 2, 1843. There are seven planets (plus Chiron) in the tenth, eleventh, and twelfth houses. This quadrant relates to thinking, the etheric body, air and light. In addition he has seven planets in three sidereal signs, which bear a relationship

---

24 Wikipedia.

25 Steiner. *The Etherization of the Blood.*

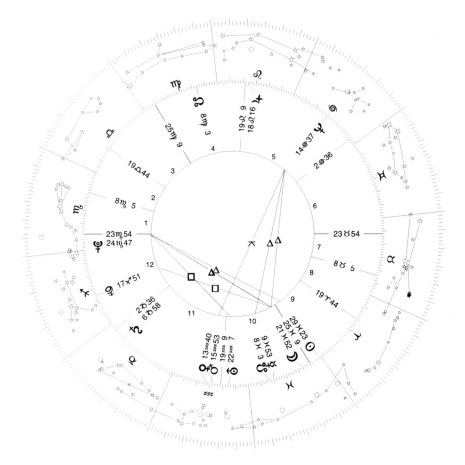

Friedrich Samuel Hahnemann
Meizen, Germany (51°N10, 13°E27)
April 10, 1755
23:45:26 LT
Vernal Point: 8° Pisces 40'29"

to water, namely Capricorn (goat with a fishtail), Aquarius (man bearing water) and Pisces (fishes). His Sun in the third quadrant (physical substance) is dissolved in the water of the fourth quadrant and like cures like. Between his given birth time and rectified birth time, Pluto shifts from the first house into the twelfth house, the realm of the laboratory worker and the individual who will uncover and overcome his secret (and not-so-secret) enemies. For he has been described as "the scholar whom

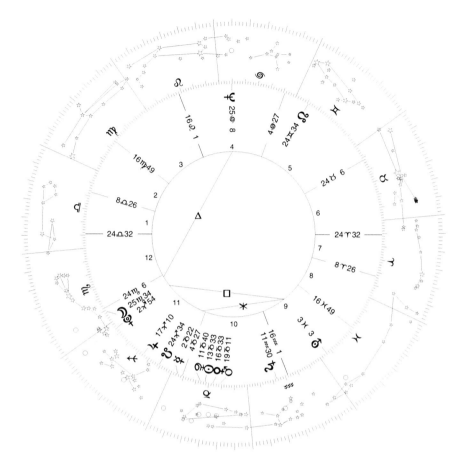

Robert Burns
Alloway, Scotland (55°N25, 4°W40)
January 25, 1759
2:20:00 LT
Vernal Point: 8° Pisces 37'18"

scholars honored and respected, the physician whom physicians feared, the philologist with whom philologists dreaded to dispute, the chemist who taught chemists, and the philosopher, whom adversity nor honor had power to change."[26]

Robert Burns was born in Alloway, Ayrshire, Scotland, January 25, 1759, at 2:30 a.m., rectified to 2:20:00 LT. He was a pioneer of the

26 Bradford. *The Life and Letters of Samuel Hahnemann.*

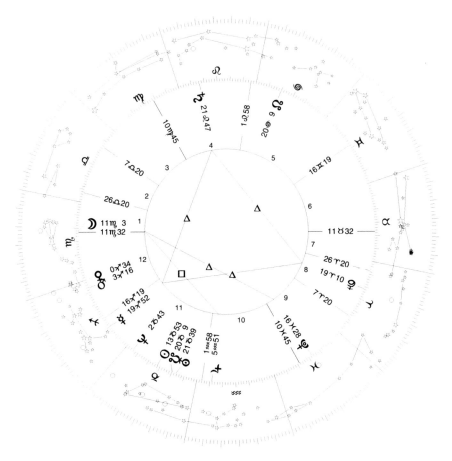

Lewis Carroll (Charles Dodgson)
Daresbury, England (53°N21, 2°W38)
27 January 1832
3:49:46 LT
Vernal Point 7° Pisces 36'13"

Romantic Movement, collecting folk songs from across Scotland and composing many famous poems. Known as "the peasant's poet," his forms were not elaborate and he wrote in the vernacular. There are eight planets (plus Chiron) in the fourth quadrant, divided between the tenth house (his Scottish heritage) and the eleventh house (intimate friendships). He had many friendships and affairs, both casual and serious. The two planets, which are not in the fourth quadrant, are in appropriate houses—Uranus in the ninth grants sensitivity, receptivity and intuitive faculties and Neptune in the fourth gives exceptional inspiration but a tendency toward scandalous behavior.[27] He died July 21, 1796, in Dumfries.

Charles Dodgson, better known by his pen name **Lewis Carroll**, was born in Daresbury, England, January 27, 1832, at 4:00 a.m., rectified to 3:49:46 LT. Besides the presence of seven planets in the fourth quadrant, the Moon is slightly (29') above the Ascendant. He was a mathematician so I would think his imagination came more from the realm of the fourth quadrant of thinking rather than out of feeling or willing. The emphasis of the eleventh house of associations and friendships—including those of a secret or intimate nature—together with the Venus–Mars conjunction on the Galactic Center in the twelfth house of secrecy reflects the mystery of Alice in Wonderland. Is it merely a coincidence that Alice shared the name of one of the daughters of a close friend? Although his Saturn is in fall in the fourth house, he did not suffer any fall from grace during his life, perhaps because Saturn is supported by a trine from Mercury in the eleventh and a trine to Chiron in the eighth house. And what about the hallucinatory experiences in the story? Authorities doubt that Dodgson himself indulged in any illicit substances other than the tincture of opium in laudanum, one of the common painkillers of the time. The size changes Alice experiences manifest in connection with various conditions such as epilepsy and migraines.[28] He died in Guildford, England, January 14, 1898. When I finished writing the first draft of this thumbnail biography, I opened the Saturday Guardian magazine and there was an article about a man who suffers from Alice in Wonderland syndrome. (Editor)

Jan Vermeer was baptized October 31, 1632, in Delft, Holland, and according to one authority was born at 3:00 a.m. on the same day. When I rectified his time of birth to 2:57:13 LT by the hermetic rule and a consideration of his biography, it appeared that he was born premature, which no doubt

27 Wikipedia.

28 Wikipedia.

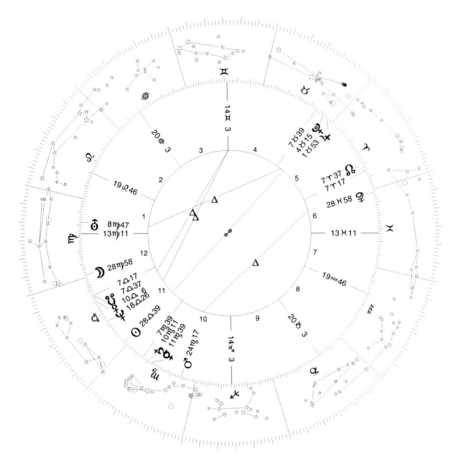

Jan Vermeer
Delft, Holland (52°N0, 4°E21)
October 31, 1632
2:57:13 LT
Vernal Point: 10° Pisces 22'52"

led his Catholic family to baptize him as soon as possible. This places eight planets in the fourth quadrant, the etheric quarter. Like his father, Jan was active in the art trade. Inasmuch as this quadrant begins with the tenth house, which represents the house and home, it is not surprising that his paintings portray figures in interiors engaged in everyday activities like pouring out milk or fastening a collar about her neck. In addition, Venus conjunction Saturn in the tenth house forms a Royal Yoga because Venus rules Taurus and Saturn rules Capricorn, the two earth signs in trine with the Virgo Ascendant. One critic ascribes to him "a keen sensitivity to effects of light and color and an interest in defining precise spatial relationships."[29] He died December 15, 1675, at his birthplace.

Pierre-Auguste Renoir was born in Limoges, France, February 25, 1841, at 6:00 a.m., rectified to 5:51:49 LT. He has seven planets in the fourth quadrant (etheric body, water element). His joyful paintings of social occasions (eleventh house), sensual nature and nude women do not necessarily reflect his character. He was often anxious and unsettled, frequently besieged by self-doubt over his direction as a painter, and at times insecure about his working class origins. He felt that painting should be an escape from the dark and depressing aspects to life. Four planets were in the twelfth house: Neptune unafflicted; the Sun trine Mars; Uranus and Mercury square Jupiter. Renoir and Monet, working together beside the River Seine studying the transient effects of light, atmosphere and weather conditions on the surface of the water, produced the first revolutionary Impressionist works.[30]

George W. Bush was born at New Haven, Connecticut, July 6, 1946, at 7:30 a.m., rectified to 7:28:21 EDT. He has seven planets and Chiron in the fourth quadrant (etheric body=thinking) and three planets in the first quadrant (astral body=feeling). When all the planets are within the span of a trine (120°), Marc Edmund Jones calls this pattern a "bundle." He is the "creator or proponent of an exclusive and well-integrated world within which his own immediate competence or superiority may have a constant manifestation of its powers. When such an exceptionally personal world is created by a person of real stature, it may have an enduring impact on the whole course of history."[31]

The Sun and Saturn rising in the first house helped him to attain power and Uranus in the second house trine Moon and Jupiter in the tenth house gave him family wealth. Mars in the eleventh tends to go headlong into

---

29 Wikipedia.

30 Renoir, *Renoir by Renoir.*

31 Jones. *Essentials of Astrological Analysis.*

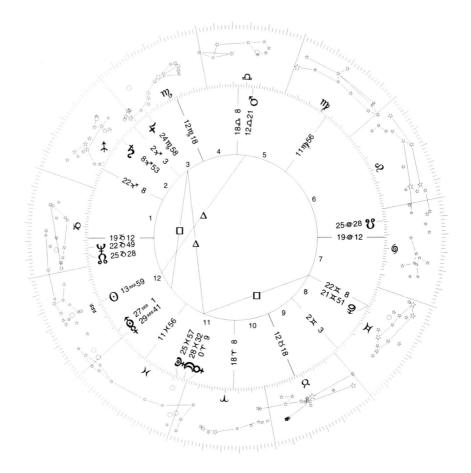

Pierre-Auguste Renoir
Limoges, France (45°N50, 1°E15)
February 25, 1841
5:51:49 LT
Vernal Point: 7° Pisces 28'37"

projects without reflecting upon the possible consequences. In addition Mars rules the Midheaven and the entire ego quadrant. Mercury in the twelfth often cannot express oneself properly. Venus in the twelfth is compassionate toward the sick and looks for peace and tranquility. Pluto in the twelfth house will uncover his secret enemies, dominate them and triumph over them, thus eliminating them as if by a miracle.

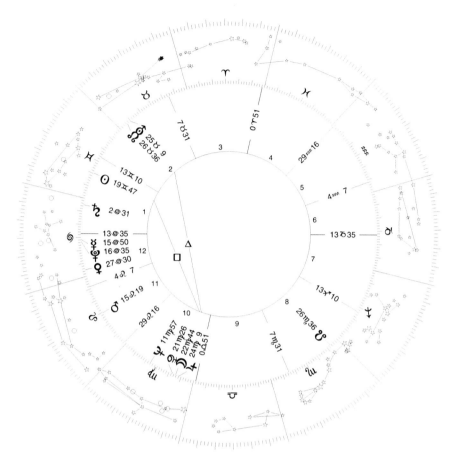

George W. Bush
New Haven, Connecticut (41°N18, 72°W55)
July 6, 1946
7:28:21 EDT
Vernal Point 6° Pisces 0'24"

At this moment in time we do not know the whole story behind 9/11, the collapse of the twin towers of the World Trade Center on September 11, 2001. There are many conspiracy theories floating about. Bush has been criticized for failing to react to the message about the attack while he was reading a storybook in a classroom in Florida. Moreover, he retired to his ranch in Texas. Perhaps he withdrew from his advisors and from the media to seek inspiration from the forces of Nature, which are far more

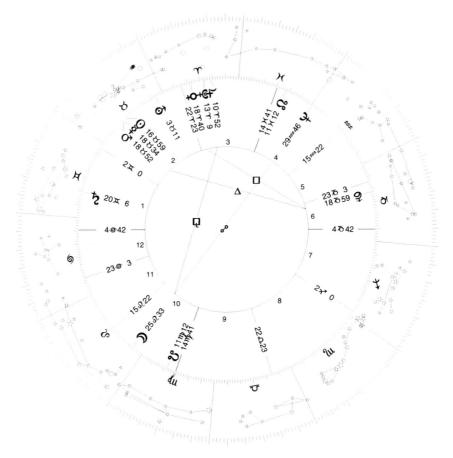

Pope Pius XI
Desio, Italy (45°N37, 9°E13)
May 31, 1857
7:52:22 LT
Vernal Point: 7° Pisces 15'0

powerful and regenerating—that is, from the life-filling etheric world (fourth quadrant).

This is reflected in Bush's horoscope by Neptune, Chiron, the Moon and Jupiter in the tenth house, the home. For those who have studied Robert Powell's *Chronicle of the Living Christ*, [32] the IC, which commences the tenth house, is in precise conjunction with the Sun at the Baptism of

---

32 Anthroposophic Press. 1996.

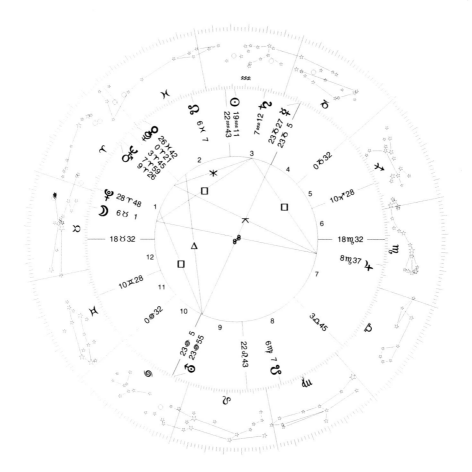

Pope Pius XII
Rome, Italy (41°N53, 12E29)
March 2, 1876
10:32:08 LT
Vernal Point: 6° Pisces 59'18"

Christ. He may have become a born-again Christian but his deeds certainly cannot be considered to be Christian.

ASTRAL/FEELING/AIR AND LIGHT QUADRANT

Pope Pius XI (May 31, 1857, in Desio near Milan, at 8 a.m., rectified to 7:52:22 LT) offers us an example in which the first quadrant (Ascendant to the Midheaven) contains eight planets. It is worth noting that this very same dominant Quadrant is present in the case of **Pope Pius XII** (born March 2, 1876, in Palestrina near Rome, at 10:27 a.m., rectified to 10:32:08). This corresponds very well with recognized authority, pomp and ceremony, huge gatherings (even if *conclave* means "locked up"), public acts and meetings with heads of state. Bearing this in mind, let us remember that Pius XI and Mussolini met and came to an agreement over the constitution and recognition of the Vatican State, while Pius XII openly condemned Freudian thinking, existentialism and Marxism. Pope Pius XI died February 10, 1939, in Rome, and Pope Pius XII died October 9, 1958, in Rome.

Nikolai Rimsky-Korsakov was born in the Novgorod district in 1844, on March 6 (Julian) or March 18 (Gregorian), at 10:30 a.m., rectified to 10:34:01 LT. He died June 21, 1908. He has eight planets within a sextile of Mercury and Mars in the first quadrant, which is related to the astral body, air and light. The other two planets are in the second quadrant so they are all above the horizon within a span of 96°. Rachmaninoff described Rimski-Korsakov's scores that "There is never the slightest doubt about the 'meteorological picture' the music is meant to convey. When there is a snowstorm the flakes seem to dance and drift from the woodwinds and the sound holes of the violins; when the sun is high, all instruments shine with an almost fiery glare; when there is water, the waves ripple and dance audibly through the orchestra. The sound is cool and glassy when he describes a calm winter night with a glittering starlit sky."[33] He has a Royal Yoga of Venus square Saturn. He died in Luga, Russia, June 8, 1908 (Julian calendar).

Béla Bartók was born in Nagyszentmiklós, Hungary, March 25, 1881, at 9:20 a.m., rectified to 9:19:24 LT. All the planets except for the Moon and Uranus are in the first quadrant (childhood, feelings). He could play forty songs on the piano by the age of four. The family moved frequently in his childhood and later he traveled around Europe, including Turkey, in search of traditional folk music. He thus brought to light

33 Schonberg. *The Lives of the Great Composers*, pp. 306–35.

Nikolai Rimsky-Korsakov
Novgorod, Russia (59°N30, 33°E29)
March 6, 1844 (Julian Calendar)
10:34:01 LT
Vernal Point: 7°Pisces 26'3"

original Hungarian folk music. He went his own way regardless of circumstances and he would not swerve from his ideal of truth, whether he
was resisting the Nazis or refusing offers to teach in any university in his
adopted country, the United States. Uranus in the ninth house of long
distance travel opposed Mercury in the third house of short journeys
and trined Venus and Neptune in the second house, which explains
his extensive travels and income from work in foreign countries. He

Béla Bartók
Nagyszentmiklós, Hungary (47°N58, 22°E52)
March 25, 1881
9:19:24 LT
Vernal Point 6° Pisces 55'4"

retained his childhood forces (the first quadrant) and some modern psychologists have diagnosed him with Asperger's Syndrome. Neptune, Chiron, Venus and Pluto in the first house breaks away from tradition, in the case of Bartók, with unusually toned music.[34] He died of leukemia September 26, 1945, in New York City.

---

34 Ibid., pp. 506–15.

Vincent van Gogh
Zundert, Netherlands (51°N28, 4°E40)
March 30, 1853
10:51:25 LT
Vernal Point: 7° Pisces 18'29"

Vincent van Gogh was born at Zundert, The Netherlands, March 30, 1853, at 11:00 a.m., rectified to 10:51:25 LT. He had seven planets in the first quadrant of air and light. Before he became a painter he was a passionate preacher. His artistic technique also grew more and more impassioned in brushstroke, in symbolic and intense color, in surface tension and in the movement and vibration of form and hue. Fusion of form and content is powerful, dramatic, lyrically rhythmic, imaginative and

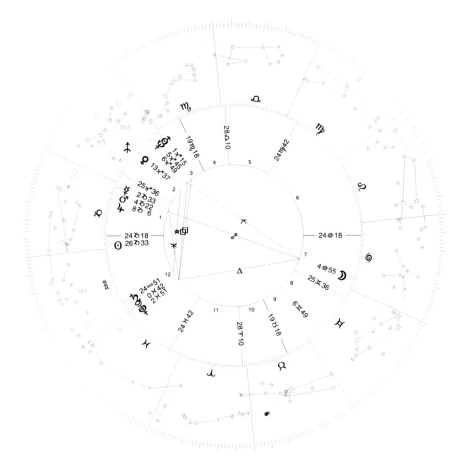

John Ruskin
London (51°N30, 0°W10)
February 8, 1919
7:30:00 LT
Vernal Point: 7° Pisces 47'04"

emotional.[35] There have been many theories put forward concerning his health problems (temporal lobe epilepsy, thujone poisoning, lead poisoning) and madness (bipolar disorder). His Sun at the midpoint of Uranus and Neptune, indicates, according to Reinhold Ebertin, "lack of vitality, a sensitive physique, impressionability, unconsciousness, illness,

---

35   Online at www.vangoghgallery.com.

Franz Kafka
Prague, Bohemia (50°N05, 14°E26)
July 3, 1883
6:53:25 LT
Vernal Point: 6° Pisces 53'10"

lifelessness, impassiveness and epilepsy."[36] He took his own life July 29, 1890, at about 1:30 in the morning.

John Ruskin was born in London, February 8, 1819, at 7:30 a.m., rectified to 7:29:35 LT. He had six planets in the first quadrant. He was an art critic, social critic, poet and artist. His essays on art and architecture

---

36 Ebertin. *The Combination of Stellar Influences.*

Antoine de Saint-Exupéry
Lyons, France (45N45, 4E50)
June 29, 1900
9:00:41 Meridian 2E30
Vernal Point: 6Pisces38'56"

were extremely influential. He started the Arts and Crafts Movement and founded Utopian colonies. Marcel Proust was a Ruskin enthusiast; Gandhi was influenced by him and Leo Tolstoy recognized that Ruskin thought with his heart (feeling quadrant). Uranus and Neptune in the third house square Pluto and Chiron in the twelfth house, and the ruler Jupiter in the first house, confirm his extensive literary abilities. Venus in the second house quintile Saturn, the ruler of his Ascendant, improves his chances of earning an income through art. In addition, Venus rules the tenth house of buildings, construction and architecture. He died January 20, 1900, in Coniston in the Lake District.[37]

Franz Kafka was born in Prague (then in Bohemia) July 3, 1883, at 7 a.m., rectified to 6:53:25 LT. All of his planets except for Uranus are in the first quadrant. Neptune, Mars, Pluto, and Saturn in the third house fit the hatred he had of a rigid, unimaginative early education, which often turned him into a nervous wreck. He eventually became a Doctor of the Law, and so was assured of a steady income (five friendly planets in the second house). He had known from early childhood that he wanted to be a writer, and in adolescence he wrote plays for his sisters to perform (four planets and Chiron in the third house). Although most houses are empty, an examination of their rulers gives an excellent picture. For example, the rulers of the fifth house, Neptune (through sidereal Pisces) and Uranus (through sidereal Aquarius) being in trine may help to describe his love affairs. In addition Uranus is square Venus, Mercury and the Moon. The lone planet outside the first quadrant, Uranus, in the eleventh house stands for his unusual friendship with Max Brod who encouraged him as a young writer and helped to save Kafka's work for posterity. He was unknown outside of Prague but over the years his work has been absorbed by nearly every culture across the globe. His spiritual quest is ours. The problems he faced in his life and illustrated in his work are the same that we must face today.[38] Kafka is a writer who appeals to our feelings (first quadrant). He died at noon, June 3, 1924, in Prague.

Antoine de Saint-Exupéry was born in Lyons, France, June 29, 1900, at 9:15 a.m., rectified to 9:00:41 Meridian 2°E20. There were seven planets in the first quadrant (astral = feeling) opposite to three planets in the third quadrant (physical = sense perceptions). The opposition between the third and ninth houses as well as Neptune, the Sun and Venus in Gemini, the third sign, stresses travel and literary achievements. *Wind, Sand and Stars* describes, among other things, he and his navigator's crash in the Libyan

---

37   Wikipedia.

38   Jeff Nowak and Allen B. Ruch (website).

Cecil B. DeMille
Ashfield, Massachusetts (42N30, 72W48)
August 12, 1881
5:15:04 LT
Vernal Point: 6° Pisces 54'44"

Sahara desert and their miraculous survival. His most famous book, *The Little Prince*, no doubt emerged from the same experience. He died when his plane was probably shot down in the Mediterranean south of Marseilles, the night of July 31, 1944. Saturn the ruler of the eighth house of death opposed the Sun and Neptune, and Jupiter the sub-ruler of the same house in the ninth house opposed Mars in the third house. In fact this opposition formed a Royal Yoga.[39]

Cecil Blount DeMille was born in Ashfield, Massachusetts, August 12, 1881, at 5:14 a.m., rectified to 5:15:04 LT. He had eight planets and Chiron in the airy, emotional first quadrant. Cecil started off to work as an actor but lacking any acting opportunities, he took up directing feature length motion pictures based on popular plays. He developed an ability to produce blockbusters (ambitious Saturn on the MC). The Moon, ruler of his Ascendant, sidereal Cancer, is in his fifth house of entertainment. Neptune, ruler of the fifth house is one of the five planets in the third house, which gave him the energy and ability to make so many successful films. Uranus, sub-ruler of the fifth house through Aquarius is precisely on the Placidus cusp of the eleventh house (radio, television, movies) and twelfth house (revolutionary views) and trine Saturn on the Midheaven. He defied McCarthy (who undertook a fervent witch hunt for anyone vaguely sympathetic to Communism) and hired several blacklisted people.[40] He also had a Royal Yoga formed by the wide conjunction of Jupiter, the ruler of Pisces, and Mars, the ruler of Scorpio. He died January 21, 1959, in Hollywood.

"I," Willing, Warmth, and Fire Quadrant

Sylvia Plath was born in Boston, Massachusetts, October 27, 1932, at 2:10 p.m., rectified to 14:13:14 EST. She was a poet and novelist, who was famous for her passionate marriage to the poet Ted Hughes. She has six planets in the second quadrant. True to this fiery quadrant, she was very intense and wrote about her anguish. Sun in the fifth house can be very jealous of any romantic competition; the stellium in the sixth house describes her perception of her husband; and Mars in the seventh house confirms the role of collaboration in her writings and a marriage overly founded on baser instincts. Her writings imitated her life and her life imitated her writings.[41]

39 Wikipedia.

40 Wikipedia.

41 Wikipedia.

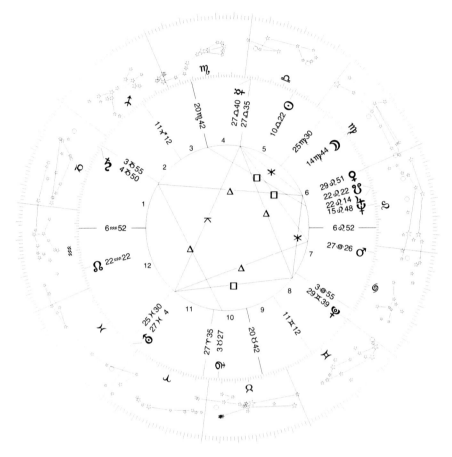

Sylvia Plath
Boston, Massachusetts (42°N21'30," 71°W3'37")
October 27, 1932
14:13:14 EST
Vernal Point: 6°Pisces 11'52"

She was one of the first poets to celebrate childbirth and breastfeeding. Mercury in sidereal Libra and the fourth house (the mother) squares Mars (the classical ruler of the fourth house through Scorpio) in the seventh house (marriage) in sidereal Cancer (the mother). Mercury also trines Pluto in the eighth house (death) and both sextile Venus in the sixth house (marriage partner). By the way, I wonder if Vedic astrologers consider the sextile between Mercury and Venus to be a Royal Yoga? Moreover, the

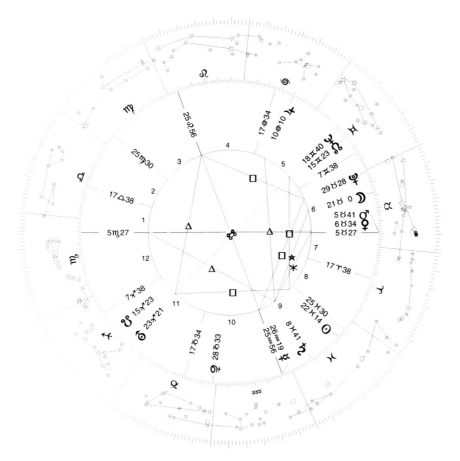

Herbert von Karajan
Salzburg, Austria (47°N48, 13°E1)
April 5, 1908
22:33:48 CET
Vernal Point: 6°Pisces 32'26"

only major aspect that the Moon (in the sixth house) makes is a wide trine (orb 10°6') separating from Saturn. Geoffrey Dean[42] found that the psychological effects of an unaspected Moon could be the most personally traumatic of any planet. Such a person can feel "markedly unstabilized or uncommonly vulnerable" and feels "an unnatural sense of disconnection with the immediate environment…and therefore appears restless,

---

42   Cited in Tierney. *Dynamics of Aspect Analysis. New Perceptions in Astrology.*

unsettled and not at home." Having made certain that her children were safe, she took her own life late at night, February 11, 1963, in London.

Herbert von Karajan was born in Salzburg, Austria, April 5, 1908, at 10:30 p.m., rectified to 22:33:48 CET. He was a child prodigy pianist but was encouraged to study conducting. In the late fifties and early sixties he was nicknamed "the general music director of Europe" as he was leading the Berlin Philharmonic, La Scala in Milan, London's Philharmonic Orchestra, the Vienna State Opera and the Salzburg Festival. He made over 800 recordings, more than any other conductor, and played an important role in the development of the original compact disc with its digital format.[43] His six planets in the second quadrant confirm his enormous energy and clearly delineated vocation. His strength of will, characteristic of the second quadrant, showed up in his bitter arguments with the Berlin Philharmonic and earlier in his career, his controversial joining of the Nazi Party, which was not for ideological reasons but as a precondition for attaining a directorship of an orchestra in Aachen. The sixth and seventh houses should be very important for the interpersonal connections between the conductor and the orchestra. The Mars–Venus conjunction sextiles Saturn; the Moon quintiles Saturn; and Pluto trines Chiron. Uranus in the eleventh house in a T-square with Neptune and the Sun explains his unusual friendships and accomplishments. He died in Paris, July 16, 1989, at 2 p.m.

Niels Bohr was born in Copenhagen, October 7, 1885, at 1:15 p.m., rectified to 13:20:16 LT. He has seven planets in the second quadrant, of which four are in the fifth house, which shows vital energy being prolonged into the following generation. Niels's father was a University Professor and his mother came from a family distinguished in the field of education. All four of his surviving sons have also pursued academic careers. The fifth house is not just entertainment and speculation, but also rules literary, artistic and scientific works. His studies concentrated on the structure of atoms on the basis of Rutherford's discovery of the atomic nucleus. Bohr also showed how deeply the challenges in the field of quantum physics have affected fundamental

---

43 Wikipedia.

Niels Bohr
At Copenhagen, Denmark (55°N40, 12°E34)
October 7, 1885
13:20:16 LT
Vernal Point 6° Pisces 51'16"

features of our scientific outlook and how the consequences of this change of attitude reach far beyond the scope of atomic physics and touch upon all domains of human knowledge. The transcendental planets, Neptune and Pluto as well as Chiron, in the physical quadrant, trining planets in the fifth house in the ego quadrant, took Niels Bohr into the super-physical realm. He won the Nobel Prize.[44] He died in Copenhagen, November 18, 1962.

---

44 At www.nobelprize.org.

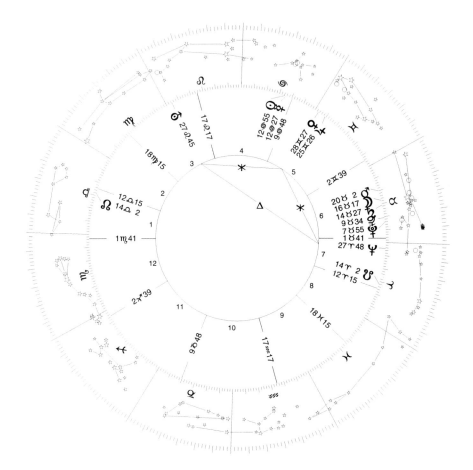

Benito Mussolini
Dovia il Predappo, Italy (44°N06, 11°E58)
July 29, 1883
14:20:12 LT
Vernal Point: 6° Pisces 53'6"

Benito Mussolini, the dictator of Italy during World War II, was born in Dovia il Predappio, Italy, July 29, 1883, at 2:00 pm, rectified to 14:20:12 LT. A mob killed him April 28, 1945, at Lake Como. Sidereal Scorpio had just begun to rise. He demonstrates the willpower, egotism and fiery nature of the second quadrant, which contains eight planets as well as Chiron. The Sun and Mercury in the fourth house undoubtedly gave him his authority; Venus conjunction Jupiter in the fifth house made him appealing to the masses; but Mars and Pluto in the sixth warn us of conflicts within the work sphere. Moon and Saturn in conjunction with Aldebaran (15 Taurus) adds an ominous note to his character and circumstances. According to Marc Edmund Jones, "His unabashed self-esteem, made possible by his lack of oppositions, proved to be extraordinary weakness when it came to any development or ordinary refinement of moral character. It also proved to be very real strength in the gyroscopic power of self-perpetuation through the one-man dictatorial rule he helped to shape and to show how it could be sustained by propaganda and mob appeal working hand in hand with the tyrannical repressions and exploitations known to man since the night of time."[45]

Edgar Cayce was born at Hopkinsville, Kentucky, March 18, 1877, some say it was at 3 p.m., others at 3:30 p.m., rectified to 15:31:32 LT. He earned a living from a modest photography business. After he lost his speech on April 18, 1900, a hypnotist was partly successful in 1901 in getting his voice back. Later Al Layne asked him while under hypnosis to prescribe himself a cure. And so began his path of healing while in a trance. The Moon Node, Mercury, Saturn and Venus are in the sixth house of health and illness. In 1923, Cayce suddenly revealed to Arthur Lammers, a curious psychologst, how his present situation derived from earlier lifetimes. Saturn, the planet of memory, is in conjunction with Venus, Mercury and the North Node; sextile Mars in the eighth house of birth and death; and sextile the Moon in fourth house of vocation. Jupiter in the eighth house trines Neptune in the fourth house and squares the Sun in the fifth house as well. Cayce has Pluto on the Midheaven in the first quadrant and six planets plus Chiron in the second quadrant ("I"). Paradoxically, it did not seem to be Cayce's "I" that was giving the psychic readings, but a group of beings. Cayce explained his lack of consciousness was due to a mistake made in an earlier lifetime. However, he had a Royal Yoga between Mars and Jupiter. He died January 3, 1945, in Virginia Beach, Virginia.

---

45 Jones. *Essentials of Astrological Analysis*, pp. 40–1.

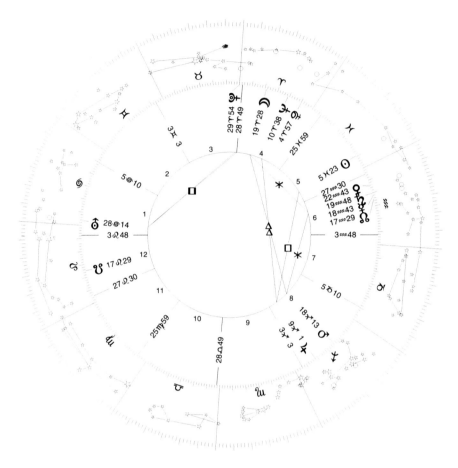

Edgar Cayce
Hopkinsville, Kentucky (36°N52, 87°W29)
March 18, 1877
15:31:32 LT
Vernal Point 6° Pisces 58'26"

Mother Teresa, whose name at birth was Agnes Gonxha Bojaxhiu, was born in Skopje, Yugoslavia (now the capital of the Republic of Macedonia) on August 26, 1910, at 2:25 p.m., rectified to 14:21:42 CET. She died in Calcutta, September 5, 1997.

With seven planets in the fourth, fifth and sixth houses, she is a perfect example of the working of the higher Ego in the quadrant of the will. At the time of her death, the Missionaries of Charity had over 4,000 sisters, a

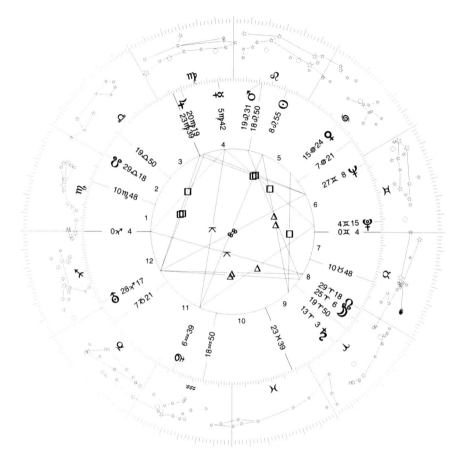

Mother Teresa
Skopje, Macedonia, Yugoslavia (42°N01, 21°E28)
August 26, 1910
14:21:42 CET
Vernal Point: 6° Pisces 30'26"

brotherhood of 300 members, over 100,000 lay volunteers, operating 610 missions in 123 countries, including hospices, homes for people with HIV/AIDS, leprosy and tuberculosis, soup kitchens, children's and family counseling programs, orphanages and schools (Sun and Venus in the fifth house, respectively trine and square Saturn in the house of foreign countries).[46] Neptune and Pluto in the sixth house of health and illness and Uranus in the twelfth house

----

46 Wikipedia.

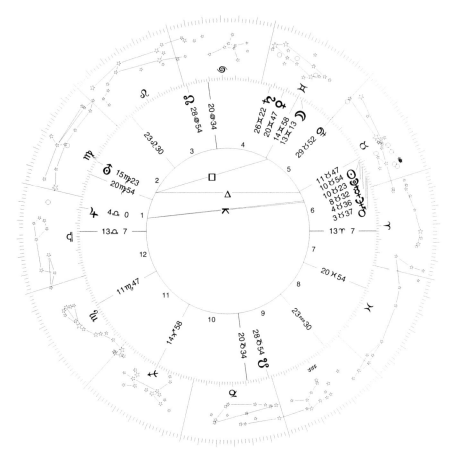

Padre Pio
Pietrelcina, Benevento, Italy (41°N12, 14°E51)
May 25, 1887
15:53:44 GMT
Vernal Point: 6° Pisces 49'54"

of hospitals, clinics and homes for the outcast were working in their highest octaves, especially with the T-square of Uranus-Neptune to Jupiter in the fourth house where it is exalted. There is also a Royal Yoga in her chart if you consider the conjunction of the Sun and Mars to be within orb.

Padre Pio (Francesco Forgione) was born May 25, 1887, at 5:00 p.m. Rome Time, in Pietrelcina/Benevento, Italy, rectified to 15:53:44 GMT (16:43:40

Rome Time). At the age of sixteen he joined the Capuchin order of the Franciscans. In 1916 he was conscripted by the army. One day he fell ill with a fever that climbed to 47.7 C (118 F), leaving the military doctors gasping. He was moved to the monastery at San Giovanni where he fully recovered. Of the eight planets in the second quadrant, five planets are in conjunction in the sixth house of health. His first stigmata appeared September 20, 1918. In the sidereal zodiac, transiting Pluto was applying to a conjunction with the Moon (14' orb), transiting Mars opposed his natal Mars and the Moon Node was separating from a conjunction with his natal Saturn. Human nature being what it is, it is not surprising that his superiors put him into confinement and eventually decided to completely silence him by moving him to another monastery. However, the entire populace revolted, preventing this from happening. While Padre Pio was in solitary confinement, people reported that he was seen at different bedsides of the ill and stricken, even hundreds of miles away. He was seen to levitate while saying the Mass. He could read the akashic chronicle and prophesied that a Polish priest, visiting the monastery to make his confession, would some day become Pope.[47] Eight planets plus Chiron in all three houses of the second quadrant demonstrate the relationship between the Ego, the element of fire and the blood, which manifested themselves right down into his physical body. The midpoint between Mars and Saturn (29°59.5' sidereal Taurus) is in conjunction with Chiron the wounded healer. Moreover, Chiron the Wounded Healer coincides with where the Midheaven was in the horoscope of Christ's Crucifixion, Friday, April 3, 33 (Julian), at Golgotha in Jerusalem.[48] Padre Pio died September 23, 1968, at 2:30 a.m., in San Giovanni Rotondo.

---

47 Wikipedia.

48 Robert Powell. *Chronicle of the Living Christ.*

CHAPTER 11

OBSERVATIONS AND MISCELLANEOUS APPLICATIONS

MAKING INTERPRETATION A LITTLE EASIER

As the reader will have noticed, I have centered my choice of illustrations around the charts that contain stellia. Since we only have ten planets and twelve houses, it is obvious we have on average, less than one planet per house. However, it is more or less evident that if one of them contains several planets, then the house in question stands out very clearly.

If the houses provide enlightenment as to certain domains of life—and this is most definitely the case—then we cannot imagine anything other than the fact that the stellium provides one of the beacons that assists the interpreter in his orientation.

So here you have yet another valuable experiment at your disposal. It is an easy and rapid one, which is not the least of its advantages. It is enough for you to have a look at your collection of horoscopes and to halt when you come across a house that stands out by dint of the fact that it contains three planets or more. You will arrive at your appreciation by considering the two possible directions, which are so much in question during the course of this book; and you will reach your own conclusions according to the results obtained in this experiment, in which the order of rotation provides the best interpretation according to what you know of the subject.

So many students have told me about the difficulties they have experienced when it comes to interpretation, especially in the beginning and, above all, when they are face to face with a total stranger. Here is a trick of the trade that will help you to discover a dominant theme. Take note of whether the majority of the planets are above or below the horizon; whether they are to the left or right of the midheaven, and draw your conclusions from this. If the planets are sufficiently distributed so as not to stand out at this first examination, which will only take a few seconds, look for the house where the ruler of the Ascendant is placed. This is an excellent orientation. If the planet(s) ruling the Ascendant are in the same house, the domains ruled by the latter are certainly of great interest where the native is concerned. For example, if Libra is on the Ascendant then some stars of Virgo will also be therein, hence Venus and Mercury will be rulers of the first house. You can complete the process by examining those houses where the rulers of the ninth (idealism) and the eleventh (hopes, aspirations, plans) are found. Note well that here we are talking about the subject (that is, his personality and psychological nature) that he represents and aspires to.

Then go on to the subject of destiny by examining the planets, if any, which are found in the fourth house (the one that starts at the MC). If this house is empty, have a look to see in which house you can find its two rulers. You will already have a very valuable outline. The rest follows.

DERIVED HOUSES

Though this system is used by some and criticized by others, I am not in the least bit perturbed to declare that it is one that I frequently use in the interpretation of the horoscope. Certain authors, such as Eudes Picard and Tinia Faery are known for having juggled them around to their greatest satisfaction. I must recognize, myself, that I owe them some of the most astonishing declarations that I have ever made to any consultant concerning facts already known to him. Some would say that this is not scientific. I take the liberty of pointing out that very often we go so far as to forget the etymology of the word *science*. Is this practice a divinatory art? Quite possibly it is. But just where do we actually draw the line between scientific astrology and the art of interpretation? Our entire discipline, beyond any shadow of a doubt, rests upon the postulation according to which the horoscope represents the state of the heavens at birth. However, as soon as we launch ourselves into interpretation, we generally find ourselves up against those who consider themselves to be rationalists.

First of all, it is worth drawing attention to the fact that in certain manuals, in the chapter that deals with the significations normally attributed to each house, even if the expression "derived houses" is not actually mentioned, they are already being used, unknown to the reader, and sometimes even, to the author. The eighth house certainly evokes death; not only because it corresponds with the sign represented by an animal whose sting can be deadly, but also due to the fact that, in antiquity, it was the final section of an eightfold division that took its starting point from the Ascendant. Well now, when influences over the fortune of the spouse, or the financial situation subsequent to marriage, are attributed to the eighth house, then we are no longer involved with the subject of death (since, under the circumstances, we leave the matter of all inheritances aside). Here, then, it only concerns the second from the seventh.

Editor's Note: It should be obvious that in counting "the second from the seventh," the first from the seventh is the seventh house itself, the second is the eighth house, the third is the ninth house, and so on.

Thus having stated this, whether we like to admit it or not, we have already ventured into the labyrinth of the derived houses. In the same way, when we say that the fourth house is the one of the memory, it must be translated by the second from the third house, that is to say, by gains from intellectual activities. When we authorise the ninth house to instruct us on relationships with the family-in-law, then we are bound to have recourse to the third from the seventh house, that is to say, the person's relations to whom he is bound by contract.

In my opinion, the legitimacy of using the derived houses is confirmed and justified by the correct developments obtained in the interpretation, and this is precisely what happens as soon as we practice the technique of counting the houses clockwise (in opposition to the signs). This technique cannot be developed here, although we would like to. It yields eleven times twelve (132) different combinations, each of them permitting different interpretations. What we can do is to be precise on two points and leave the rest up to you. On the one hand, we advise you to put the technique to the test by using the horoscope of someone known to you, be it someone in your immediate entourage or a celebrity; and on the other hand we suggest that your choice be, more or less, limited to a chart that contains a stellium or a group of planets close together. Well now, we really do claim that such an attempt using the system of the derived houses, certainly will surprise the interpreter as he will realize all the more strongly, that he can only arrive at a conclusion by considering the houses in accordance with diurnal movement. In order that the reader, yet unfamiliar with this system, really understands what I am driving at, let us say for example, that the fourth house, as well as all the significators that are normally ascribed to it, becomes thus equally, the second house from the third, the third from the second, the fifth from the twelfth, the sixth from the eleventh, the seventh from the tenth, the eighth from the ninth, the ninth from the eighth, the tenth from the seventh, the eleventh from the sixth and finally, the twelfth from the fifth. In the last example it could mean ordeals involving children, this interpretation being only one among many.

Please let me tell you about a conversation, which I had with Mrs. Colette P., a resident of the countryside close to Nice, versed in astrology and who gave me a celestial chart to interpret:

"The brother-in-law?" she asked me.

"But isn't he dead?" I replied.

"Yes, he is," she said, quite amazed, "but the other brother-in-law?"

"Well, I think he's dead, too."

So Colette also thought I was gifted with clairvoyance. Not by any means whatsoever. The fourth and sixth houses were strongly afflicted by anerets (planets, which provoke death). Well, the fourth is the eighth from the third from the seventh, that is, the death of the spouse's brother. In the case where the practitioner considers that the third house is the brother's house, thus already entering into the system of derived houses, he takes the fifth as being the third from the third, that is to say, of the following brother; we shall be able to say that the sixth becomes the eighth from the third from the third from the seventh. In other words, the death of the spouse's brother's brother.

However, having said that, I join Gouchon in his opinion as expressed in his dictionary under the heading "Derived Houses," which states that although this system can give impressive results, it can also be extremely disappointing. This practice obliges us to recognize that the more we wish to extract results from the horoscope, the more we run the risk of making mistakes.

Moreover (especially when we involve ourselves in practices that depend more on divinatory art than on so called scientific influences), everything rests on the practitioner's intuition, and notably, on his intuitive faculties at the time of the consultation. I, therefore, warn all beginners to stay away from this rather hazardous and dicey practice.

TRANSITS OF THE SLOW-MOVING PLANETS

The planets, especially the slow ones, will manifest themselves gradually in their transits in the houses: they will enter through the final point of the house and, little by little, they will exercise, all things being equal, a maximum influx when they finally arrive closer to the cusp of the said house.

More often than not, whether it be a question of an improvement or deterioration in health, or in the professional or financial situation, things will come to pass gradually or progressively rather than suddenly. There are obviously a great number of exceptions; for example, if it is Uranus that intervenes.[49]

CATEGORIES OF THE HOUSES

We know that there are angular or cardinal houses and succedent and cadent ones about which we have already had occasion to say a few words. The fact that there are also personal and material houses, social and occult ones, as well as fortunate and unfortunate ones, will also be considered. Here, I shall limit myself to pointing out that when the

---

49 EDITOR'S NOTE: In my experience of using the Placidus House system there are occasions when a planet transiting the cusp at either the beginning or the end of a house coincides with a significant event related to either house the planet is just leaving or just entering.

houses are considered as unfolding in the same direction as the signs, and that authority over the professional and social life is given to the tenth house, then it is obvious that this same house is in square with the first one.

We have insisted on the fact that the third house is the one pertaining to the chosen profession and the reader will certainly not fail to notice that it is thus in sextile, that is to say in a harmonious angle with the Ascendant, the first house. In the same way, if a certain environment, especially at the starting point of existence, is imposed on us by actual events, the fifth and eleventh houses, those of love affairs and friendships respectively, are said to be in harmonious trine and sextile aspect with the Ascendant, then we are eager to recognize that this is equal, as it were, to the rotational direction attributed the houses. However, if we consider that the third one is well and truly the sector upon which deliberately chosen activities depend, we notice that this third house is found to be in harmonious sextile and trine aspect with the fifth and eleventh houses. We shall notice that the first, third, fifth and eleventh houses exchange harmonious relations among themselves, thus appearing to leave a great deal up to free will; whereas the square between the first and tenth houses, when they are considered as being in the same direction as that of the signs and when this tenth house represents the career, seems to leave less liberty in the choice and practice of the profession.[50]

APPLYING AND SEPARATING ASPECTS

Of course, this does not in any way change the rule concerning aspects, namely that preference is given to the applying over the separating aspect. We mean that we estimate the applying as being stronger than the separating. If the Moon is 3° from Jupiter and runs toward it, the conjunction is applying; roughly twelve hours later, after having completed its

---

50 EDITOR'S NOTE: Here Dorsan is employing the archetypal equal house system. For all house systems that are dependent on the MC–IC axis as well as the Asc–Desc axis, this may not always be the case. However, I think it would be a valuable addition to chart interpretation if in a particular chart, two or more houses, which should be in a harmonious relationship, were not.

exact conjunction with the Great Benefic, the Moon will still find itself at a distance of 3° from Jupiter, but in a separating conjunction. In the first case, all other configurations being equal, it is classical to consider the applying Moon–Jupiter conjunction as being stronger than the separating. At first, this conjunction is applying, afterward it becomes separating. Of course it goes without saying, that this configuration was made because of the Moon's movement toward Jupiter in the direction of the zodiacal signs. By counting the houses in a clockwise direction absolutely nothing is altered as far as this law is concerned. Finally, it is a good idea to state that in this example it is a matter of the planets being in direct movement, which goes to show why we chose the Moon, since it is never retrograde.[51]

THE RULERS OF THE HOUSES IN THE HOUSES

Students often encounter serious difficulties when they wish to form an opinion on a domain, which depends upon a house that is empty of planets.

First of all, the general significators of the question ought to be examined; then the nature of the zodiac sign where the cusp of this empty house falls. After this, the planet whose domicile is in this sign, namely, the ruler of the house. Quite naturally, one is led toward the consideration of the position in the houses of the rulers of this house.

However, this technique can also be used on houses containing one or several planets and I strongly advise you to utilise it to your advantage. The ruler of the Ascendant will fall within one of the twelve houses; besides, it could even fall within the first one. The same goes for each of the rulers of the eleven other houses. Theoretically, then you have the possibility of 144 different combinations open to you. Actually, you have 288, in practice, for you will do the same for the second ruler of each house. As a matter of fact, this wonderful technique will bring you replies to a good many problems for, the position in the houses of the two rulers of one house, can alone furnish several tendencies.

---

51 EDITOR'S NOTE: For example, if Mars is retrograde then it could be applying to say Jupiter, even though Jupiter is in an earlier degree of the zodiac to Mars.

Thus, for instance, if the ruler of the Ascendant is in the fifth, it will be necessary to choose between one's love of children and that of risk. If the second ruler of the Ascendant is in the ninth, that can attract one toward further studies, but also toward overseas travels. Here, one would be more inclined toward studies as this is a common trait to the fifth and ninth houses, in which are respectively found the two rulers of this first house.

This technique is not new, far from it. However, I think one has little recourse to it. Here we come back to the fact that certain practitioners, disappointed by rules that they find to be ineffectual, have gone so far as to abandon the rulers. But how on earth could we expect good results with rulers, which were adulterated by the incessant staggering effect produced by the precession of the equinoxes? Even more so when we attribute to a certain sector of the Heavens a house completely perverted, or misrepresented, by an erroneous rotation.

Of course, we must advise that a great amount of prudence be exercised, especially in the early stages. Rather than playing the fortune teller on a horoscope that is unknown, it is better to try it out first on a person who is known and thus seek confirmation of the psycho-physiological dispositions that appear evident to you, or of events in the past. With a little experience, this will allow you to develop and finish off the interpretation, as long as you act gently and do not show yourself to be too demanding. As always, wanting to draw too much from a celestial chart is the sure path to erroneous results.

The Wedding Date

In an article entitled "The Wedding Date According to the Horoscope,"[52] the astrologers J. Bucco and Henri-Joseph Gouchon put forward the first hint of statistics (I use this terminology because a law was established from a restricted number of charts), showing the position of the progressed Moon (secondary directions) in the radical house at the time of marriage. This is what they found:

---

52 *Les cahiers astrologique*, no. 1. January 1938.

Counterclockwise House	I	II	III	IV	V	VI
Number of Moons	4	6	8	7	3	3
Clockwise House	XII	XI	X	IX	VIII	VII

Counterclockwise House	VII	VIII	IX	X	XI	XII
Number of Moons	3	7	2	3	2	2
Clockwise House	VI	V	IV	III	II	I

At the time of the wedding, the Moon was thus most often in the traditional third, fourth and eighth houses. The fact that it was in the fourth house (that of the home) is fair enough, but in houses pertaining to movements, trips, and loss when marriage is an acquisition—well, we really do have to admit that this does not correspond to anything we hoped for or anticipated.

However, on the contrary, if the houses are counted clockwise, the fullest ones will be the fifth, ninth and tenth, or more precisely, in the same order, the house of the love life, that of profound aspirations and finally that of the family life, since the traditional meaning of roots or home is conserved in the IC.

Once again, by inverting their order of rotation, the houses live up to our expectations entirely.

SERIOUS CONTRADICTIONS AVOIDED

Up until now, most manuals tell us that the fourth house enlightens us as to the end of life. Moreover, as already seen, a great number attribute it to the father, the protector, who is actually linked to the beginning of the subject's life. Of course, in this case, this fourth house is considered as starting at the IC and climbing up toward the Descendant when the same rotational direction as the sign is followed.

In opposition to this, through following the rules that we have expresssed in this work, the house that represents the father finishes at the IC. The first part of life, as we have seen, is mainly determined by the first Quadrant that goes from the Ascendant to the MC and the end of life will be determined through the last Quadrant that goes from the IC to the Ascendant and, above all, through the first third of this last Quadrant, which we call the tenth house. Consequently, there is no more confusion between the sectors upon which we depend, on the one hand the beginning of life, and on the other hand, the end of existence.

PLANETS AFFLICTING DEATH

In Hindu astrology, our Anarets, or death-inflicting planets, are called Marakas. I was greatly struck to see that the second and seventh houses are named "houses of Death," and that the planets in them may become Marakas, this is to say planets that kill; and we insist on the fact that the second house is more forceful than the seventh when it comes to inflicting death. The cusp of the seventh house remains the seventh whatever the order of rotation given to the houses.

But how can we logically attribute to the second house what represents gains, a decisive role in the greatest of all losses, namely, the loss of life itself?

For the reader who is now accustomed to the mental gymnastics that we have imposed on him, the reply to this seemingly inexplicable paradox, is one of the most simple: the cusp of the second house becomes, if we invert the direction of rotation that we recommend, the beginning of the twelfth and last house; and it is classical to study the eighth, the IC and the twelfth when we tackle the problem of death.

THE FIRST AND TWELFTH HOUSES

We have already devoted quite a lot of time during the course of our introduction, as well as in our illustrations in Chapter 10, to the subject of the two houses that are separated by the Ascendant, whatever the system of gyration adopted. And we have also said that our way of operating is, in practice, a great deal less revolutionary than it appears at first glance, notably for the very reason that the four main axes retain their essential significations. Here, we merely wish to draw attention to the fact that where the sectors of the heavens are concerned and, in so far as they enlighten us as to certain pathological weaknesses, we can often arrive at identical conclusions by following very divergent paths. Indeed, supposing a native has his Ascendant in Libra (the Scales) for a Western practitioner accustomed to working with the tropical zodiac. Let us also assume of course, that the houses are taken as evolving in the same direction as the signs. For this reason our practioner will tell his consultant that there may be a risk of chronic intestinal problems since the twelfth house is found in tropical Virgo. If after following our suggestions, this same astrologer becomes, first of all, a siderealist, and secondly he sees the houses as unfolding according to the natural direction, the cusp of the twelfth house no longer falls in tropical Virgo but the Ascendant, from a siderealist's viewpoint, falls in sidereal Virgo. We shall then arrive at exactly the same conclusion as far as the diagnosis of intestinal weakness goes.

A HORARY HOROSCOPE IN FIVE MINUTES

At the beginning of this book I showed you how I managed to convince some people, who were already slightly initiated into our science, that it was possible to correctly draw up a celestial birth chart in less than five minutes (provided that it is not necessary to know the longtitude of each planet very exactly). And now, in order to thank you for having so kindly read my exposé right to the very end, I am going to give you a present: how to draw up an horary horoscope in less than five seconds. Yes. You read correctly. In five seconds, and why not? This really is the drama of our profession: we see the profane believe in a lot of cock-and-bull stories, which are connected to astrology in name only, and then very often, when you state the truth you are not believed. However, as for me, I am well and truly immune to this paradox that is, at times, difficult to bear, we must admit. I tremble with indignation when I read in the pseudo-horoscopes of the common press, that the natives of such and such a sign will be strongly influenced today, this week, or this month, by the sextile Neptune–Pluto. Does the author really know that these two planets have formed this aspect since the thirties, with an orb of less than 10°, and that they will still be forming it well after the turn of the century? However, please note that there are those horoscopes in the press that are in fact drawn up by competent and honest colleagues, who would never write such garbage. While we are on this subject, I shall say, once again, that the Board of Directors of a daily or periodical, publishing horoscopes, should demand three things:

1. That the article state straight away the period covered;
2. That it be sprinkled with the minimum amount of technical references;
3. That, above all, it be signed.

I have been using the technique, which I have wished to teach you for decades, that is to say, well before electronics came to our aid in the matter of computations; but even now, I advise very strongly that it be used, for it gives an image of the heavens that is easy to interpret, since you see the planetary bodies fixed on the circumference of our celestial charts. You only need three tools that are not at all costly. First, you ought to get yourself a little portable clock or alarm clock that you will keep close to you at all times, be you an amateur or a professional. You would be advised to choose an old-fashioned model rather than one that is ultramodern and operating with electronic precision. Indeed, you will ask your watchmaker to make sure that this little clock gains time rigorously by four minutes every twenty-four hours. The salesman will probably think you are a bit weird, but that is completely secondary; in the practice of astrology, "You ain't seen nothin' yet!" Be very insistent on this point, and leave it with him under observation over a period of several days in order to be sure that it gives you total satisfaction. Then, at your home, taking legal time into account, as well as, quite possibly, the (stupid) so called daylight saving time, the longtitude of your place of residence and the usual small rectification normally required, you will then set your clock at the sidereal time of the place and moment. If it is well regulated, as explained above, it will not be necessary for you to add the daily 3 minutes 56 seconds, that you know so well. Now for the other things, buy a large ring binder capable of containing 360 perforated Celestial Charts. I assume, of course, that you regularly reside in the same geographical longtitude and latitude. At the top right-hand side of each sheet, mark the sidereal time in the following manner: 00 hr 04 min, 00 hr 08 min, 00 hr 12 min, and so on up to 24 hr 00 min.

Then on each chart, mark very legibly, the Ascendant and the MC as well as the cusps of the succedent and cadent houses, according to the method of domification, which you have adopted. Finally, it will be enough for you to have before you, or possibly behind your interlocutor, a large circle made out of the material of your choice, whose diameter can be in the vicinity of 40 centimeters. However, these tricks of the trade are largely outmoded today by electronic calculators suited to astrological work. Nevertheless, this process as outlined above, does have one advantage: it is cheaper. As far as I am concerned, for a great many years I used a large horoscope made of mahogany, clearly divided up into twelve equal sectors, with 360 holes pierced toward the circumference. My secretary's first task, every morning, was to move the Sun one degree, the Moon roughly 12° to 15° and the rest as necessary, leaving the slow planets untouched most of the time.

It is enough to flick over the right edge of the 360 semi-blank charts with the aid of your thumb, after having had a quick look at your clock, then mentally project the position of the planets onto your Celestial Chart, thus selected, and where you have opened your ring binder. There you have an horary horoscope, which is one hundred per cent scientific, and which has been set up in the twinkling of an eye. With a certain amount of practice, you will be able to guess the object of the person telephoning you.

At one time, right at the beginning of my career, I was in a particular town taking the waters, and I was able to pay for my cure with a few consultations slotted into my timetable. One fine morning I received a phone call, in the presence of my companion (who was later to become the mother of my children), and I made an appointment for 3 p.m. on the very same day. I said to my girlfriend: "Later on, just after 3 p.m., could you go down into the lobby in order to welcome someone who may seem to be a little lost?"

"Before three, you mean?"

"No, it won't be necessary; she'll be late."

"But how will I recognize her?"

"You will see at the entrance, an elderly woman, not very attractive to look at, who will be limping badly and who will be wearing glasses."

A little after the time set for the appointment, the consultant in question arrived. She corresponded perfectly with the above description. She was carrying a walking stick and was wearing very thick spectacles. Your secret, then?

What secret? There is no secret. I have told you all. The Ascendant of the hourly horoscope at the time of the telephone call was strongly afflicted by Saturn, which generally gives elderly people a rather unattractive face. Saturnians are known for being late. Pretty little things are usually born under a Sun–Venus conjunction, or with an aspect that Venus projects onto the Ascendant or onto the ruler of the Ascendant. Sometimes Venus is in conjunction with the Ascendant and so there is no risk of your making a mistake. While we are on this subject, be on time if you have an appointment with a Martian, for these people are always in a hurry and they will arrive a little before the appointment time. Saturn of the lady's horary chart afflicted the two luminaries that gave rise to the troubled eyesight. Finally, the Sun–Saturn affliction put Leo and Aquarius into the picture; consequently, she suffered from a spinal column condition. The ninth house was afflicted; but this person could not have come from very far away, since, on that very day she was in the same little town as I. Thus, through analogy, this drew attention to the ninth sign, Sagittarius, thus the lower members. You will therefore admit that it is not at all a question of clairvoyance, and you will understand why astrologers, the real ones, do not like to be known as fortune tellers. Of course, I am not aiming at any particular seer who, often, uses astrology for assistance in his work.

CHAPTER 12

PARADOXES CORRECTED

To put it in a nutshell, the change in direction that we have been advocating and putting into practice for many long years, allows one to correct numerous paradoxes. We have insisted upon the exchanges between the first and twelfth houses (vitality and lack of vitality), the fact that the house of gains in our system corresponds to the first hours of activity in the day of a human being and is not at all analogous to a period of total inactivity; we have restated and adjusted the difference that exists, for all that concerns the social and professional life, between the planets that climb toward the MC and those that descend; we have given a logical and quite natural place to the sectors of the father and of the mother. We have established an appropriate resemblance between Gemini and Sagittarius on the one hand, and short and long journeys on the other. But you will notice very quickly that in practice the above list is by no means limited. Indeed, in certain manuals one can read that the fourth house, if well-aspected, leads to success in foreign lands; as far as we understand things, this is rather the domain of the ninth house, through its correspondence with Sagittarius.

In the same way we have seen, in certain cases, death attributed to the fifth house; for us we know that it really involves the eighth house. We have explained why very grave afflictions, which are apparently in the second house in the sector of fortune, really came into play in the eleventh house. Through analogy, with the signs of Virgo and Libra and the sixth and seventh houses, we have established a very clear-cut difference between the sector of the spouse and that of legal ties. In short, we think that we have demonstrated to the reader that if he contemplates the unfolding of the houses according to diurnal movement, that is, in a clockwise direction, in opposition to the direction of the signs, then he will find a solution to a great many problems, anomalies and points of weakness, which he has had occasion to meet during the capital phase of the execution of our art; by this I mean, in the interpretation.

I beg you to forgive me if I have repeated myself, but I was adamant that in these pages, that I would provide an answer to the question that is so often asked, "But how do you organize yourself in order to see through a celestial chart and arrive at such an interpretation?"

They wanted to make a perfect horoscope where signs and houses blended into each other. This is doubtless an analogy. But to juxtapose them in the way that it has been done up to now, I mean by this, to go deliberately and completely against the grain as far as the most elementary rule of cosmography is concerned, constitutes, from my viewpoint, a very serious error. It is very difficult to believe that for countless generations intelligent human beings have been overlooking such an obvious truth, as it cries out for recognition. Above all, do not let yourself become a part of, or be influenced by those whose main argument will be to claim that I say "Bah" to a multi-secular practice. But the problem does not lie here; the main thing is Truth itself. Well, if astrology wishes to remain logical, then it can only depend on the observation of the stars in the very first place, and on the cosmography of the Solar system.

JUDGE FOR YOURSELF

Moreover, the sole judge in the matter is not he (or she) who allowed himself (or herself) to be led astray, with all the extenuating circumstances that we very sincerely allow him (or her), but you, and only you, dear reader. Nothing is worth more than your own personal experience. Once you have seized the twofold mental gymnastics that we have imposed upon you from the very start, a large veil will be rent before your very eyes, and in no time at all the interpretation of your celestial charts will undergo considerable improvement. After surmounting the first difficulties, to a point where you become quite accustomed, a certain amount of spade work involving and leading up to predictions will be rendered a great deal easier. Just to give one single example, the transits that the slow planets make in the radical chart (that of birth); let us suppose that a slow Jupiter–Saturn sextile comes about in your second house (gains) and in the fourth house (profession); it is quite simple and rapid to conclude that your professional income will progress for the months during which this sextile is maintained. Previously, you would not have arrived at a prediction as exact as this since the significations attributed to each of these two above houses, were falsified. This examination alone, repeated in several horoscopes, will convince you of the rectitude of my method.

And I really do speak from experience. In my work, *Return to the Stellar Zodiac*, I insisted that the reader arrive at an opinion completely on his own, and that this be done through the examination of the horoscopes in his very own collection. The mail that I received straightway, especially its tenor, encouraged me to publish as soon as possible, the details of my operating technique. "For twenty years now, I have been practicing astrology. I have been saying to myself that it should work, but somehow something is not quite right. Thank you for having reestablished the balance," is what one Franco-American astrologer wrote to me on the subject of the error first committed seventeen centuries ago and that was certainly due to Ptolemy. There is hardly any doubt that the error concerning the direction of the houses is just one, among many others, that can be attributed to him. The least little observation of the heavens will demonstrate to you that if you give the planets in the signs, as well as the succession of the signs, a leftward direction—quite justifiable at least in the Northern Hemisphere—then you can only, quite logically, give a rightward direction to the unfolding of the houses, starting from the Ascendant.

The Sidereal Zodiac and the Clockwise Houses

I really do believe that, now you have two good working tools at hand, which will allow you to progress in this royal art that is astrology. I hope that this same art will permit you to communicate better with the Universal Power, to better serve those who come to you for guidance, as they seek their real place in this world. Not an easy task, as the practice of astrology teaches us that we are all, or at the very least, born unequal. Having said this, I am thinking about the reply a young female American student once provided when she was asked point blank in the street by an opinion poll: "What is the use of astrology?" After thinking for a minute, she said: "It helps everyone to find his true place." I thank the heavens with all my might for having allowed me to write these two works (this one and my previous one), for very sincerely, and without any false modesty, I have the impression that I feel very deeply, within myself, a great joy to know that I shall have left a little something behind me when I have "shuffled off this mortal coil."

Jacques Dorsan's Horoscope

Jacques Dorsan told Robert Powell that he was born on December 22, 1912, in Orleans, France, at 12:35 a.m., rectified to 0:34:19 GMT, and he died on September 8, 2005, in Nice, France. Mercury is the ruler of both his Ascendant (sidereal Virgo) and his Midheaven (sidereal Gemini). Robert Hand considers Mercury to be the planet of astrologers.[53] Mercury in the tenth house presages many changes in residence, which is true for Dorsan. In addition, Venus and Uranus are in the ninth house of long distant travels. Mercury forms a sesquiquadrate to Neptune in the third house. This excellent position for Neptune gives a prophetic sense and an ability to produce literary works out of the ordinary. Moreover, Jupiter and the Sun are in Sagittarius, the sign of prophecy, opposed to Pluto in the fourth house. Dorsan described himself very well when he described the fourth house Pluto: "He could experience success through the destruction of an inheritance, even a spiritual inheritance."

53 Email communication.

Jacques Dorsan
Orleans, France (47°N55'0," 1°E54'0"
Sunday, December 12, 1912, Gregorian
0:25:32 GMT
Sidereal Time 6:33:56,
Vernal Point 6° Pisces 28'29"

Although his ideas did not immediately catch on when he published in French, with this translation into English, it is our sincere hope that Ptolemy's error will be finally reversed and that the opposite rotation of the houses to the zodiac will be fully recognized in astrological interpretation.

REFERENCES

Blavatsky, H. P. *Isis Unveiled: A Master-Key to the Mysteries of Ancient and Modern Science and Theology*, vol. 1. "Science." Pasadena: Theosophical University, 1988.

Bouché-Leclercq, Auguste. *L'astrologie grecque*. Toronto: University of Toronto, 2011.

Bradford, Thomas Lindsley. *The Life and Letters of Samuel Hahnemann*. New Delhi: B Jain, 2004.

Bradley, Donald A. *The Parallax Problem in Astrology*. St. Paul, MN: Llewellyn Publications, 1986.

Cahiers astrologique, Les. Paris: Dervy-Livres (periodical).

Dreyer, Ronnie Gale. *Vedic Astrology: A Guide to the Fundamentals of Jyotish*. York Beach, ME Samuel Weiser, 1997.

Ebertin, Reinhold. *The Combination of Stellar Influences*. Tempe, AZ: American Federation of Astrologers, 2000.

Gauquelin, Michel. *Dossier des influences cosmiques*. Edition Denoël, 1973.

———. *L'hérédité planétaire: notre naissance et l'horloge cosmique*. Paris: Edition Planète, 1966.

———. *Les hommes et les astres*. Paris: Denoël, 1960.

———. *Neo-astrology: A Copernican Revolution*. London: Arkana, 1991.

Gouchon, H. J., and J. Reverchon. *Dictionnaire astrologique: Supplément technique pour simplifier ou supprimer tous les travaux mathématiques concernant la carte natale, les révolutions solaires et surtout les directions*. Paris: H. Gouchon, 1947.

Hand, Robert. *Horoscope Symbols*. Rockport, MA: Para Research, 1981.

Heline, Corinne. *Sacred Science of Numbers*. Santa Monica, CA: New Age Bible and Philosophy Center, 1975.

Herbst, Bill. *Houses of the Horoscope*. San Diego: ACS, 1998.

Jones, Marc Edmund. *Essentials of Astrological Analysis*. New York: Sabian, 1960.

———. *The Scope of Astrological Prediction: An Introduction to the Dynamic Horoscope*. Stanwood, WA: Sabian, 1969.

Kolisko, Eugen. *Reincarnation and Other Essays*. Bournemouth, England: Kolisko Archives, 1940, 1978.

Lasson, Léon. *Ceux qui nous guident* (Those Who Guide Us). Paris: René Debresse, 1946.

Leo, Alan. *Mars, the War Lord: Being the Substance of a Course of Public Lectures Delivered before the Astrological Society*. York Beach, ME: Samuel Weiser, 1970.

———. *The Progressed Horoscope*. New York: Cosimo, 2005.

Manilius, Marcus. *Les astrologiques ou la science sacrée du ciel. Illustré d'une suite complète des gravures du "Livre des fables astronomiques" de C. Julius Hyginus, Selon l'édition de 1578*. Paris.

Manilius. *Astronomica*, G. P. Goold, trans. Cambridge, MA: Harvard, 1977.

Néroman, Dom. *Traite d'astrologie rationnelle*. Paris: Éditions Sous le Ciel, 1943.

Powell, Robert. *Chronicle of the Living Christ: The Life and Ministry of Jesus Christ: Foundations of Cosmic Christianity*. Hudson, NY: Anthroposophic Press, 1996.

———. *History of the Houses*. San Diego: ACS, 1996.

Ptolemy. *Tetrabiblos*. F. E. Robbins, trans. Cambridge, MA: Harvard University, 1980.

Raman, B. V. *Hindu Predictive Astrology*. New Delhi: UBS, 1993.

Renoir, Pierre-Auguste. *Renoir by Renoir: Artists by Themselves*. Rachel Barnes, ed. New York: The New York Review of Books, 2001.

Sepharial. *The Manual of Astrology*. Slough, UK: Foulsham, 1962.

Schonberg, Harold C. The Lives of the Great Composers. New York: Norton, 1997.

Schonberg, Harold C. The Lives of the Great Composers. New York: Little, Brown, 1970.

Steiner, Rudolf. *The Etherization of the Blood*. London: Rudolf Steiner Press, 1980.

———. *The Inner Nature of Man and Our Life Between Death and Rebirth*. London: Rudolf Steiner Press, 1994.

———. *Life between Death and Rebirth*. Hudson, NY: Anthroposophic Press, 1968.

———. *Man's Being, His Destiny, and World-Evolution*. Spring Valley, NY: Anthroposophic Press, 1984.

———. *The Riddle of Humanity: The Spiritual Background of Human History*. London: Rudolf Steiner Press, 1990.

———. *The Riddles of Philosophy*. Great Barrington, MA: SteinerBooks, 2009.

Sucher, Willi O. *Practical Approach towards a New Astrosophy 1972–1974*. Meadow Vista, CA: Astrosophy Research Center, 1985.

Tabula smaragdina Hermetis: The Emerald Tablet of Hermes. R. Steele, D. Singer, trans. Proceedings of the Royal Society of Medicine 21, 1928.

Tierney, Bil. *Dynamics of Aspect Analysis: New Perceptions in Astrology*. Sebastopol, CA: CRCS, 1983.

Treadgold, Peter. *Astrofire* (astrological computer program). Sophia Foundation of North America (see below).

Volguine, Alexandre. *L'ésotérisme de l'astrologie*. Paris: Éditions la Grande Conjonction, 1995.

Zunin, Leonard. *Contact: The First Four Minutes*. New York: Ballantine, 1994.

COMPUTER PROGRAM: Peter Treadgold, *Astrofire* (distributed by the Sophia Foundation of North America, Palo Alto, California). *Astrofire* has a comprehensive research module for data storage and comparison charts, a star catalog with over 4,000 stars, and a database of birth and death charts of historical personalities. It is capable of printing out geocentric and heliocentric/hermetic sidereal charts and ephemerides throughout history. With this program one can compute birth charts in a large variety of systems (tropical, sidereal, geocentric, heliocentric, hermetic); calculate conception charts using the hermetic rule, in turn applying it for correction of the birth time produce charts for the period between conception and birth; print out an "astrological biography" for the whole of life with the geocentric and heliocentric planetary systems; work with the sidereal zodiac according to the definition of your choice (Babylonian sidereal, Indian sidereal, unequal-division astronomical, etc.); work with planetary aspects with orbs of your choice. Included are eight house systems and a variety of chart formats. It includes an ephemeris program with a search capability. *Astrofire* runs under Microsoft Windows. If you are interested in *Astrofire*, please contact:

> Sophia Foundation of North America
> 525 Gough St, #103
> San Francisco, CA 94102
> Phone/fax: 415-522-1150
> sophia@sophiafoundation.org
> www.sophiafoundation.org

Astrofire can be purchased online from the Sophia Foundation website:
sophiafoundation.org/astrosophy/astrofire/

Journal for Star Wisdom

Robert Powell, editor

The *Journal for Star Wisdom* includes articles of interest concerning star wisdom (*Astrosophy*), as well as a guide to the correspondences between stellar configurations during the life of Christ and those of today. This guide comprises a complete sidereal ephemeris and aspectarian, geocentric and heliocentric, for each day of the year. Published annually, new editions are available beginning in November for the coming new year.

According to Rudolf Steiner, every step taken by Christ during his ministry between the baptism in the Jordan and the resurrection was in harmony with—and an expression of—the cosmos. The *Journal for Star Wisdom* is concerned with these heavenly correspondences during the life of Christ. It is intended to help provide a foundation for cosmic Christianity, the cosmic dimension of Christianity. It is this dimension that has been missing from Christianity in its two-thousand-year history.

Readers can begin on this path by contemplating the movements of the Sun, Moon, and planets against the background of the zodiacal constellations (sidereal signs) today in relation to corresponding stellar events during the life of Christ. In this way, the possibility is opened for attuning, in a living way, to the life of Christ in the etheric cosmos.

The main focus of the journal in 2011 is the significant year 2012, with 2011 as a stepping stone to this pivotal year in the history of humanity and the Earth. Apart from articles by David Tresemer and Robert Powell more directly concerning 2012, The journal for 2010 will be an special, expanded issue, with in-depth articles on this key year in human and earthly evolution.

Journal for Star Wisdom 2011

www.steinerbooks.org | ISBN: 9780880107280 | 154 pages | paperback | $25.00

Journal for Star Wisdom 2012 available November 2011

THE ASTROLOGICAL REVOLUTION

UNVEILING THE SCIENCE OF THE STARS
AS A SCIENCE OF REINCARNATION AND KARMA

ROBERT POWELL AND KEVIN DANN

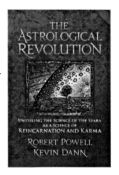

The basis, the tropical zodiac, emerged through Greek astronomers from what was originally a calendar dividing the year into twelve solar months. The fact that ninety-eight percent of Western astrologers use the tropical zodiac means that contemporary Western astrology is based on a calendar system that does not reflect the actual location of the planets against the background of the starry heavens. In other words, most astrologers in the West are practicing a form of astrology that no longer embodies the reality of the stars.

Drawing on specific biographical examples, *The Astrological Revolution* reveals new understandings of how the starry heavens work into human destiny. For instance, the book demonstrates the newly discovered rules of astrological reincarnation through the previous incarnations of composer Franz Schubert and his patron Joseph von Spaun—respectively, the Sultan of Morocco, Abu Yusuf Ya'qub, and his erstwhile enemy, Alfonso X, the Castilian King known as "El Sabio" (the Learned), along with their sidereal horoscopes. Rudolf Steiner's biography is also considered in relation to the sidereal zodiac and the rules of astrological reincarnation.

After reestablishing the sidereal zodiac as a basis for astrology that penetrates the mystery of the stars' relationship to human destiny, the reader is invited to discover the astrological significance of the totality of the vast sphere of stars surrounding the Earth. *The Astrological Revolution* points to the astrological significance of the entire celestial sphere, including all the stars and constellations beyond the twelve zodiacal signs. This discovery is revealed by studying the megastars, the most luminous stars of our galaxy, illustrating how megastars show up in an extraordinary way in Christ's healing miracles by aligning with the Sun at the time of those miraculous events. *The Astrological Revolution* thus offers a spiritual—yet scientific—path of building a new relationship to the stars.

www.steinerbooks.org | ISBN: 9781584200833 | 254 pages | paperback | $25.00

CHRIST & THE MAYA CALENDAR

2012 & THE COMING OF THE ANTICHRIST

ROBERT POWELL AND KEVIN DANN

Despite the explosion of books, videos and TV shows that claim to penetrate the mystery of "2012"—the numerical shorthand for the completion on December 21, 2012, of the thirteenth B'ak'tun cycle in the Long Count of the Maya calendar—consensus about its meaning seems to remain elusive. As metaphysical speculation mounts, professional astronomers and ethnologists dismiss the whole body of modern interpretations of the Maya calendar as New Age gobbledygook. Among the supposed seers themselves—including José Arguelles, Carl Johann Calleman, and Daniel Pinchbeck—doctrinal disputes worthy of academics are now the norm. The scholars have every right to be miffed at the sometimes sloppy thinking and exaggerated claims of the seers, which tend toward enthusiastic proclamations of an imminent, universally accelerated psychic evolution, while the seers themselves have legitimate critiques about the limits of scientific inquiry when it comes to the prophetic traditions of ancient peoples.

Christ and the Maya Calendar approaches the significance of 2012 by spiritually penetrating phenomena of today. Drawing on the book of Revelation—which provides an archetype for understanding spiritual history, as well as Rudolf Steiner's Apocalyptic indications—a completely new context for grasping the end date of the Maya calendar emerges.

In addition to penetrating the spiritual background of our time in relation to the coming of the Antichrist (the incarnation of Ahriman), the authors explore the significance of the Mexican mysteries and present a wealth of new research with the intention of helping the reader to navigate the Apocalyptic scenario currently shaping up, with the global financial crisis as one important expression. Most important, the authors refer to the Second Coming of Christ as the true event of our time, with the incarnation of Satan/Ahriman as its shadow. The authors also show the significance of Divine Sophia as the antidote to negative consequences of Ahriman's incarnation.

www.steinerbooks.org | ISBN: 9781584200710 | 280 pages | paperback | $25.00

ELIJAH COME AGAIN
A PROPHET FOR OUR TIME
A SCIENTIFIC APPROACH TO REINCARNATION

ROBERT POWELL

The research presented by Robert Powell in this book shows that a new science of the stars is possible, based on a study of reincarnation and karma. Willi Sucher did much to pioneer the development of a new star wisdom, or astrosophy, as a scientific tool for the investigation of karma. Powell has discovered that applying the science of astrosophy to the findings of karma research reveals—through the discovery of astrological reincarnation rules—the foundations underlying star wisdom. Once these foundational findings relating to astrological reincarnation research have been assimilated, a reformation of traditional astrology will inevitably take place. Once the new astrology is established, there will be a similar feeling in looking back upon traditional Western astrology that modern astronomers have when looking back upon the old geocentric astronomy.

The purpose of *Elijah Come Again* is to contemplate the incarnations of the prophet Elijah, with the goal of laying the foundation for a new "science of the stars" as the "science of karma." At the close of his last lecture, after discussing the sequence of incarnations of Elijah–John the Baptist-Raphael–Novalis, Rudolf Steiner spoke of this individuality as "a radiant and splendid forerunner...with whom you are to prepare the work that shall be accomplished at the end of the [twentieth] century, and will lead humankind past the great crisis in which it is involved." These words indicate that, from the end of the twentieth century and into the twenty-first century (that is, now), the Elijah–John individuality is to be a "radiant forerunner" for humanity in the next step underlying our spiritual evolution.

Elijah Come Again presents a scientific approach toward unveiling the mystery of human destiny.

www.steinerbooks.org | ISBN: 9781584200703 | 260 pages | paperback | $35.00

CPSIA information can be obtained at www.ICGtesting.com
263664BV00003B/1/P